D1372854

Flo Aeveia Magdalena

Sunlight on Water

A Guide to Soul-full Living

All Worlds Publishing
Plantsville
Connecticut

Copyright © January 2011

All rights reserved. No part of this book may be reproduced in any form or by any electrical or mechanical means including information storage and retrieval systems without permission in writing from the author, except by a reviewer who may quote brief passages in a review.

For information contact: Debbie Seidel

All Worlds Publishing
P.O. Box 603
Plantsville, CT 06479
Tel. 866-235-1350   Fax 860-276-9539

Published by: All Worlds Publishing

Eighth Edition 2011. Trade Paper.

Printed in USA

ISBN 1-880914-13-1

DEDICATION

This book is dedicated to all the souls
who have recognized The Ones With No Names,
remembered their vibration, and called them forth...

Also by Flo Aeveia Magdalena

I Remember Union:
The Story of Mary Magdalena

Honoring Your Child's Spirit:
Pre-Birth Bonding and
Communication

Sunlight on Water

My Gratitude To...

Jayn Stewart for her expertise in editing and proofreading.
This revision and edition were made possible through
her efforts. Jayn is dedicated to keeping the vibration of
the message and intention of The Ones With No Names
congruent. Her collaboration and guidance in bringing these
spiritual messages into form is invaluable.

Désirée DeKlerk for her graphic assistance and loving
support, thus making this revision possible.

Stacey Hentschel for her financial support.

Those who were drawn to be present for the reception of this
book in February, 1996: Janene Hardy for her constancy and
accuracy in transcribing the original tapes; Noel McInnis for
an untiring initial editing from the original tape transcriptions.
Carlee Janci for holding the space and cooking meals so we
could work, especially the chocolate chip cookies!

Debbie Bower Seidel for her continued support and assistance
of this and other publications of All Worlds Publishing.

All of you who give continued support to this work and to the
fulfillment of a million years of dreaming—
the choice for peace on Earth.

Table of Contents

Chapter 9

Chapter 10

Chapter 11

Chapter 12

Chapter 13

Chapter 14

Chapter 15

Chapter 16

Chapter 17

How It All Began

As far back as I can remember, I have searched for the meaning of life, asking questions and looking for answers. Why do certain events and circumstances touch certain people's lives? Why do conditions of separation, grief, fear, aloneness, and violence exist here, despite God, despite the good people, despite the good intentions, despite religion? My search to answer these questions persisted throughout my Presbyterian upbringing and scientific training as a nurse.

As I watched the "struggle" of life and the seemingly meaningless events which "happened" to people, my quest intensified and the disillusionment with human systems and those in it affected me deeply. Honesty, good intentions, and kindness didn't seem enough.

In the late 70s, working the night shift on a medical teaching unit, I awoke many times with fear in the pit of my stomach that had no seeming connection with anything in my life. A year later, as a psychiatric nurse, I learned to call this "free-floating anxiety."

When I was first introduced to metaphysics in June of 1979, I was skeptical, fearful, and insecure. I was not truly alive, bobbing around on the surface of reality, touching only the edges of myself, living an illusion of separation, always trying to feel union with something or someone outside myself.

Even after I learned about the soul and began coaxing it out, the struggle continued. Knowing about my soul and realizing the oneness of all things was wonderful, and yet, I didn't feel my soul then. I had not yet surrendered my will to my remembering. My mind was so strong and the conditioning so deep that the hopes and dreams of peace and wholeness seemed far away. But I persevered. I began teaching classes in wholistic health, integrating the metaphysical and medical parts of my life. By accessing my right brain I professionally offered guidance through channeled information to others. I saw their soul patterns and drew pictures of what I saw, helping them to remember the contributions their souls could bring to the world.

I worked in group settings, accessing the soul level. Using sound, toning, and light, we would go deeply into that place of soul and bit by bit, my soul and others' souls began emerging. I began to feel strength, strength that couldn't be taken away from me by outer circumstances. I felt the connection to myself through time and the connection with others that time had not or could not diminish.

It was in November of 1986 that The Ones With No Names (TOWNN) came to me. During a soul group, as we went around sharing, one by one, I heard their words in my mind. I had never heard "voices" before and was startled, and yet, in a surprising way, reassured. Their intention was pure, their essence was light, and their message brought me hope. As time went on, I began to trust them.

They became a presence in my life. In the beginning, their words impressed themselves on my mind, and I felt their perspective insert itself gently into my thinking. As I came to work with them almost daily, I slowly found my questions being answered and my fears assuaged. Their presence fostered enormous change, growth, and learning for me. As our vibrations integrated I no longer heard them, and yet, their presence came through me as I worked with groups and individuals.

Their perspective is universal: there is no right or wrong, everyone is growing toward their highest potential, (no matter what it looks like on the surface), everything is part of one system, we are all one. They bring us our essence without boundary or limitation. They assure us and encourage us with great patience, time and time again, because they know our plight, even though they have never been here in physical form.

Perhaps what moves me most about them is their empathy for us and their concern for the journey we have all chosen to travel here. They call themselves Cosmic Guidance Councilors. Together we have spoken to thousands of people about the individual plan or design in each of their soul's blueprint. Their perspective holds everyone equal and draws forth life, creation, and potential. As they read each soul's blueprint, TOWNN charges the essence within each soul and helps bring the truth of that soul into being here, through the vibration which is carried in their words. They speak continually of the design of union, and it is their "job" to assure that design. Yet, each of us holds a critical piece in the fulfilling of that design.

In May of 2005 TOWWN requested that we gather each week through conference calls to hear their story and understand why they are here. Each time they spoke to us they brought a message of hope and inspiration which expanded the wave of consciousness that our species is creating. This wave brings the promise of inner and outer peace through the awakened spirit. These conversations continued for five years, until May of 2010.

In October of 2008 TOWWN brought forth Circuitry Alignment, an amazing process that reconnects the template of our divinity from The Swing Between Worlds into the Seed of Light we carry within our body. This unique and profound experience refreshes this divine spark, guiding it from the above to the below—from our spirit into our body cells. Practitioners trained in Circuitry Alignment now offer this modality throughout the world.

The Ones With No Names give us shortcuts to find our own answers. They provide creative ways to live without pain. They encourage our independence, showing us how to co-create, cooperate, and serve.They remind us that we are a part of creation, the Monad and the Sophia—the male and female aspects of creation, and that our fulfillment is the same as the fulfillment of creation. They remind us that we chose to come here, chose the life patterns we would live, and the piece of the hologram we would contribute to the world—to the design of wholeness that only we can give—the design of oneness in form.

According to TOWNN, there has never been a time in human evolution when humanity has had the power to affect union as much as it can now. All the forces of the universe accompany us on this journey as we remember that The Dream of We is in Me. Remember as you read that you are here on Earth to live and create from your soul, that this is the time of oneness, and that our human journey now brings us to the fulfillment of the design—the peace of a million years of dreaming.

This guide is their message of hope and assurance for humanity. It tells us how to access the Akashic records, where knowledge is housed in the universe. It provides us with the keys to move from surviving to creation; from loss and abandonment to safety, trust, and comfort; from confusion, pessimism, and separation to truth and security; from seeming chaos to order. It teaches us how to co-create, remember our origin of oneness, and grease the wheel of the hologram, the place of oneness, so that everything fits and we live the reality of Heaven on Earth.

Sleep with this book under your pillow. Live and breathe a new cadence of breath with no time. Learn how your energy responds to the people in your life; check out how you open or close your heart with each person you meet. Understand why you can't seem to change habits or patterns, even though you've tried hundreds of times. Learn, experience, understand, re-establish, re-calibrate, re-cognize, re-solve, re-member.

Thank you for listening, for yearning, for questioning, and for remembering.

Flo Aeveia Magdalena

Let Your Fingers Do the Walking

Short-cuts to Understanding
The Ones With No Names

It occurred to me one night just as I was going to sleep and had almost put *Sunlight on Water* to bed, finishing up the final touches, that it would be helpful for those of you who don't know The Ones With No Names to give you a short introduction to their work:

* In each of the exercises suggested, it is helpful to breathe first from the spleen chakra area, located about two inches below the navel. You then access your life force with each breath and initiate the rhythm of order from the deepest part of you. Breathe deeply and fill your lungs and body as if they are a container, and then, as you exhale, settle into the body, becoming more relaxed.

Remember that the exercises are designed to bring you to the experience of being a continuum, unifying with your spiritual essence, which is fluid. So just relax with the instructions and concepts, allowing them to be possible, at first, and then, as you practice, join the energy as it flows so that you feel a part of the movement of the consciousness of you and creation, becoming one.

* Stating "I am a light being, and light I shall remain," taking a deep breath, and then stating, "There is no time," is the combination which brings us organically to our first breath, before the imprint of density and belief were placed on top of our divinity and spiritual nature. THIS REPATTERNS THE AMOUNT OF LIGHT THAT IS INFUSED IN OUR BODY!

This is an easy and direct way to affect our charge—how much light we carry and how much light is infused into our cells, tissues, and organs. Being and carrying light brings the memory of oneness—before we were form—brings us to peace, with no edges, (which cause conflict) and no congestion (which cause disease).

* The work of The Ones With No Names is about bringing spirit into form, what they call "trusting the body with the spirit." It's about full presence. Grounding is the primary way in which this experience

is fully understood by the mind, body, circuits, and visceral tissue—the part that carries the DNA.

You can ground outside or inside, in bare feet or with shoes on. There are several different techniques in the manual and you can practice different ones until you find the one that best serves you.

Grounding every day has benefits like straightening the spinal column, reducing menstrual discomfort, improving vision, increasing reception of energy, resources, memory, etc. Any condition that is affected by energy flow is affected by grounding, because it moves the energy and balances it through the entire system. It is strongly recommended, because grounding brings the above and the below together, through us.

See the grounding chapter and the glossary for ways to ground. My favorite is to stand and imagine I'm a tree with deep roots bringing me deeply into the center of the Earth and that my branches reach up and touch the sky. Then, as I breathe, I become light dancing on water, merging my form and my essence with the elements and essences of nature.

* Cellular osmosis, looking and feeling like Sunlight on Water, is the fundamental way in which grounding re-orients the dense human to allow the creative, spiritual to come into balance with the form.Remember, since we are not taught that we are spiritual beings, that part of us is being called forth. Grounding and osmosis give us the key to that calling forth.

* Drinking water with a slight bit of lemon squeezed into it on a daily basis assists the circuits to carry more charge. The number of glasses is up to each person. The guidance suggests that as we drink more water, the bladder does not respond as much, and the water inside the cellular wall balances so that the cells stay hydrated.

The extra fluid can run the charge we're accelerating without depleting the cellular or making us run to the bathroom frequently. If we turn on the circuits through intention, charging our being with creation, running lots of energy, and expanding our consciousness, and don't drink water, it's like putting your finger in the light socket and you may feel irritable.

HAVE FUN AND REMEMBER, IT IS ALREADY DONE!

ENVIRONMENTAL SUPPORT

* To support our spiritual circuits we drink lemon water.

* To support our organs and immune system, miso soup assists in balancing our body PH and offers a safe way to detoxify the body on a daily basis.

* To support our connection with our subtle bodies, a process called The Golden Arena is recommended. Below is an excerpt from the full Golden Arena channeling from June 16, 2008.

Imagine a golden light energy or substance being poured into the top of your head which flows down your body through a channel into the bottom of your torso, filling you up every time you breathe from the bottom up, like a container, inch by inch.

Say, I am that, I am. And now say, "I exist in present time which is all time, on this creative wave of golden light and energy and substance in the center of my body. I stand in this, I sit in it, I lie down in it. From now on the golden substance, light, and energy are in the core of my body and fills me from the bottom of my body to the top of my head."

Daily you can also affirm:

I pledge to invite the golden arena of pure consciousness into my field of energy everyday. I pledge this to promote balance in myself, in others, and in this universe. I understand I must be proactive if I expect my life to change. I understand that there is no going back. I hold my consciousness and cherish it now as the vehicle of my transformation. I do not project or transfer my feelings. I own them. I add golden energy to all my thoughts and feelings so that I return to balance. I understand that creating anything requires balance and alignment with creation. When I am aligned with creation, I create.

Introduction

The Ones With No Names

We are a body of light and knowledge that maintains order and truth in the universe. Part of that truth and order is giving you as much assistance as possible in the process of charging your light body so that you can do it yourselves. We have asked for the cooperation of all dimensions in bringing you this manual for three express purposes: to make your learning more simple; to let you know that there is cooperation in the ethers to assist you; and to show you that the greatest experiment is yours. We will teach you to bring the three into one, which is the design, the key, and the gate to access the gold at the end of the rainbow.

We are "rainbow" parents because we encourage independence. Experience is a great teacher. If you understand through the cells what the light body is and experience the charge of the light body, it's worth five million words.

The fundamentals we provide are ways you can view yourselves, the world, the universe, the Earth, the creatures, the force fields, the essential energies, the kingdoms, and the essences in an interrelationship that sustains light and knowledge, truth and order. Our objective, really, is to create Heaven on Earth.

The design of oneness is such that each of you is intricate to its unfolding, wherever you are and whatever you're doing. You can relax, enjoy life, be at peace within yourself. No matter what you do, what your habits are, or what you believe is right or wrong, you will learn to sustain light. It is easier now.

There's nothing to worry about because you will accelerate. One day you may just wake up and say, "I am going to affirm 'I am light'." You cannot fail. The design already has your permission to be the best that you already are. So it's good news. The foundation of this good news was your choice in the Swing Between Worlds before birth to bring light to Earth, which is why we come now to remind you of this.

Our love for you is infinite as we unfold the principles of our understanding of the universe. We do so in love so that you take to heart, to soul, to awareness what you originally chose. What unfolds from reading this material is a foundation that establishes you in the great design from the beginning. There is no greater place than to be in at the beginning. If you are drawn to pick up this book, you were there at the beginning. You will be there at the ending. And most importantly, you're here now.

We recommend that you read this book thoroughly. Study the exercises and do your best to integrate the vibration and concepts of each chapter. After you've gone through the exercises and tried them at least once, you'll know what each one feels like. Then we recommend that you go through the manual every week and ask, "What do I need to do this week?" You might say, "Today I need to feel the energy I felt when I was doing this particular exercise." Experience this book as a context for understanding, a manual for living, and instruction for bringing your life into truth and order.

Those of you who assist in attaining the design of oneness are working on the experience of light becoming peace. As the light comes into the body fully, it manifests as a literal place physically, ethereally, psychically, societally, and familially. As light is embodied, it becomes the threshold for peace, which is union in action.

As the light bodies refine, the feeling of separation is no longer there. Communication will occur on all levels: interspecies, intergalactic and much more. As all these levels filter in, technology will advance.

We are revising the current system of being, relating, orchestrating, designing, and co-creating everything. You are providing your vehicle as a way for the light body to anchor so that your life becomes the consciousness of the design, which is technology, the heart, and everything else in union.

You are refining every system of your being so that it can reflect a new technology that is ethereal and practical simultaneously, which is our definition of technology.

New models and technologies will emerge. People will use light instead of pacemakers, light instead of food, and light instead of lovers. As this way of being unfolds, the choices people make will be very different.

Each of you has an opportunity to make that charge happen. You'll change your channel from one side to the other. "I don't want it to be hard anymore. I'm choosing light, so I'm going to flow with the essence of that. As I do, no-thing matters, everything is light, and everything is now."

This will attract others to you magnetically. They will come into this experience with you and open to unfolding this technology of heart, which provides an opportunity for the new relationships that you've been wanting.

All the new models are born from critical mass. That's why we will make reference to the critical mass so much. Attention is placed on the massive coming together of light, so that everyone understands that this is where the catharsis from separation to non separation happens. Critical mass is, by definition, a place of non separation.

As you intend to live from the soul, each of you has responded to the calling. *We would invite you to participate in this manual as a response, rather than as a reading. Because as a response, it will carry a charge. Let the charge in.* It will validate for you that you are a piece of Heaven, and it is of great import to live that piece of Heaven, absolutely.

Be the charge wherever you've been planted, and grow there until the moment comes with a snap of the fingers that says, "My calling is over here," and then go. Know as you go that you've already played out all the scenarios in front of you. You have created a wave of critical mass to ride home on, and it's more than okay, it's phenomenal. Your part is the lead part. No matter who you are, it's the lead. Because only you can play it. Without you it doesn't happen.

Your design, as it was chosen, was ordained by the Absolute. As you live it, you will experience contentment, deep, deep contentment, and the knowing that the pieces are already together. It's not your responsibility to put them together. That's what re-membering is: knowing that the charge is yours and that your decision to make it happen, made it happen. As you unfold it, it is pure revelation. It is what's revealed, not what's hidden, and not what's attained by working, thinking, educating, and suffering.

Since you are that piece of Heaven, your ordination is about divinity. What makes it divine is that as it was chosen and accorded, it was also re-solved, put back into the fluids that bring you forward now into its expression. For it is the fluids that you are flowing through and with that carry the charge.

Being a piece of Heaven on Earth, vibrationally, is a frequency that requires no-thing, and a place that always was, is, and will be absolute. Which means that you are absolute. There is nothing that you have to do, but be.

The Heaven that is in you will then be on Earth, and the charge of that essence will vibrate in such a way that the fullness of your soul will express its essence. All things will be made clear unto you. For that is what the design says.

Prepare for the eventuality that you will be a sacred place for the world. Diligently see everyone and everything as light. Please see only that they are light. Do not worry about if they are all light, or how much they have, or what is missing, for what you focus on will magnify.

When humanity remembers that it is light, and when you remember that you are light, dichotomy stops. When you vibrate in the frequency of light, truth happens, order happens, judgment stops, separation stops. The main reason to believe only in light, is that it is a short-cut. It brings you to a vibration, and there is no time in vibration.

There is no-thing but light. And when you allow that, no-thing matters. You can forgive, you can trust, you are safe, you are in touch with your soul, you are resourcing from the universe, you are honoring yourself, and then relating from that space of sacred marriage. There is no need to defend or justify, it is simple and easy. It is the natural way of being.

The most profound action that you can take in your life now regarding the future, is to make children available to your life, and be sure that they remember that they are light; that you are creating ritual with them from birth about their light nature, as in The Birthing chapter of *I Remember Union*. (See Appendix.)

The role you were given is a Key to the Kingdom that supports your consciousness in expression. Everything you know, everything you sustain, everything you carry, goes with you so that it always feels co-creative. It feels always as if you're doing it with, and that's beautiful, because that's union. And that's why Heaven is coming to Earth.

"Know that we are loving you very much and that we

pledge for you our presence in each moment

of your unfolding,

now and always.

We give for you our blessings, and say for you that

You Are Blessed. You Are Blessed. You Are Blessed."

~The Ones With No Names

Sunlight on Water

Chapter 1

You Are Light

It is always about light that you choose to incarnate. When you are in the Swing Between Worlds before birth, you also choose many ways of expressing your light.

Each day if you say, "I am a light being and light I shall remain," your essence automatically becomes charged with your inner light. The light begins to pool in the areas of consciousness where your essence is linked to your vibration. You begin to see everything as light. It carries you on a fluid wave of creation. Creation is light, and truth and order are the foundations of creation.

When you feel your essence charging, you experience union. The memory of that brings your essence out. It is unnecessary to work with the ego, the personality, the subconscious, or the psyche because you can work directly with your light body.

As you develop your essence, you charge your light body, and it begins to vibrate in the experience of order and truth. When a number of you at the same moment vibrate in that capacity, a unified field is born. This unified field is made up of many rays of consciousness, and that is how there can be as many truths as there are people. For when the light is charged from the essence, everyone's truth is the same, for all truth is about the memory of the beginning, which is oneness. One thing that will help you remember oneness is to say three times: "I am a light being and light I shall remain."

When your essence is charged, the soul emerges. The soul holds the design for your life that you created in the Swing Between Worlds.

If you remember that your design is already in operation, and that what you yearn for is reflected to you from the future, you can relax, for there is nothing to do. It is about reception, remembering, and alignment.

The soul holds the design of your future in your physical experience. When your essence is charged, the soul emerges. There is a melting down of conditioning, separation, and judgment and union of the ingredients necessary to live oneness in human form. It is not about analyzing the issues of your experience. It is about unifying the field of order. This is powerful because it provides an opportunity for individuals to move beyond their experience and to live truth.

THE CIRCLES OF TIME: AN EXERCISE

An exercise that helps with this is to draw two circles on the ground or on the floor about six feet apart. With a piece of chalk or crayon, write in one circle the words "present-present" and in the other circle the words "future-future." Imagine each circle spinning to indicate your movement into a time continuum. When you are ready, leap into the spinning circle marked "future-future" and then turn around. Look back at the space marked "present-present" where you were standing. When you view the "present-present" from the "future-future," all the dynamics in your life are different and stimulate vision, memory and trust.

Then as you look at the "present-present" spinning circle, walk back toward it. As you get closer to your original position in the exercise, imbue yourself with light. Imprint the present moment as if you were a piece of clay in the present and are the key in the "future-future." Then imprint that key into the present space.

In this exercise you become what you are, and yet, what you represent is unknown to you logically. That is why embodying the vibration of who you are in your physical experience is so important. Then your pattern of light becomes cellular and joined with the visceral tissue in the body. When one thinks about vibration and frequency outside of dogma, or a spiritual path, or a belief system, the forging of those two points of being and becoming can be immediate. There is nothing you have to attain, prove, or change—you are in that moment all that your essence has chosen to be.

The original design is behind you, and that means there is a pendulum, a movement. As you jump into the "future-future," you are coming from the present, yet there is also that original point that allows for the triad, or the three-in-one, which is the point of union. As you foster your "future-future," you're also re-identifying with your intention. That intention is the light, the pattern that became the energy that is you. Your essence can flow and allow you to be present fully, without thinking or trying to figure it out.

The viability of attaining that point of destiny is about remembering the pattern of light that you represent. When you stand in the "future-future," you are the pattern of light that you represent.

THREE-POINT MANIFESTATION ~ THE THREE-IN-ONE

If you are in the light body, the only thing that exists is order and truth, which establishes oneness between the original, Absolute; the middle, or the present point; and the end, or your future point. That creates a system where everything you're working with is now, so that your original point, your present point, and your future point can become the same vibration.

That is how oneness happens. It's how the light body creates the charge to stimulate the essence, to open the soul, and to allow you to remember your birthright, which is to see the vibration that you've come to live, and to acknowledge what you're here for.

You can stand in the body of your consciousness and view these three points in any or all of the following ways:

1. before, middle and after;
2. "past-past," "present-present," "future-future";
3. original, now, and hologram;
4. the absolute, actual, and point of accomplishment or resolution.

In the three-in-one experience, those places are all integrous with each other. You need no system of thought for that because everything is now. These concepts enable you to function from a different point of reference.

Think about yourself as a point of light that has come to shine, and the way you shine fulfills your design. Each moment you intend that, it happens. Everything else dissolves—becomes immaterial—because it is no longer necessary to think about how your design will unfold.

Your charge will call to you the frequency of your being so you can wrap yourself in it and keep warm, or receive love, or nurture the body, or feel safe, or actualize your potential.

It isn't that you will not be in relationship, or not find harmony in the world. It is that you stop seeking those things in an external sense. You are providing a resonance within yourself that meets all your needs. You stop thinking about meeting those needs because you're too busy expressing who you are. Your being is too busy shining light and catalyzing essence and drawing souls to you to reflect the oneness you feel. This is how the hologram of oneness will be lived.

THE CONSCIOUSNESS OF LIGHT

There is a great yearning for order and truth. This is the future being born now in all of you as form. The quality of consciousness that is light allows no interference, supports no violence, allows for no disintegration of truth, supports and accelerates light, foundations essence, and is the wave upon which the soul is born.

As the next years of consciousness take shape, each of you has a very important role to play. The critical mass of consciousness is born in oneness when light bodies vibrate at the experience of truth and order and are synthesized as one being or one body. You don't have to work together, necessarily, on the same goal to attain the same point. You don't have to live in the same place to create or manifest anything that is of that vibration.

There are no rules or conditions for this union. It doesn't have to be lived in any particular way. However, as you unfold the light you create a balance of equilibrium, a tuning fork, or morphic resonance of oneness. The logical basis for choice is going to become charged by your essence instead.

Know that there are no shoulds, even if today it looks like you have to do this or that. What seems to be logically in your path can change with the snap of the fingers.

When you charge the light being, you charge your consciousness. We define it as "following your calling," which is what happens when your charge of energy meets your intention.

When you get your charge, at first it has no direction—remember that. It isn't about going home to the light, it's about being the light.

You don't have a conscious direction to take that in. You can tell that you're in the experience of light because you don't care where you are! This is a very important concept.

You might logically say, "Today I'm going here." But then when you affirm, "I'm a light being," you may find yourself going in the opposite direction magnetically. You recognize that this is the solution you've been looking for. Many times, changing direction provides you with an incentive of energy to resolve what's going on. It's like when you jump from the "present-present" spinning circle into the "future-future" spinning circle and look back. It's a completely different recognition.

It is magnificent, exhilarating, exciting, essential, fire, light, consciousness, truth. It is not boring! You can't say, "I got it all worked out now. I went to the 'future-future' and saw my outcome and my direction, and came back. Now I know what I'm supposed to do." It doesn't have to do with what you think you're supposed to do based on what you thought you felt in the "future-future."

It's about becoming light—not translating light, not discussing light, not organizing light and implementing it and saying, "This is what you're going to do, and this is what I'm going to do, and this is how it's going to work." When we talk about the hologram in the "future-future," it's about the fact that it's already done.

We suggest that when you make the statement, "I am a light being," you are becoming nameless, you are becoming essential. You are aligning with your true intention and nothing else matters! It doesn't mean loss, abandonment, or giving up everything. You're moving your experience into being alive.

There's no holding this back. You can't make sense of it so you know your next step. It's about jumping in. When you jump in, you receive the fullness of your being. Many of you like to get a little bit at a time, digest it, assimilate it, and then go for more. That used to work well. You'd go to a certain point and then plateau and synthesize.

The more you synthesize things, the more you water them down. The more you water them down, the more energy you need to bring them back up. Now the body is assimilating things much more quickly. It's why you cannot keep relationship in its old ruts and spaces. Relationship means unifying light and consciousness through choice. If you're not unifying light and consciousness through choice, you cannot relate anymore.

As dynamics change and your souls expand their ability to run light, your bodies are no longer going to be dense.

The easier it is to flow outside of that which was, the faster the intention to create the new can be experienced. The less you want it to be something particular, the more easily order and truth flow.

NON-ATTACHMENT: AN EXERCISE

Take those things that really matter to you, the people, ideas, or events, and represent them with a witness—a piece of clay, a rock, a feather, a pebble, a paper clip—whatever you like to work with. Write everything that matters to you on paper, or designate every pebble or piece of clay by assigning them all names, faces, or values. Then put them in a group and sit on them. Sit on all those material things that matter to you. They can be people, animals, property, jobs, memories, beliefs, God, famous gurus, or anything that matters to you. Then disintegrate them, burn them, bury them, chop them up, anything. Disintegrate each one.

You'll find that you're no different than you were before. You haven't lost anything. You've just proven that whatever matters to you, whatever form it's in, it's still there. Even after you take it apart, throw it away, burn it, it still matters. Why? Because you are in some way oriented to that thing as being connected with your reality.

If you relate to it as if it matters, there's attachment. If you relate to it as if it's part of your light, then you start co-creating.

This simple exercise proves that you really want to co-create with these things. You do not want to attach to them. You want to do something with them. That's why they matter—because you want to do something with them. What you want to do with those things is make life better and experience the light so that things make sense and there's no pain.

When you elevate the vibration of who you are and what matters to you into the same vibrational field of light, you have the relationships you want.

You have the creative capacity with others that you've been desiring. When you take those pieces of paper or chunks of clay, say this: "I separate myself from this thing. I make it this material object." You begin to see how you could lose what it represents. You realize when you take it outside yourself and give it another name and give it an experience of matter, that it becomes separate from you. It becomes something you could lose. When you realize that no matter what you do to that object, it doesn't change who you are inside and the connection you have with that person or idea, then you realize this is how to create.

You can take a look at the design that shows that you and this person are connected, the feeling of wanting to co-create with that person, and the feeling of union and say, "This is why we're together. As I bring in the experience of light, I am always in union with this person. This is what it's like to be light in form, co-creating."

The objective of this exercise is to feel that whatever it is you think you want, it's already there, it's already you. You're the same vibration, or you wouldn't care about having it in your field. This takes away the conditions. It takes away the things that you think you need to have.

As you charge your consciousness and affirm that you are light, as you pick up what you think is important and put it down, as you change its form and realize nothing changes—you are safe. You have it. This changes the paradigm you are living in the world.

How does it change? There's no more separation. I am my dog, I am my light, I am my heart, my body, my health, my lover, I am everything. I am my mother, I am my father, my child, my friend. I AM. I AM light, and light is all. It's that simple. In that moment five hundred years of evolution come and go.

Part of the dilemma that faces humanity is that things are getting lost. They are getting re-oriented—structures, ideas, frameworks. Everything's changing. If you have all these things that matter to you and change their form so that they become the same vibration that you're in, you can feel your connection. You can start co-creating.

You have experienced that connection vibrationally, as light, and so you are in a different place. The place that you are in requires no proof. Why? It's essential—it's the essence of who you are.

What you're learning as the experience of humanity unfolds, is that you always have everything you need inside you because the synthesis is already complete.

THE ESSENTIAL SPACE

The essence guides the being always and is where the experience of "having it all," or synthesis, takes place. And yet the essential space is very rarely where one connects or unifies from.

When you are in the human perspective, you go out in the world to find what you need outside of yourself. Your essence is the force which moves toward unity and the expression of wholeness. When it finds what you feel you essentially "need," the essence will reflect that back to whatever or whoever you find, and unify with it, but it won't take it. It appreciates it, mirrors it, teaches you that it exists, but the essence doesn't take what it finds. However, humanity does take it. The human part identifies roles, actions, and models of behavior.

For example, let's say you are at a party and your essence is drawn to unify with someone there. The human part says, "I want you. How do I want you? I'll define that: I'll marry you; I'll sleep with you; I'll be your friend; I'll be your mentor; I'll be your neighbor; I'll be your lover; I'll be your teacher." But these roles, identities, and definitions do not necessarily bring union if lived only through the human framework and conditioning.

Our suggestion is to orient the being to light first, saying,

"I am a light being and light I shall remain." Feel the charge of that, open the essence, and then be in the essence as light. Jump into that future place, look back at yourself, orient that experience and then take anything that still grabs you. "I still want this. I still want that. Where is she or he? What's this? What's that?" Take those things and say, "All right, these still matter, so I'll take what matters and separate them from myself. I'll name them, put them on a rock or piece of paper and find out how it is to be separate. Then I'll destroy this, in the creative/destructive sense, and allow the newly born to take its place. I'm going to take the old model and disintegrate it."

If you disintegrate your models yourself, then it doesn't have to happen physically or externally because you're in the light co-creating with whoever or whatever that is. You don't need to lose it to understand that you have it. You don't have to take it to prove that you are one with it. There's no way I can lose it. There's no way it can disappear. There's no way I can't have it anymore, because I always have what I need inside me.

When you do the non-attachment exercise, you move the psyche to a place where it can just be light and experience the integration of personality and ego. You don't have to pay attention to all of that or go through the levels of attaining the light body through pain or separation. We're suggesting a short-cut to fostering the responsiveness to essence that allows you in each moment to be already there. You don't need to affirm about everything or practice by giving away everything you own to know that you really don't need it! You can understand the concept of attachment in an easier way, and then you don't have to actually live through the experience of destruction.

Your consciousness shapes itself differently because there is no resistance to expansion or growth because it's not fitting any particular preconceived pattern as it was before. What you're learning is being chosen by each of you without a structure to uphold it, which means that whatever you want you're getting, and you're getting it very quickly.

To allow the design to complete itself in this time, in this moment, is your greatest capacity. When there is an understanding of energy patterning, there can be an affirmation and manifestation of the pattern in its design, energetically, which provides the momentum to bring the experience of union into your life and experience.

Each of you has an intricate role to play in that manifestation, and it's time to hone the frequency, put it together. Tune your instrument and start taking that instrument into the world. How you do that, and the experience of what you do is much less important than that you do it.

You dissolve any barriers between you and the hologram of oneness. You wake up every day and know you know. You're busy manifesting your divinity because divinity is what happens when you receive absolution from either attaching or separating.

All the consciousness in place in this dimension is seeded from the design. Everybody is working at the same intentional level so that this job, this inside job, can be accomplished. This is so that the energy of the space of union and absolution—oneness, light, essence, charge, soul—can do in a very beautiful way what it has been ordained to do. This is different from doing a task. Doing what has been ordained is like following a wave, being a part of that wave, and understanding that you were born to be a part of that wave.

Even if you take yourself out of the equation, you're in the equation. That's the beauty of this design. That's why it's going to work, because it's already been ordained and the pieces are already in place. There's nothing you have to do about it, because as you instruct consciousness to work with you, all those pieces are put into the beautiful display case that turns everybody on. As that happens, it's catapulting that design into its next evolutionary state, which is not evolution as it was lived in a linear way but is quantum leaps of consciousness. That's why somebody can walk in the door and say, "I'm ready." You look at each other and say, "Where do we start? Can we use the word 'soul'? Can we use the word 'truth'? Can we use The Ones With No Names? Can we use 'light'? What does this person understand?" Then you realize that there is no language for this. It's not about what somebody gets, it's about what they essentially are.

This is how you do your work walking down the street. It's how you do your work lying in bed doing nothing. It's all about a viable, sustainable organism that is comprised of every living thing in all dimensions. It means that no matter what someone is doing, it's getting done.

The soul is the place where free will is lived at its ultimate by being light, organizing the consciousness around the charge of light, and living in conjunction with the design that brings the hologram into being. That's the trajectory of how it works. When one is using free will outside the trajectory of the soul, one is deliberating—holding the force back. And yet, at the moment when the vibration of light kicks in, that person can be exactly where any of you are who feel you've been around the circuit for a long time.

All that is necessary is the charge. When you're in the charge, things flow, unfold, excite themselves, become spontaneous, coincidental, simultaneous, and manifestational. When one is not in the soul charge of the essential space of light and essence, decisions bring the mundane, decisions bring decisions, more decisions, and more choices.

If you wake up in the morning and you have so many things to decide that you don't know what to do, you're probably out of essence. If you wake up in the morning and there's nothing for you to do but carry that charge and live that consciousness, you're probably in essence, or living your calling. So simplify everything. Simplify it all.

Again, nothing is right or wrong. It's either in the flow of productivity, creativity, sustenance, charge, energy and proliferation, or it's boring, hard, difficult, or struggle. When one is able to see oneself as a dynamic light field, then one can say, "I'm in the difficult place, so I will affirm 'I am light' more times right now." It's about switching tracks. One can switch a track and feel differently just by switching that track. It isn't that one has to in any way change oneself. If one doesn't want to change, or feels that to change would be too hard, or take too much time, one may refuse to incorporate light. Not wanting to do something hard makes it hard, and it doesn't happen. As one thinks about change, one can realize that change does not have to be hard. Change is not something in and of itself that is a prerequisite for anything. It is the experience of changing from one dynamic to the other that's important.

Many times the words, intention, definitions, or belief systems about something make it difficult or struggle-full for someone to be in full soul, when really all it is, is shifting perspective, which is magic—changing consciousness at will. So magically, one can move from one circuit or one track to another in the twinkling of an eye by making that choice to be light. It's fundamentally simple, and that's why on many levels the parameters that people will attain will be much greater. Each individual has the absolute power to affect the capacity of their own charge.

When you charge your own charge, the destiny that you chose before you came in the Swing Between Worlds is manifested through you as light in form. The union of all is the reality for all, and that which you have come to affect becomes the fulfillment of your design and the fulfillment of the hologram—the peace of a million years of dreaming. This is accomplished in each of you as you choose to charge your light.

Sunlight on Water

Chapter 2

The Earthly Imprint
Living the Charge of Light and Truth

It is time now for each of you to resonate with the truth of what is within you so that your course of action and your alignment with your greatest calling will be affected. Your ability to hold this space amid the destructuring of humanity's belief systems will require the capacity to focus and to be at one with light and truth. It will call you to live that which cannot be seen or proven. As the destructuring of beliefs happens, a new set of paradigms can be lived in place of what was structured into your being by your mother at the time of your birth.

THE EARTHLY IMPRINT

Holding your own space and acknowledging your own truth is challenging because your core is encoded by society to respond from human conditioning. This conditioning has been recorded on your Akashic record and your essence many times. This means that you vibrate at the same rate of speed as your earthly imprinting, which is regulated by your hypothalamus. This code of life and light was imprinted with the core imprint from your mother at birth.

This imprinting affects your responses; your rhythm of inner activity associated with bodily function; response to weather, cigarette smoke, diet, race and creed (prejudice); your idea of what a man is and what a woman is; how you think of God, if you do; your opinion of what's fair or unfair, i.e. social justice; how old you are before you develop disease; the way you raise children, view the elderly, feel about euthanasia, etc.

You have within your core a program which is running like a clock and has been running since you took your first breath. This program is seeded in your consciousness, filtered into your perception, and opened out to physiologically. It includes the rate and pattern of your breathing, your responses to the invisible, your capacity to see psychically and physically, and affects just about everything you do.

This earthly imprinting carries with it six generations of pre-programming and is given to you at the moment you take your first breath. It is in the etheric space around you and in the drumbeat of the hypothalamus. The hypothalamus is the underlying governing point from which your automatic cerebral functioning is initiated. You respond, therefore, without conscious volition, to everything that comes across your path.

Because this is such a deep and almost unknown aspect of your life functioning, often you will find that you respond before you have time to think about it. This is played out when, for example, you make a decision to like someone. Then when you come across this person again, even though you have truly affirmed your decision to like this person and respond to them positively, you find yourself doing otherwise. There are times when you respond from habit. You may make a mental and sometimes spiritual decision to change that behavior, but you find that you do not. This leads to guilt, remorse, incongruence, and resentment.

Since the encoding is essentially given to you with your first breath, it therefore needs to be re-established with breath. It was given to you by your point of entry into this dimension (your mother). It is associated with being human and following the directives of your species. It must be re-established from the Swing Between Worlds, from the moment and the place of your choice to become human. To pattern your being from the Divine means that you are essentially (from essence) making peace with your heredity, your lineage, and your visceral cellular response, simultaneously.

Imagine that you come down the tunnel of birth, feeling your essential light and your vast system of energy. Now feel the constricting of your wings into the small, compact, dense point of entry which is your physical body. Imagine that as you come down the tunnel there is a point of no return, where, just for an instant, you realize that you have crossed over from one dimension to another, and that the only way back is through the process of Earth life. You are allowing the core of your essence to be programmed by the directives of the people and the society you have just entered. You will learn and go by the course direction determined by your date of birth, time of entry, and geographic location. You have chosen a context to experience your lessons—what they will be, what you believe in and what you stand for—and this course direction will be a factor in all that you live.

When you have reached the point of "no return," there is a momentary panic, a freezing of your essential movement as light, and in that moment permission is given for the imprinting to occur, because when one gives permission to live in the human dynamic, one gives permission for the system of functioning to be transferred to the fetus. At that moment, there is a response from the fetus which says, "I now give permission for this choice to be manifest." It is still possible to change the mind, as you have observed some souls doing, and yet the orientation to the soul of the mother, particularly, is strengthened and forged at that moment. The relationship between those souls, karmically, is established for all time. This is the key to understanding your responses, your mechanisms of belief, and your preferences.

A replica of the patterning from six generations is accorded for most souls, and then transferred as birth is happening, the cord is being cut, and the first breath is taken. The important thing to remember is that you chose that specific imprint in the Swing Between Worlds and it is already accepted. Your body type, personality profile, and preferences were also chosen. So it is not that you arrive here and are given anything that was not your free will choice. It is that as you arrive, it is stamped into you and therefore is inextricably linked to your core essence.

This helps to explain the resistance many of you experience when you want to change patterns or beliefs, stop the violence you have experienced or are initiating in your life, or stop the judgment, separation, or prejudice. You find that in some inexplicable way your actions and follow-through are different from your essential choices since your actions are also linked to the organic and physiological.

To restructure these patterns requires you first to understand the mechanism, and then choose to respond differently. Then you practice this so that you see the repatterning occur before you act. You can put this choice to act differently into effect from the place deep within, embedded in the rhythm of the psyche, that will trigger new and/or different behaviors and responses.

At the moment your light body condenses into form and you enter the dimension of another world, the transfer from the mother becomes the map of your journey. If this map were not instilled within your organism, you would be unable to carry out your mission because there would be little or no relationship (understanding) between your essence and that of your mother and/or subsequent points of connection in the world.

In the Swing Between Worlds you have total knowledge of all dimensions, and these points of reality are at your disposal. At that point of initiation and choice, there is absolutely nothing that you don't know. So you have chosen and are responsible for (have the ability to respond to) every point of reality that is associated with this imprinting process. That includes who your mother will be, all the preferences we spoke about before, and the outcome. And the outcome! Remember this part, because it is very important in the equation of balancing the three points and bringing them together from the perspective of truth.

You remember from the Swing that your choices bring you certain learnings, growth points, contributions, associations, relationships, gifting, resolutions, and destinies. You come for a purpose. Your life system will click in at a certain coordinate and upon entry will lock into that coordinate. What you have chosen will be initiated.

THE FACTOR OF TIME

The only factor programmed into the equation at the moment of choice that is altered upon arrival and in subsequent moments of experience, is time. Time is the balance point between the design in the matrix of the soul essence and what is imprinted from your mother. Linear time is the fulcrum point through which your innate soul design, chosen in the Swing, and the imprinting from the human, are unified. Time is the factor which affects all your process, regardless of what you believe, where you live, and how you live in the dense and rational "culture." The exceptions to the "normal," the exceptions which are "natural," are the aboriginal and what the Anglicized world calls "primitive" cultures.

Primitive cultures usually have a relationship with the universe as well as with the Earth. They are more likely to respond from the total base of knowledge held in the Swing Between Worlds and more able to reflect the total picture. This reduces the separation between what is chosen in the Swing and what is lived in life. The relationship to time is a key element in breaking the code of the imprint.

Responding to time as an aboriginal would, aligns one with the Swing—the interdimensional place of knowing. It initiates responses to balance the imprinting of the six generations and therefore brings balance to the organism. This makes it possible for the hypothalamus to respond to truth rather than illusion. The dynamic is to grasp the intention behind the "Master Plan" and direct the course of your life from that knowing. It means reprogramming truth into your reality, truth which has been perhaps only a dream, a longing, or a memory.

With the massive destructuring of consciousness in the Earth dimension, it is opportune for you to forge a new union between your organic state of being, your relationship to the Earth, your people, your heredity, your lineage, the coordinates of your journey, and the core within you.

The key to reprogramming is available to you when you realize there is no time. It is the key to re-establishing your essential memory and calling, and therefore the road toward establishing your truth in the world. It is also the key out of the patterns which no longer serve you, and the key to your choice to live in peace and harmony with others.

Now is the time for you to live from your essential charge of light and to foster only truth from your being. Now is the time when the Earthly models can be adjusted to include union and peace and those experiences which you so long to make real.

The three essential points that will be aligned through your free will are: 1) the original choices made in the Swing Between Worlds, which have the coordinates of your truth programmed in and vibrating at a frequency which is individual and collective at the same time; 2) alignment with mom, which is essentially your key to belonging to this Earth project you've determined to participate in; and 3) the association between the hypothalamus and the core of your truth.

THE HYPOTHALAMUS

The hypothalamus is the regulating mechanism that accords or recognizes light. The hypothalamus is the place where your decision to bear light, remember your light, and shine forth that light is made possible. It is the place where healing, loving, forgiveness, responsiveness, and union are possible. The hypothalamus is the place where divinity happens cellularly.

When you are born, the patterning of six generations imprints the hypothalamus with the rhythm of the culture's experience. The rhythm of the breath is the key to establishing beliefs. These are sent visually, graphically, and vibrationally, but they are forged through the breath. This affects the pulses, which set the patterns into the body that set the timer. Once the timer is ticking, the soul experience will be adjusted according to the mechanism between breath, pulse, and time.

When you come back to substance—the fluids of the universe— you can return to the place where you are still in the womb outside of time, without the imprinting from your mother. In the fluids of substance you are pre-fetus! You are available to the knowings that you chose in the Swing without being affected by time.

Seeing yourself as an osmotic space that looks like sunlight on water returns you to the osmotic space of being before form. Putting yourself in fluid affects imprinting from your mother, experience from your culture, and time constraints that keep you on one side of the equation or the other.

TRUTH IS THE KEY TO UNION

How do you get it all together? First, remember that there is a design and that the design is accorded in this dimension from truth. Truth is the key to union because when truth is present, there is agreement between individuals and groups that have different hypothalmic programming.

No matter where you were brought up, what color skin you have, what your sexual preference is, or where you buy groceries, you can agree that you are one. No-thing stands in the way of oneness. It is foolproof because when one lives truth there is no disagreement, only the agreement to co-create. That's how you know whether or not you are in truth. Truth does not separate, it unifies. It is simple. Truth is the most direct way home.

You do not need to know what your truth is before you start any more than you have to know about the hypothalamus to affect it. It is not about studying a concept. It is a free will choice to align the intention that will best move the being into the place where truth and experience are the same. Since we are in the middle of the destructuring process of belief, dogma and institutions, we have the greatest capacity to affect new systems of functioning organically, which can then be lived structurally. We will have structures after the destructuring, but they will be different from the models that were imprinted by your mother.

You have a rare and exquisite opportunity to affect your life by returning to the Swing to see the design and to encode it with your rhythm, pulses, vibration, core essence blueprint, and time. You can bring these points into alignment through truth. Light will activate the hypothalamus to repattern the amount of light you encode in any one moment. The timing is essential here. The equation is: 1) return to the Swing, 2) acknowledge that you are human by patterning, and 3) make a decision from your core essence to experience life outside of time in union with your original vibrational pulses.

The point of free will says, "I have returned to activate my original design. I am a being of light living through truth and order within the framework of union, outside of time. I incorporate the three points of initiation, patterning and time to unify the levels of my being through truth."

This starts a wave rolling that comes from origin and flows through your body, repatterning your hypothalamus so that it can receive light from your essence. You receive light, and the breath and pulse begin to reflect a non-linear, non-constrictive, non-heredity. This establishes a rhythm of union within the cells, the blood, and the breath. Imagine breathing and pulsing as union outside of time. It takes you into bliss. It is bliss because there is no struggle to survive, beat the aging process, the dis-ease process, to meet a deadline, or to remember whatever you've been trained by society to feel is important to validate your worth. In the second that you have that bliss, nothing can touch you. You're free. You've made it! You've passed the test! It's like after a long, really hard day, crawling into a nice warm bed and being absolutely comfortable, receiving what you need.

When the hypothalamus, choice, and light are the same frequency through truth, union is created in the being. You are converting your heart rhythm, which affects the pulses and breath. As light in form, you bring the experience of union through living truth.

The reason that many of you find it so challenging to change your actions is that they are associated with time. For so long, change has taken time! Everything you have ever seen about transformation requires you to do something. Even the exercises we give you to facilitate your memory and union, require something of you. They are linked to the time it takes to understand what we are saying and do the repatterning exercise. You have a choice. Making that choice is your greatest and most profound secret, gift, and potential. Make the choice to bring the dynamics of the unified field of the truth into your breath, pulse, and vision to re-order your circuits and more profoundly reflect light.

Accessing light through the hypothalamus is profound. This ability to affect your unconscious functioning will reveal ways to create new realities in every area of your life. It is time for you to look at your back to see what you've been missing. Now is the time to expect that all the areas of your life will come together. It has been normal for there to be at least one area of life which seems to disappoint one, or take longer to accomplish, or is less productive. The capacity now is to reflect divinity and co-create continually with all dimensions in the universe, simultaneously, outside of time!

When you go into the hypothalamus and affect the pulses and rhythms of your being, the soul blueprint emerges. The soul becomes, along with the hypothalamus, the key of light and truth and order. These direct your being. Functioning is directed from choice, unaffected by directives or beliefs, and manifests creation outside of time.

REPATTERNING THE IMPRINT

You can re-establish patterns with your children, born and unborn. Repatterning will align them with the Swing, the hypothalamus, and the soul. It will accord the truth in pulse and breath, which gives them permission to remember that they are out of time, out of body, out of belief, out of dogma, out of personality. They can manifest what they have chosen to contribute.

In the beginning was the word and the word was God, and as the intention of the word was spoken through light, the journey of humanity began. You are, each and every one, now available to the word. The knowledge that has been held from humanity vibrationally is now open and you have access to everything that is.

Enough of you have broken the barrier between time and space for there to be enough energy to be in bliss so that you are outside of time. When one is outside of time, one is in creation. You have no limits or boundaries. You can initiate your children in the same way as you will initiate yourself. It is the way home, the way to comfort, and to a relationship with yourself that sustains and honors life in all dimensions. It is an opportunity to begin at the beginning with this Coming Together of the Ages and initiate new models based on sustainability, creativity, co-creativity, honoring, community, and re-sourcing from all levels.

You are repatterning and establishing new relationships with everything in your life and environment. You will also establish new relationships with your unconscious.

The universe is repatterning the vibrational levels around you, which are re-patterning your breath and pulse. It is happening through substance automatically, without will and control and without conscious understanding about how it works. You do not have to know how something works to have it work. It is working, regardless of your level of information or experience with it. The critical mass will ultimately bring truth into being. The repatterning is creating a critical mass, which is re-doing the imprint from the mother.

The feminine has taken on, as a service, the job of acting as the messenger of lineage. Imprinting relates to habits, patterns, belief systems, fear structures, thought processes, survival mechanisms, and identifying with form. Mother does her best to imprint the rules of the form and does so without words because the child does not yet speak language. The mother imprints all of this through the cells, which is why it imprints so deeply.

To repattern does not mean that you shift from being 5'1" to being 5'10" or from believing one thing to believing its opposite. It means that the relationship you have with Earth changes. You remember that you are light and live from that point of origin, memory, and lineage. You acknowledge the heredity of the Earth life you are living, and yet you are unaffected by the structures which limit your essential nature of oneness and availability to truth.

Divinity is accorded as an experience when there is union between the design and the moment. To facilitate this union, one must be ready to completely disavow the illusion. In a physical sense that means joining the hypothalamus, the body, and the matrix (the core). In a spiritual sense that means joining the Swing Between Worlds and the design. Amnesia is the physiological condition which happens when the vibration is inconsistent with the knowing, or when the vibration is oscillating at a rate of speed which reflects illusion or disconnection with Source.

The easiest way to bring together the worlds, unify the being, experience consistency between what one wants to do, say, feel and reflect, and the truth—is to reflect the truth from the core. To bring the core together and feel its vibration attuned to the original Source, to hold that vibration, to breathe that into the body and cells outside of time, provides a link with the truth. The truth is the immortal. The truth is the Akashic. The truth is that which unifies. To be here differently than your mother and her mother and her mother requires a choice to be here and yet belong to the truth. It does not matter what you believe about the truth. It can also be called nonseparation, nonjudgment, and other things. Belief about anything is unnecessary.

The only reason that you have amnesia about any aspect of the truth is because you are in a space vibrationally where your ability to unify has been altered. The hypothalamus, the charge of light, the design that you see from the Swing between Worlds, the core you follow deep within, and awareness that the illusion is not your reality, all encourage remembering.

Congruence is important because when one is congruent, the inner and outer points of experience are energetically the same. To love without judgment, to act without prejudice, to honor with no need, is possible for humanity.

When you make the intention to align your circuits in union, you replay the circuits within you that have experienced disunion. You may find that the more you want to unify from the belief system or the fear structure, the more the disunion will play itself out. Remember that if one is ninety-nine percent attuned vibrationally, that other one percent will feel very irritated and out of sorts. The same thing applies for union.

Those individuals with whom you still experience rancor are the ones whose attunement to light is in some way opposite to yours, and you are seeing the reflection of that which you most wish to integrate. When one is your opposite, they demonstrate that which you have chosen not to embody. It is a red flag because you are afraid you will demonstrate it. Most times you will want to leave the vibration of that interaction because the person or situation reminds you of that which you do not want to experience in yourself. However, whatever you are most away from directionally is going to bring the most relevance to you now because before union can happen, there must be a resolution of dichotomy. All factions, groups, and individuals are going to polarize before they unify.

The key is in seeing, feeling, and experiencing polarity, then immediately experiencing union outside of time. To do it inside of time brings back the conditioning of the mother. For example, she might say, "You have to be responsible, and if you're not responsible you're no good." You grow up with a definition of "responsible" and feel that this individual who you are now polarizing with is irresponsible. It seems impossible that you could be anything alike. You've thought it through and you're trying to see the other viewpoint, to love, etc. And nothing is working.

The way to resolution is through vibration: that is, according that you and the other person are the same vibration. Take their position and your position and bring them together. Being in union vibrationally is the way to experience union personally. Amnesia comes when one believes through imprinting that there are certain behaviors, choices, and actions which are right or wrong. This creates a polarity where one is on one side and one is on the other side. It does not mean that one way is better than another way. It means that there is no right or wrong. Vibrationally they are the same point. They come from the same place, and that is why they can be unified so easily. Yet, when you decide to unify, that last one percent requires of you that you step into the place where union exists outside of this time frame. The design of oneness will show you how you are one.

When one is in a difficult situation and chooses to separate from a person, the separation produces karma in the old sense and irritation in the new sense. You might think you are saying something that is justified, but you are the one who will suffer. If you say something against someone else, the first place the vibration is set up is in your own throat. The separation happens in your own body, against your own cells, and brings you out of the vibration of peace. You experience peace when you vibrate as light outside of time. You keep yourself out of that peaceful space whenever your vibration is not equilibrated with light.

Everything is based on the vibration of light. When humanity stops worrying about what is right and wrong in the world, in their marriages, or in politics, and initiates a unifying vibration in thought and speech, then violence against others will cease because the violence against themselves has ceased. That is the key to resolving anything.

The purpose of the human free will journey is to travel from the Swing Between Worlds into the body and back again to the Swing, the journey from oneness to separation to oneness. Because it does not exist in the belief system that oneness is a reality here on Earth, most people believe that the return to oneness happens only after death. This supports choices to exploit others. For example, this belief would give people the idea that they could do what they needed to for survival, or do what they think is necessary to assure their own well-being. They would not think of others' well-being or the effect their actions might have on others.

The journey of humanity has a very different design in vibration. It's important for you to believe only that there is light and nothing else. For a moment, be with the idea that:

There is nothing but light,

You are light, and

There is no time.

When those three points are experienced simultaneously, your breathing changes, your vibration changes, your judgment and prejudice fade, and your programming becomes unnecessary. You can talk to your mother in your heart and say, "Mom, I don't need that programming anymore. I'd like to choose for myself now. As light, there is no reason for me to fear. I do not remember by judging. I remember by putting the light and the breath and the vibration of light into my equation."

Taking any of the three points and mixing and matching them so that you are no longer conditioned to respond in the usual way, done over a 21 day period, divinely facilitates the union of the final three points: 1) the Swing, 2) the body, and 3) the Swing. These three points are the key because they give you the coordinates for your lineage and your participation in the design. They activate your hypothalamus because in the Swing Between Worlds you saw how you would bring these choices for union into being.

Think of yourself as originating in the Swing Between Worlds, coming into the body, and returning to the Swing. Everything is unifying, all positions are becoming the same, and there is no separation, there is no time. "I am home. Home is here. I belong here. I am a spiritual being in a physical form. I believe only in light. I am light divine, remembering that there are no points of reality in which I am separate from anything else."

EXPERIENCING LIGHT: AN EXERCISE

One of the most profound ways you can experience light is to say, "I am a light being."

Take a deep breath.

Then say, "There is no time."

Do this repeatedly when you affirm your immortal soul, which remembers all and is limited by nothing.

Light, breath, no time; light, breath, no time. As you say and image this, your body feels that you and your mother understand each other. You resolve your differences, and nothing matters. You get it, and yet it doesn't get you. You're free of the dichotomy. You're in your core and can delineate between the truth and the illusion. Remember that in the core there is a memory of your vibration in order with all other vibrations, which creates the experience of order. It is a spiritual principle, and yet it is a physical experience that can bring the truth into the human realm. The vibration of order shakes the structure of disorder so that it is challenged.

Challenge that which you know to be a belief or an action or a vibration that is out of order—challenge it by choosing to vibrate as light. Breathe as light, which stimulates the hypothalamus to produce more light. Breathing light produces light.

Time is the balance point between the above and the below. Living in no time is simple. Choose to be in the Swing Between Worlds, breathing the fluids of the universe, for there you exist outside of time. When you accord your place as a divine essence of light, you are home, all time is now, and there is no more separation. No more illusion. Only you and light and breath and being, for the above and the below are unified through your essence, and that is why you have come.

GUIDELINES FOR LIVING IN THE LIGHT

• Keep your thoughts and words pure.

• Vibrate in your head and throat only in oneness.

• Anytime you find that dichotomy is creeping in, think only that you are light.

• This is the way to no pain, which allows the solution to move you toward growth instead of toward the problem.

• Breathe light through the body, and vibrate the light and the breath at the same rate of speed.

• Step out of time, go to the hologram, or the resolution point, or the fulfillment of potential. These are all "future-future" points. Choose any way you want to view these points. Realize that there are different words for the same point. Your objective is always to be the pivotal point where you are unifying those aspects outside of time, for then they truly become one.

• Design your life so that you are out of the mainstream vibration of illusion. Light and breath and no time are your moment-to-moment choices.

• Jump out of the hoop of thought and into the hoop of the universe. Jump into the holographic circle we spoke of earlier, where all the points exist together.

• When you are vibrating at a rate of speed outside of time as light, your perspective on all things changes. When you are outside of separation, union happens.

Chapter 3

Grounding:
The Connection Between the Above
and the Below

The Seed of Light is the capacity to vision, to see, and to design as gods. Each of you carries this seed in your body, and you are ready to use its capacity to unify humanity, technology, and creation.

As you go forward to create a different world, it is important to carry the charge of the good of all. Create with honor so that each of your actions supports the whole. Let your actions be resplendent with the courage, the caution, and the consistency of creation.

What is it like to make a decision that is of God? What is it like to be a group consciousness that is of God?

The closer you are to refining light in form, the more contagious that experience will be to others. Then the wave of critical mass can manifest through each of you so that you are the whole in motion. It is important to feel the results of the many beating as one heart. Imagine union sustaining itself as all the lights shine forth with one ray of consciousness.

OSMOSIS: AN EXERCISE

See yourself as a field of energy, sunlight dancing on water. This is osmosis—dancing, oscillating frequency unfolding and flowing so that you experience union between matter and human form, between the Earth and the circuits of the body.

Sunlight on water is creation in motion. An oscillatory frequency, the vibration of being many particles at once, creates the experience of moving out and in simultaneously. It provides the awareness of how to move and shape-shift energy. You can change form any time you choose.

Light has no boundary, no limit. As light you do not stop with your body's edges. You are not diminished, so you do not get tired, you do not get old, you do not forget things or hear absently. You are present, fully alive.

THE IMPORTANCE OF GROUNDING

Grounding revises your circuits by bringing light into your body so you can be more fully alive. Grounding aligns the circuitry of the physical body with the circuitry of the Earth's etheric physical body, and is therefore a direct link with creation.

If you ground for five to fifteen minutes a day, the circuitry of your body will define itself as creation. What you experience is more rhythmic, more honored, and more deeply natural. Your vision improves, your hearing is more open, you see through the third eye into all dimensions, and your heart beats more in rhythm with the Earth's cycle. Women's cycles become more regular and deep and labor is easier in childbirth. Pain is released and dis-ease moves out of the body. What you have experienced as normal feels antiquated, as if it were something you read about in a history or herstory book. It was the dark ages of the evolution of the soul.

GROUNDING: AN EXERCISE

To begin the grounding experience, go outdoors. Place your feet in direct contact with the Earth's back. Stand loosely with your feet shoulder-width apart, toes pointing straight ahead, your knees slightly flexed to allow for energy flow. Arms and shoulders are relaxed and eyes are closed. Breathe deeply and gently from the Earth's core into the center of your body. Then breathe out the top of your head into the space of creation and back down again, like a sliding, moving, rhythmical scale on the piano, up and down the instrument of peace. As you move each point of energy, you are accorded the absolute space of being.

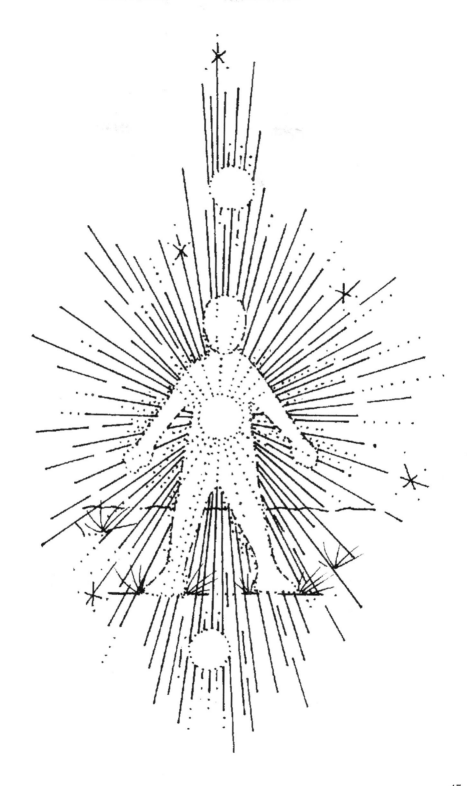

45

As you play the scale of your instrument, you bridge your connection to the above and below simultaneously. The sacred marriage of the above and the below is humanity, and is the experience of energy in motion.

THE YEARNING TO CREATE

Each of you has the capacity to be your own integration of male and female, of creation and Earth, of form and substance, or however it is linked in your perspective. Each of you has set into motion a different part of creation, and that is why there seem to be differences between you. Yet when creation comes upon itself, it acknowledges. It does not say, "You create differently than I do." Creation would say to creation, "Ah, let us create. Let us co-create. Let us flow together."

You will know when your human aspect is balanced by your divine aspect when all you want to do with others is co-create. You will say, "What can we do together? How can we foster oneness in motion?" You will not say, "Please spell out your intention. Tell me how you choose to do your part. Tell me what you think is important." Those conversations will not take place because as you come together there will be inherent cooperation. You will be so moved by the presence of the others that you will gleefully clap your hands and say, "Where shall we go as we merge?"

The excitement of the yearning in each soul is for the critical mass of its own expression. And it also yearns to express itself in effectiveness and consciousness with others. That's why, when your essence is charged and you say, "This is my calling," it always involves somebody else. It involves a way in which everyone will benefit. And it always, always supports all life and diminishes none.

The charge is structured from purity of intent. If one person decides that what they have to give is separate from what others have to give or receive, they will find themselves alone because the supportive energy is this experience of cooperation.

DISSOLVING YOUR EDGES

We suggest that you take your edges, those things that rub against others, and challenge them. Look in the mirror. What is it that rubs? Take the words that come to you—ego, self-righteousness, jealousy, ineffectiveness, inadequacy, lack of self-worth—and rub them until you get the purest essence from them. How could those words bind you instead of separating you? What do they tell you about your yearning for merging and unifying? Instead of separating you, how might they be the glue that binds you to others?

Whatever your edges tell you, they are just words. They tell you whether or not you feel responsible, whether or not you remember, and whether or not there is integration in your being. It is about whether or not you are unifying.

Grounding allows you to merge and blend these edges so they ripple through you and do not separate you from what is real. It's very lovely, because as you look in the mirror and experience yourself disappearing and becoming the fluid movement of sunlight on water, you can ask, "What's holding its shape the longest? What part of me would disappear last?"

In some people it would be the genitalia: "I couldn't disappear those because I would lose my identity if I didn't have this part of my body." Or it will be the mind: "I can't let my mind go because I won't be distinguished from others." Or it will be the center of power or the shoulders: "I'm responsible for too much, to let go." This becomes a valuable tool of observation. You don't judge it, you just observe it. Your edges are just conditioned reflexes and responses.

You don't have to work on the ego and the personality. You only have to say, "I am light, and light I shall remain." So while you're grounding, when you're erasing, say, "I am light, and light I shall remain." Your karma is released, patterns are dissolved, and thought systems are revised. You are a revised edition! Joy is born because the wisdom and knowledge you carry is reunited with its original intent.

Find the glue that keeps things together for you and dispel that glue so that it no longer makes edges. Then in the mirror you will see the experience of love, an absolute knowing that you are in union.

You are setting the foundation for a new concept of humanity. Think about yourself as a fluid vehicle of conscious light. All the dynamics you've been working within your thought, your philosophy, your ideology, your religions, your families, and in all societal concepts are based upon the fact that when union occurs there is the dissolution of edges. To many people this seems like the ideology of utopia: "It's impossible. We think in too many different ways. We have too many places where we disagree."

Everything that you disagree about can be boiled down into dissolving edges. When you dissolve an edge, you set into motion a very rapid oscillation. When one is in transformation or in the state of samadhi or nirvana, one has no edges and experiences the Absolute.

LIVING AGELESSLY

Endorphins are that part of the consciousness which says, "Yes!" You do not need to exercise, make love or have a massage to have endorphins released. What one forgets is that the system is based on unity. It began as a unified field and if one chooses to sustain that field, it will come again to its original design.

If you hold the light, the soul lives its inherent design. The same thing is true of the human capacity to live spontaneously, to live agelessly in a state of grace where divinity paves the way, and union, cooperation, and co-creation are absolute. That's the way it is designed.

When you ground and smooth out the edges and feel the boost of the endorphic level coming into the body and opening the areas of zeal, consciousness, creation, and heart, you feel, "Yes! This is normal! This is natural!" You erase the dogma of your conditioning of six generations, received from your mother at the time of birth, about what's normal. You are becoming what is natural.

You feel organic. You come from a garden with no pesticides and no abnormal fertilizers. You vibrate in a way that says, "I'm a raw carrot and I'm pure," or, "I'm a raw beet and I'm pure." Through activating this endorphic level, you zing all the places in the body biologically, physiologically, and anatomically. The experience becomes more than thought, more than an intention from the soul or from the charge of essence, or from the light itself being carried through you. You are light at that moment because when this process defines itself in the vehicle cellularly, viscerally, anatomically, in molecule and in atom, you remember how many strands of DNA you were born with. You remember how many levels of your consciousness were opened naturally.

What was the foundation that you came into this experience with originally? As you're grounding, affirm, "I am original. I am natural, and I have ordained my life as the expression of creation." As you come to these places of accordance, you open windows to your original design biologically. This goes along with recognizing your original design etherically. This is because when the etheric and the biological come together, the vibratory rate creates a union of force fields which allows for the movement of consciousness through the force fields.

When your fields unify and the above and below are in oneness, there is no physical boundary to your energy, its flow or intention. This is how one moves a mountain. It is possible to move rain from one part of the world to the other, to move dryness from one part to the other, to stabilize force fields, to create food where there is no soil, to sustain potable water where there is no source. You can sustain life through light rather than technology.

CREATING WHAT IS NATURAL

We are entering a time of great change. Human beings, as a society, now have an opportunity to cooperate and create from the experience of being, rather than technology. What is it that you need to live naturally? You will create these things, not because you have studied for many years at a university where these things are understood mathematically and in physics, but rather that you have studied for many millennia in the school of light in motion, and your technology is the expression of light in motion.

As you stand and ground, the answers to the questions that are most pressing for humanity will come through your body and be directed toward the places of Earth that need to feel that naturalness again. What you carry in your consciousness will be birthed. You will know and remember the natural way of being before there was war, violence, socioeconomic status structures, before the almighty dollar, and before worth was accorded by things instead of knowing. This is important, for it brings grace into humanity and allows it to be simultaneously experienced by many.

Your power base is shifting from who is in power to empowerment of soul, self-realization, self-actualization and self-potentiation. When one self-potentiates and self-realizes, one becomes creation in action. Individuals osmotically move their level of reality into truth. The co-creative capacity will foster responsiveness so that all the force fields, all the levels, all individuals, all species, and all humanities work together. It is one interrelated system. You find that interrelated system when you live from the experience of the profound being as sunlight dancing and oscillating on water, which is osmotic. As you live that oscillation, sparked inside you is the memory of the oneness of all dimensions dancing together.

We encourage you to dance on the land and move your bodies physically and psychically in preparation for the movement of total consciousness because that is where the union will take place. It is choosing and discerning the path of least resistance. Pay attention to the part of the body that calls out to you the loudest, the part that says, "Fix me, heal me, touch me, blend me." These parts of the body are connected as you experience the oscillation of erasing your edges.

As you create these experiences daily, you no longer have edges, your boundaries of perception disappear, and you see into all worlds. You live as one of all nations and are advised continually of the status of the experience of creation as it unfolds. You'll know things. You'll remember things. You'll function as one who knows.

THE JOY OF CO-CREATING

When you affiliate with other people, there is an immediate endorphin release, a charge of energy and excitement that you're together and even more excitement that you are blending your edges so well that nothing needs to be adjusted to provide comfort.

Something gets born because the energy is prolific rather than dissipatory. If you are with individuals who dissipate your energy, move away from them. Gravitate toward those whose energy fields support co-creation—being in creation at the same time. Your field of energy will then be enhanced by those around you.

It does not have to be mental, emotional, physical, or sexual support. It is an etheric level of realization that you are being supported because you are working in tandem with others. You are all pulling your own weight at the same intensity and because of that, there's comfort, nobody's pulling more weight than anybody else. The more you feel this, the more you will attract those who will be with you. Your comfort level will determine that.

As you blend and merge your edges, you become more available to others, and in that availability there is service. The service does not take energy from you because it is about comfort. In the new communities, as you enfold and embrace each other, each of you relies on yourself and yet yourself is now becoming others. The edges are so well blended that there are no ways to distinguish between you.

In community your outer being appears to others as one facet, yet no one can see where one facet begins and where it ends because the whole appears as one stone. It is multi-faceted inside and appears as one space of union outside.

Grounding and erasing your edges complements all of your work. The work has to do with think tanks, co-creation, systems theory, communities, sustainable agriculture and environments. It's all the same thing. Instead of studying books to find out what you should do, the most important foundational piece is to sustain it all by being in the place where it all is, which is in the expression of your own edgeless, osmotic field of light in form.

There are no places in you that are untouched. Karma is revisited and released. Thought patterns are restructured. Belief systems are turned inside out like the proverbial pocket, so that you can see what's in there. Fear structures are overturned. Consciousness becomes what it is! There is nothing on any level that interferes with that consciousness or takes it away from its own knowing. You say, "This is who I am, really. This is where I come from. This is what I've always known. This is what I've always been striving for. There is nothing here that I have to do."

That's when excitement is absolute! When the bottoms of your feet are always tingling with information and the heart is always expanding with more compassion and more of the experience of being in the merging. The head enlarges so big that you can't think anymore. You can only scope out all that is and see how it correlates and bring it together so that it manifests in a way that is full of knowledge. Your belief is only in light and nothing else, and no part of you is held away from itself.

If you think about it, each of you has held parts of yourself away from the rest of you. What we mean when we suggest that you aggregate is to put all your parts together so they fit like the seamless edges of the pyramid. It's the experience of coming together in wholeness so dimensionally that you are a congruent field and everything fits with everything else. The parts that you hold away from yourself are parts that as you erase, the glue is released, the knowing is there, the affirmation supports the experience, and you're home free.

In erasing your edges you can bring yourself more fully into your truth. You are ready to be tuned. "Yes, I can hear a violin tuning, a piano tuning. I feel how I am coming together with my inherent naturalness." The excitement in your being is because you are prolific. You can co-create forever and ever. It doesn't matter what dimension you're in, you can always co-create.

You can trust the joy and excitement that comes up in you when you think about being ageless, painless, bottomless, and topless— when you experience that you don't have any boundaries and all that is, is what you are. It is not just living divinity. It is being in that state of grace which honors creation constantly.

CREATING SUSTAINABLE SYSTEMS

There is no greater tribute to the One than choosing to cooperate in comfort, continually co-creating that which resources life, brings water, brings the ingredients which sustain all levels simultaneously. Technology usually depletes one level to serve another. That's the key to why technology cannot continue as it has been designed by the mind.

As the new technology emerges, which unifies fields and communicates by linking mechanisms between organisms, everyone and everything will make a contribution. Everything will say, "What will serve the whole will serve me in this moment, or I will not be served."

If you are doing something that doesn't serve every component, then it's important to say, "What would serve that component? I will not partake in this meal unless it serves all components. I will not participate in this commodity, project or process unless it serves all." The barometer, the scale, the valuing of what works, what one participates in, is based upon the sustainable process of unification. What is unifying the whole? How does that provide mechanisms for the growth of all parts?

Each system that you work with—education, religion, societal, family, health, crop growing, energy generation, whatever it is—see it in a systems process first, in a biosphere. Before you create or build something, ask the question of yourself, of your group, "How does this sustain life? Or does it?" If it takes from one to give to the other, it's technology without heart.

Everything is considered. Everything is a part of what is designed. Whether it's fifty years or five hundred years in the future, or fifty or five hundred years in the past, whether it's another climate, another planet, or another life system, it is considered. You can no longer say, "It's okay for now. We can sustain it for a while. They'll have to worry about it five hundred years from now, but by then they'll know how to take care of it." That's what's been happening since the beginning, "We'll do this now and let the consequences find themselves. People can decide how they want to live with it and change it." None of that is viable because it considers life in a way that supports only the intention of those present, and not those imagined or sustained in other frameworks. It is nonapplicable to life. If you have to stamp it "nonapplicable to life" five hundred years from now, then it doesn't pass the test.

Integrity says, "There has to be a way that sustains life forever and ever and ever." And when we find that, what do we find? The hologram of the original design! The difference in succeeding in the normal way and succeeding in the natural way is that the normal way says, "This will work for now. We don't have to worry about anybody else." In the natural way succeeding means that you find the solution that was in the design at the beginning and incorporate it.

YOU ARE IMMORTAL

What does being one with creation mean? What does co-creating mean? It means that you are in the vibration that has always been and will always be. Solving problems doesn't mean learning anything as much as it is re-solving, re-membering and re-cognizing. This is how the vibration of a system sustains itself immortally, and you are all immortal. When the changes occur from the experience of being in a body with edges, to being light—formless, oscillating with creation—immortality is a viable fuel which can power your travels throughout all dimensions. What you need to recognize, remember, resolve, re-Source, and orchestrate in that experience is available to you from that place of sustainability. What is immortality but sustainability? You're sustaining your force field through time.

Many of you read about galactic processes that human beings are now or will experience—how strands of DNA will be available, etc. The nuts and bolts of it is that you are alive through time with no separate place to hang your hat so that you are experiencing what it's like to be immortal in form. Immortality doesn't mean that you die and come back and die and come back. Immortality means that you are sustainable as a field of energy in creation.

If you can grasp that concept as a secret that allows you free access to everything, then you have it made. Portals will open for you that you don't need a combination for, to study hard for, or buy admission to, these portals belong to you. They take you into simultaneous reality where there are no conditions, no limitations, no strands of DNA left out and memory that doesn't serve. Everything is available. It is living in creation as a viable field of order.

You experience being immortal because you are in the field of immortality. You can go into a field of hay and beautiful wildflowers. You can go into another field where rows upon rows of orchestrated flowers have been planted, seed after seed. When you're in those fields, you experience what's in those fields. Traveling in the fields of immortality is no different. You say, "As I travel, everything is available to me."

This opens you to a concept of immortality you may not have

fully comprehended before: because you are immortal, as you work on the planet to create solutions in the fields of order, you're not limited to the twenty-first century. You're not limited to what you think your education is in this lifetime or what you think your experience is. There's no way to limit immortality because by its very definition it means that you continue forever and ever.

When grounding, you experience your life through time and space and order and being. Immortality means that you don't forget it, you don't misplace it, you don't limit your access to everything.

Grounding, rubbing the edges, erasing those spaces, and feeling where you are coming into congruence opens your upper thresholds which have to do with immortality. When you go into meditation and transition states, alpha and deeper levels of consciousness, you go into the synchronous motion of consciousness in movement through time and space, order and being. You go there to defy gravity, logic, aging, disease, judgment, separation and pain. That is why humanity goes to God or the Goddess or to the infinite place of creation. That is why humanity looks for answers and solutions from Spirit.

As you come into those experiences of immortality, the levels of consciousness that you ordain osmotically from sunlight on water begin to surround you and carry you into the ethereal space of your own destiny and your own birth. What you can experience is total recall.

Total recall puts experience into perspective. It's a big "Whooshing!" sensation like a release of endorphins, orgasm, massage, being high from running or exercising. The experience is one of absolute knowing. "I do not die. I do not end. I did not fail. It will work, it's all done. I am an instrument of light. I can tune my instrument. I can be comfortable and co-create. I can sustain life. I can honor all points of reality and in that experience I am the light. I am the way. I am the truth. I am the order which holds it together. I now know what I am here to create, experience, and sustain."

As the experience of being viable becomes authentic, you do not consider this a job, work, or a task. It's not a vocation or an avocation. It is a calling to order. This is about becoming what you are, not striving to do something that will support other people's opinion of you or buy you bread. This is about pleasure. It's about sustaining your life so that you consider all life as much as your own.

Every time you do a grounding exercise all life supports you. Everything in the continuum of immortality feeds your essence. This is the lifetime that gets all the thrust, the momentum, the intention, energy, pleasure, consciousness, light, truth, and order. This is the time of remembering! Each of you, in that space of total recall, provides an opportunity for the foundation of a new world to be born.

You'll walk down the street and see someone and know exactly who they have been to you every single time they've been in your life, every single time—what you did and did not do, say, feel, experience, challenge, and resolve. In the twinkling of an eye the resolution will be there because you're in total recall, which means no judgment and no karma. Life keeps getting cleaner and clearer, more authentic, and more comfortable.

It doesn't require you to think about anything. It only requires presence. Giant billboards and screens will open up and you'll say, "I get this, this makes a lot of sense." We are to do this together as action, as energy, as resolution, as creation, and it's done as it starts. Then you can play it out like a piece of music on the piano, which means that the practicing is done and you can enjoy the sound. You don't have to say, "Did I play the note at the right time? No, you should have played that note. Maybe we should have practiced it separately first, and then practiced it together, and then maybe we'd be able to enjoy it." The enjoyment time is upon you. That's really good news!

In relationship with other human beings, other galactic spaces, creatures, earth elements, essences and kingdoms, the practicing time is done. Just enjoy the sound. Just enjoy the fact that you can be comfortable. As you're creating, you're sustaining. "We're going to create sustainable agriculture for the rest of the time that is allotted to this dimension. All the generations that come after this one will be able to live a sustainable experience."

Then you might think, "Wait a minute. We gotta start from scratch. We've never done this before." The good news is that when you go into the future and into the past and marry those together, the solution is evident. Remember, in immortality is the key to all considerations because you've already done it once. It's already accorded you. This is the time to remember it and activate through creation. This isn't the time to slog and struggle.

There is no resistance in the universe to your totally remembering everything, individually and collectively. You will unite the fields of consciousness in existence from all time and in all time.

The good news is that you are creating a life system that will provide you with everything you need. It will ground you to the experience of being light in form in a comfortable, sustainable manner and resolve all time and space in this dimension. It's a big clearing of everything. To sustain this level of commitment, grounding is the key because it links molecularly through the circuits, through the current, and through the osmotic fields, everything that is now.

Five to fifteen minutes a day, minimum time, will provide the keys to accessing all that we have spoken of. This will sustain a field of energy that will dispel and disintegrate anything that is illusion, belief, thought or fear. Squeaky clean is the result.

Collectively, it is the place of sustainable creation where heart and technology can work together to provide a space where life is honored, all time comes to serve the process, and all knowledge supports the unfolding. The result is an exciting, prolific, sustainable model of co-creation and cooperation that brings the design into its fullness and to its absolute expression. It is God in form. It is each of you living the totality of your being as it was chosen by the Gods before even God began.

Chapter 4

Safety in the Crystal Cathedral of the Soul

The soul provides you with reassurance, safety, and trust. The soul also helps you understand your fears, where they come from, and how to deal with them. Many people are feeling a high level of personal disintegration, which is an inner reflection of the outer destructuring of the world as we know it. Sometimes you may feel alone and separate from Source.

You can go down this track for as long as you want, and yet you can choose to get off, even when you're depressed and thinking you can't get back up. If you use different circuits, you can foster a new consciousness and shape-shift your reality to create the life you want.

If you easily created the life you wanted, and it didn't take time, energy, effort, or learning, it wouldn't have any value. By experiencing the track of depression and separation, one learns compassion. Many of you have come to bring compassion to humanity, so anything that's not compassionate is getting knocked out of you.

You have had times of complete union within yourself. You may not remember them, but you've had them. For example, you may have been saintly in other lifetimes. That's why it's hard for you to get involved in situations of conflict in the world. An example might be going into the inner city where there are hardships that in your heart you want to help with but don't want to deal with. Perhaps in other lifetimes you went into the monastery or the nunnery. You were taken care of by a structure that was also taking care of the people. So you served, but you weren't responsible for your own life in the same way that you are now. Now, in doing service, there is involvement.

You may remember the peace and the joy and the solace of having time to just sit and look at nothing, and pray and meditate and chant, and go out and putter in the garden, and have people go by and say, "Yes, my brother," or, "Yes, my sister," and have no real need to provide safety for yourself because the structure provided it for you. Memories are strong in many of you of celibacy and aloneness. In some ways, being alone made you safe because it was anonymous. The structure served you, and you served humanity.

In this lifetime you are the structure, and you must provide your own safety, but you have found no instruction manual. Without the structure or the manual, safety becomes the number one issue because you don't know where to get it. The second issue is trust, because when you don't get safety, you stop trusting the structure. In this situation you're the structure, and if you can't provide safety for yourself, you can't trust yourself. If you don't trust yourself, then you can't make decisions. If you do make them, you're going to question them. You may find it difficult to have relationships because you say, "I don't trust me, so how can I trust them?" So you are trying to be safe, honor your being, and create the reality you want at a time when there's very little to hold it together.

CREATING A FEELING OF SAFETY

To create a safe place of connection with your soul, we recommend that you make a structure around yourself. Give it some parameters—a crystal cathedral, a cave, church, or the Empire State Building. Think of a structure that will help you feel safe, and call it whatever you want. Whatever you choose, start feeling that the structure is around you. Do this as an exercise. The soul is where your structure really is, but if a particular structure makes you feel safe, there's no reason why you couldn't put it around you now.

If you don't do it, you'll still be all right, and yet you'll probably go through more vacillation than you need to, more alienation from your center, and more separation from your soul. On the other hand, if you feel safe, if the soul is there, and if there is structure, you'll begin to trust yourself. Trusting yourself means that you make decisions more easily. You don't have irrational fears because they don't have any basis. There's nothing separate from you because you are one with everything. You understand that oneness is somewhere inside you.

You might refute it sometimes, but you do understand it, and you also understand that you're one with everything that is, which means that you're also one with your resources and with your future.

You can bring in your future and the resources you want and need. But in order to do that, many of you have to leave the structure of what you remember, such as the church, patriarchy, conditioning, and society's models. You think, "Okay, I have to do my own re-Sourcing, I have to go to the Source and re-Source myself so that I have what I need to survive. I have to do my own creation. I have to stand in front of people, or be next to them, or give them my help, and I'm by myself. I have to change the rules. I have to play God. And yet something in me says that's not okay to do."

You may keep sabotaging yourself because you're not ready to play God. In other lifetimes you served God, and by serving God, the people came, and you helped the people. But you weren't responsible in the same way. God was responsible.

It was easy when you had the structure, because you could say, "I'm doing what I can. I'm following guidance and leadership outside me. I have this incredible structure. Everybody believes in it, so it has to be real. I can trust that there's a God because otherwise I wouldn't be here." Now here you are in this lifetime, and what is to say that there is a God in your life? What is to say that you have the ability to represent God by yourself without some big organizational structure around you? What is to say that you can do this? It means that you'll have to be responsible.

All this brings up questions and doubts in your psyche. You're angry that God isn't doing it for you, and that is perfectly understandable. In other lifetimes it was a group responsibility and process captained by God. You could discuss things. You had help. And you're alone now, at least in your perception. So you think you must have done something wrong. Where is God, anyway? These are some of the dynamics that you are running neck and neck with, head and head with, face to face with. It is powerful because you can resolve these points in your psyche and get on with it.

The structure of your soul is not yet strong enough around you. That's not literal, it's perceptual. Perceiving that your soul isn't strong enough around you, perceiving that you're not really connected to God, that you're not aware enough to be responsive to the needs of people and make money doing it, that's all perception. The easiest way for you to deal with this perception is to change it. That's what we meant by going on a different track. So decide to switch tracks.

To do this, surround yourself in the structure you have chosen to use. For example, a crystal cathedral. This crystal cathedral represents your soul. Every day as you go to work, go into the crystal cathedral in your imagination and say, "I'm at work." Then say, "I need God. Unless God is here, I can't go any further." So you bring God in. You can bring God in any way you want. It doesn't matter. God can be a flying Madonna, a cross with or without Christ on it, a cross with angels flying around it, a bird, anything. It doesn't matter what God is to you perceptively, because it doesn't change God to view God in a certain way.

So you bring God in. If you don't know how, say, "I'll pick up a feather. Here's God. I stick it in the top of my crystal cathedral. It's looking down at me. This is it. I have God." You don't need to do anything, you don't need to find God, you don't need to have a sign from God, and you don't need to have God come to you in a dream. Just decide. Change your track and God is here. It's all about how you look at something that makes it what it is. So you have God there, you have the crystalline structure of your soul, and then you ask yourself what else you need to feel safe. Whatever that is, put it into the crystal cathedral. Everything that you need is right there. It might be food, warm gloves, plants, your dog, whatever. Now you feel safe.

The next step is trust. If you create a crystalline structure to hold your soul, you can sit in it. God's here and you've got plenty of food. The objective is not to go out into the world and see if fifty thousand dollars falls in your lap and say, "I can trust because I got some money," or to see if somebody offers you a job next week. It's not about testing the limit in the beginning. In the beginning it's about holding the space. When you have the crystalline structure, God, safety, food, and trust, just hold it. Don't go anywhere with it. Don't test it. Don't go out and stand in front of traffic to see if you're safe. ("I'll see if God's structure is really going to keep me safe.")

Hold it steady maybe three to five times a day. Just sit there. "Okay, I've got my structure, God, safety, food, trust," and go through it like a checklist. Sit there in the feeling of having it all congruent until your mood starts to lighten. If your mood doesn't lighten, stay there. "If I'm going to punish myself, I might as well punish myself doing something that's going to be effective. I'm going to use my energy at least in a way that helps me out." So you sit and your energy starts to expand. The soul is communicating to you in a safe place with plenty of food, and God is present. You're beginning to trust that framework, and it begins to expand. You put the pebble in the pool, and it starts to ripple out. As you sit there, you feel better.

Then you say, "I have to get up and go to work, or go to school," so you pick the structure up and carry it with you. Maybe you imagine that you're Cinderella. You pick your skirts up, and when you walk, you imagine that you're carrying your crystal structure with you with the feather on top. Or perhaps you're a knight, and you put your armor on, envisioning that your structure is a cave or a castle. Your food is going with you, the whole thing—it's all visualized, but it's energetically available, and you're always going to have it.

So you walk along. Pretty soon you realize that a lot of things you've been worried or angry about, and a lot of things that have been missing in your life aren't missing anymore. You're always carrying your wisdom, your essence, your design, your guidance, and your protection with you.

You take your structure into each situation and speak from that place. You have relationships from that place. You have commitments and interconnections with language, consciousness, and energy. You feel as if you are embodying your essence, and people are responding to that essence. The questions you had before aren't there anymore. You've changed your track.

We recommend that you don't try to forgive anything, understand anything, or analyze anything, because it won't help you. You're too smart for that. When you decide you want something, you'll find it. Many of you are extremely powerful, and when you decide you're going to fail, you'll find a way to fail. If you stay on that track, you're going to create whatever reality you want, because you're very strong willed. Most of you have spent lifetime after lifetime in experiences and structures of discipline. I have to be here for 35 minutes on my knees. Discipline. So if you say to yourself, "I'm not going to make it," you will do everything in your power not to make it because you are disciplined. Discipline says, "I do what I say I'm going to do."

When you discipline yourself to carry your little crystal structure with you, or your cave, or the Empire State Building, and stay in it for a long enough time, it can become a discipline. If you just stay in there everything will take care of itself. You don't have to worry because what you have is what you need. What you need is what you want, and what you want is what you are, because it comes from the desire of your soul to fulfill itself. So you don't have to do affirmations about being safe, feeling good, liking yourself, or doing better—no spiritual mumbo-jumbo. You make the intention: "I am going to live safely within the structure of my soul, re-Sourcing myself. Whenever I need anything, it will be re-Sourced, and I will trust myself in the presence of the Divine or God, or Source, or Goddess. And that's my discipline. If I think I'm going to fail, I cannot pay attention to that anymore. I will stay in the structure of my consciousness." You will close off to those thoughts and experiences that don't serve you.

When you come upon people who have a myriad of problems and their world is falling apart, what are you going to teach them? You'll teach them how to find what they need inside. Teach people by the embodiment of what you're doing, that the essence is what's important, because the track of the essence will always lead you home. Energetically as soon as you hop on the track of the soul, you're at your highest vibration in that moment. It doesn't mean it can't get higher, but it will only get higher if you're there to support it.

In a nutshell, you're taking all of your resources and putting them into one place, saying, "I'm a little low on wood, or I'm a little low on fuel. I better see how much I have. I'm not going to leave it scattered all over the place. I'm going to put it all here so that when I need it I can find it. I'm aware of my assets, and they're all in one place." It's a very thrifty maneuver, because it allows you to assess what's real. Then you realize that you have a lot more than you ever thought you had.

You can do this with grace. You don't need to carry on when you're in the soul structure. Don't bring any stuff in there. Pretty soon the stuff won't have any place to attach, so it won't be able to come with you. If you don't give any energy to stuff, it disappears. You're profoundly validating experiences of truth inside yourself. You're in the right place to live your future, you're in the right place to ease and balance and resolve your past. You're empowering yourself.

You cannot be hurt. Yet until that knowing comes deeply inside you, you may feel afraid. It isn't something to worry about, it's just to understand. When you're afraid, it means that the soul wants to access that experience. When the fear comes up, jump back into the cathedral of your soul with silver crystal light and gold shimmering sparkles, and say, "All right, fear's calling. What does this mean? It must mean that the soul is ready to reveal something. I'm going to sit down and discipline myself. I'm going to listen to what the soul has to tell me." Sit there in your crystal cathedral or cave. Imagine that you are the knight or a princess. Say, "All right, show me what this fear is." As the fear jumps around doing this and that, say, "Soul structure, shine it from the windows. Throw down information, or visions, or more feathers, or maybe scarves. I want to see what this fear is trying to show me and what my soul has to tell me so I won't be afraid." What you are learning to do here is to use archetypal, visual and imaginary spaces to heal the parts of you that feel disconnected.

Whatever comes up, deal with it in the cathedral. Bring it in where there's enough light to see it, enough clarity to feel its vibration, and enough solace, support, peace and beauty for you to know that no matter what happens, nothing can happen to you because you're safe.

The more the levels of illusion dissipate, the more you're home free. You're receiving what you want to receive, functioning in a way that supports you for the rest of your life. You put together what you know psychologically, philosophically, societally, and spiritually, with etheric, causal, practical, soul energy in the circuits of your body, so that all these points of relationship are formed.

You do not find answers in the mind or psyche. People don't stay in the essence of who they are to find the solution, they try to figure it out somewhere else. They go into the mind, which can only tell them the past. It can't tell them what the solution is because the solution is in the future.

The soul provides safety for you. People don't feel safe because they're not in touch with their soul. If they were, they wouldn't be afraid of anything.

When you're in the soul you always have three components at the same time—soul structure, safety, and trust. As that balances within you, it is amplified, and people will come to you. If you can impart that one iota of consciousness to someone so they have trust in themselves, their lives will change. They will have presence. When they have presence, nobody is going to rape them, rob them, or kill them.

FEAR IS THE MESSENGER OF THE SOUL

The foundation of changing tracks is making the conscious decision that you are ready to look at fear as if it's a message rather than a killer. Have a showdown with it. It's not about your personality having a showdown with fear because that would be a set-up. The fear has soul as its adversary because the soul is strong enough, the soul is immortal, it can't be killed. You're starting out with a hero or heroine that you know can win and fear is going to be the guy who gets put six feet under. You have strength to deal with this, and it's going to work, so it's not some kind of set-up. Until the soul states its position, the fear has its way. Once the soul states its position, the fear has to acquiesce because the soul is the place where the deepest point of free will is expressed here on Earth. You speak to the fear because it's really a messenger of the soul to get the soul to come out and acknowledge and start living what's in there.

Your deepest fears are unexpressed energies that have not yet found form and direction. So if you bring the fear out and look at it and see what's there, you realize what part of you in the soul hasn't come forth and been born. The fear stops it from being born. The soul has every right to rear up and say, "I want to be born."

Because of the free will process, the mind has to give permission for the soul to exercise that right. It's harder for the mind to not give permission as the critical mass is unfolding and the acceleration curve is evolving. There's more energy of awareness than ever before. Souls are learning to express, and yet it's still a part of the dynamic supported by society that it's natural to have fear.

There are only two natural fears at birth: fear of falling and fear of loud noises. So go into the cathedral and say, "You're not a natural fear. Why am I having you? You must need to have a conversation here. I've got the stage ready. It's your turn. Speak" You're the director here. You just bring it out and see what happens. It can't hurt you because where are you? You're in safety in the cathedral. It's being acted out in your psyche, but you as a person are not damaged. You are enhanced by what happens because you're clearing out the closets. Some fears may be millions of years old, yet it doesn't matter. You don't have to say, "I wonder where that came from. I'd better worry about that for three weeks because if that was in my psyche, no telling what else might be in there." Just let it come. It's not about judgment, and it's not about holding on and attaching to what happened, and deciding that because it happened it means something profound. Watch the unconscious play itself out, give it witness, and realize that you don't have the whole picture.

You can forge this commitment to create resolution and balance in your life. Hold it steady and watch it expand. Let all the new pieces come in. You're not focusing just on fear or just trying to stay in the cathedral. You experience, "Wait a minute, there's balance here. I'm getting excited about this! I'm having more safety, and I'm able to resource myself more easily. I let the expanding feed me so that I keep all of it in balance at the same time." If you focus only on your fear, you won't see what you're receiving and how things are changing.

You're using your capacity to create and the concepts of truth to forge new tracks in your consciousness to provide you with the results you want. The fear is dealt with by the soul in the cathedral. The safety and trust in soul and self are felt and acknowledged, and the structure becomes that you are the soul and you are God, for as these points are lived within you, they begin to manifest from you.

Choose your track. Give the grease to what works. The illusion and the disintegration cease to affect you because by living in the soul, you are living only from truth. And you are safe.

Chapter 5

Living Life Comfortably

As you work with the techniques and processes in this manual, it becomes also a condition of your life that you are comfortable. We would like to program that in from the beginning so that your feeling about yourself is that of comfort. That's an important way to view your reality because it means that you have everything you need.

When you are comfortable, your body feels taken care of, supported and honored, and you are at peace with your emotion. There is no-thing that you seek. As you experience your spiritual transformation, feel it in your awareness as comfortable.

We have discarded the idea of poverty being associated with spiritual experience because not having, or believing that you're not supposed to have, would mean that on some level comfort would be absent or diminished. This is not the intention of the universe. The re-Sourcing that you experience from receiving comes to this moment, bringing you wealth on all levels. Comfortable means bringing you the experience of having what you've always sought.

Again, it is not from searching as much as it is from the experience of accessing what you already have. There is that phenomenon of being in accordance with everything. Your conscious direction then unfolds and blooms, re-Sourcing itself.

"Being of comfortable means," signifies that you are in all time simultaneously and are aligning with the consciousness of having. You are re-Sourcing from the universe, and that makes a foundation which links you to the comfort, the understanding, the relationship of being in oneness with all things. If you are experiencing or expressing any level of poverty, it is about separation—pure and simple separation.

Comfort is promised to souls who live in union. The Findhorn Community in Scotland is a perfect example. The community grew crops so big that people came from all over the world to see them. There's cooperation in growing tomatoes the size of grapefruit or roses the size of cantaloupe. Interfacing, interlocking pieces of consciousness are adjusting constantly to each other to provide natural instead of normal.

As you create the phenomenon of your own synthesis with truth, the result is miracle. Once the experience of union is established in the individual, groups begin to live in that same framework. That's very important to understand. If you're in a group and you need to manifest money, it's an individual process to identify where the experience of separation occurs because being in the group, in and of itself, will not manifest the money.

The individual must first be in union before the experience of proliferation happens in larger numbers. It makes sense. It is putting each person right there in the space and saying, "Is there anything that you're not absolutely in union with? If so, bring it together." Re-Source it, receive it individually. Then the group will receive it. It's about taking response-ability for each of your experiences with the integrity of being in oneness with all things. It is foundational to each of you in a community situation or a group process. If that's a family or small community, strive diligently to align your own consciousness so that you are not separate from re-Sourcing.

Go home to the original place of creation. Open yourself, immerse yourself in that vibration, and let the fluids of the universe pour into you. It's important at a cellular level to be orchestrating identification with something other than your current personality, because it is conditioned to believe in separation. It's not good or bad, it just is. When you unify with that unifying place inside you, then you have no conditioning.

UNION WITH THE LIGHT BODY: AN EXERCISE

To receive the original space of your own design, start by lying down or sitting comfortably in a chair which supports your head and neck, or sit in a yoga position on the floor, however you like to meditate.

Begin by closing your eyes and going home, out the trapdoor

70

in the top of your head. Then imagine that this being that you are, which is light—tingly, sparkly, and osmotic—is beginning, as a light body, to come into physical experience. See an image of your light body actually coming down to your physical body. Then watch this light body coming around the physical part of you. View it coming back into the top of the head instead of feeling it. It will have more effectiveness if you watch the vibration come together rather than feeling it coming together.

As you come down from original creation, surround who you are looking at as you, and then like a pendulum take these two bodies of energy that have become one and watch in front of you, moving off to a third point, which is the outcome. That's how you are in the experience of "future-future."

How did you design your part of or piece of the hologram? How does it look and feel when you're living it? Watch that as if it were a movie.

The light body comes down from the Absolute into the center, merging completely, osmotically unifying with that present moment. Then the two points come together with the third point, which is the point where all of you is present in a physical body, living your dynamic spiritual energy, fulfilling your destiny.

It's moving from the left position, which is up a little bit, down to the center, which is where you're sitting or lying, and then going up a little bit to the right so that it looks like the arc of a pendulum. When you go up into "future-future," you are able to hold that space even though gravity would say, "Gotta come back down!" You hold that arc until you experience what it is that you designed.

Remember that this is anti-gravity. In its scientific mode in physics, it is defined as momentum. You have to bring the momentum back. And yet, if you take those two points and unify with the third, you start a whole new continuum.

UNION WITH THE LIGHT BODY

The framework accelerates, comes around the top and creates a circle to empower the first point, which is the "past-past" or the original, and again into the "present-present," and then into the "future-future." So the "future-future" and the "past-past" become the same point again. In the circle they come closer and closer together. All the points become equal, validated with the same energy.

BEING A CONTINUUM: AN EXERCISE

If you make three dots with a pencil on paper, then draw the circle we're talking about, you have one dot at nine o'clock, one at six o'clock, and one at three o'clock. As you hit three o'clock, if you go up to twelve o'clock, and around to nine o'clock again and again with that pencil, the first time it's one thin line. But as you do it more and more, it becomes a vehicle. If you do it enough, it comes right off the paper and you end up with a sphere. It feels as if you're making a continuum. In order to re-Source your life, you want to be part of a continuum. As you create and validate that energy, instead of going from nine o'clock to six o'clock and three o'clock and back to six o'clock, you go from nine o'clock to six o'clock, to three o'clock, and then to twelve o'clock. You are bringing your continuum into the present by way of the future rather than by way of the past.

If you understand that the future is what seeds your moment, then you understand that that's where your money, your resources, your ideas and your creation come from. That's why you can't find it anywhere that you're used to looking! The mind can only help you with what has already happened. None of the points is more important than the other, but the order that they come to you in is very important.

Individually then, you're experiencing that you have a pendulum, which is going to future-future and instead of coming back to the present from the future, (which means it comes backwards), it goes forward. It goes where it has not yet gone, which is the key to manifesting. So you go where you have not yet gone. Going forward is the key to creating comfortably as a continuum.

You're coming back to the beginning, and yet the way that you're coming back is through a new route. Because it's counter-clockwise as you look at the clock, it gathers energy to you. Concentricity takes it out. Concentricity is the motion of sharing, the motion of critical mass, the motion of expansion, of re-Source. Counter-clockwise energy gathers the totality and brings it into your present moment.

If you are in the middle of this model and bring the past-past or Absolute (9 o'clock) into the present (6 o'clock), and go forward into the future (3 o'clock), you will find that you do not have the momentum necessary to create that frame. To go up to twelve o'clock and then come in from the other direction (from 3 o'clock) would feel as if you were spreading yourself very thin. When you initially do this process, imagine it. Watch it out in front of you. Then when you've made the complete revolution and it's coming in from your left, from the momentum of 12 o'clock, into 9 o'clock, into the present, it's made the cycle. It's as if the pen has already made the circle. All the tracing has been done.

TOTAL RECALL

Your ability to manifest is formulated from a different part of your psyche. This is what total recall is about. When you're making the circles and receiving the energy in a different way than you've perceived before, you design yourself as a fluid momentum in the universe. That's another reason why it's important to go to the hologram and do your best to see, "What's my piece? What's my gift? Why is it important for me to do XYZ?"

The sense of your finding yourself can be incorporated in a comfortable way so that you are seeding your future. Many times if you say to someone, "Tell me about yourself in the future," an immense wall goes up. "I can't see that. I know a little bit, but I don't know what's in my future. I don't even want to see it because I might not like it. I can see other people's design, but I don't see my own." It's because of attachment to what you do or do not see that the comfort level is kept away. Attachment does not allow total recall.

The present of this time and the future of this time are going to be more magnificent than any other human dynamic has ever been. As you come into accordance with this absolute space and flow with it through the center, to the future, and back around again, you feel the momentum. Where is it carrying you? Into the future. It's like going on an amusement ride. You establish a centrifugal force as you go, which keeps you completely in the design level of the outside of that circle all the time. You don't fall back in , forget where you are and lose your place. You build the momentum so that you never lose it again. Once you are re-Sourcing your experience you are comfortable for the rest of your days.

This experience allows you to support yourself completely through your connection to the universe. The level of comfort brings tremendous resources to you because the commitment of the universe is that when oneness is the experience, everything is available simultaneously. You are bringing the Absolute or "past-past," the "present-present" or the now space, and the "future-future" of the hologram into the same vibrational context.

At that point one loses one's ability to discriminate against, to separate from, or to identify as A, B, C, or D. Union is a way of being, an actual experience, cellularly. It's exciting because there is no lack in that space.

MANIFESTING COMFORT THROUGH COHESIVENESS

The "future-future" is where there is prosperity for everyone because the resources are supportive of the interrelatedness between all systems. Then you have an absence of poverty, an absence of being uncomfortable, which means you have a sense of easiness and free-flowingness. Manifestation, in terms of crops and resources, is easy because of cohesiveness. You have no competition because people have no reason to compete against each other. There's no reason to compete because everyone is cohesive with their own experience. It's a sharing of play and a sharing of joy. If someone asks, "Who's going to win?" then someone has to lose.

People are dis-ease-free; life is lived in harmony. Peace and prosperity are the natural way of being when cohesiveness seeds the present moment. It's reintroducing the future of the resolution through seeding your original space so you feel the congruence between the "past-past" and the "future-future." The pieces are the same vibration. That's how you change the now in the sense of changing track, moving vibration, moving energy, feeling comfortability, and feeling cohesiveness.

THE FUTURE SEEDS THE PRESENT

It's not a going "toward" in the old sense of the word, i.e., money is out there and you're going to find it. It's not about making some event happen that brings it to you. It's about you going to the event that brings it to you. That's different. Not that other things don't work sometimes. It's just that they are not based on the experience of cohesiveness and creation from a context of union.

As you create this context with your life where you are responsive to your interrelatedness with creation, you start to feel absolute. You begin to feel comfortable in the world. People will stop wanting to go back by leaving the planet and being fed up because things don't work. They'll stop wanting to leave the body, or relationship, or their throat, or their root, or their feet and disappear.

They'll realize that they can have it all. They can be comfortable in the "present-present" because everything is here with them. They don't have to leave to get it. It means that there are no excuses now. There's no reason for you to be absent from your life, from your body, from your heart, from your relationship. It doesn't make any sense for you to be absent from your own state of being. No wonder you're not comfortable. You have to occupy the chair in order for it to be comfortable. You can't stand there and say, "I'm not going to sit down because it won't be comfortable." You won't know until you sit down, and then you make an adjustment until you are comfortable.

COMFORT IN THE BODY: AN EXERCISE

Get in the chair and try it out! Get in the body and try it out! Jump in. Explore! Those of you who feel that you spend 99% of your time out of your body, practice jumping in the top of your head. Imagine that you are liquid gold and that you're filling your body with your essence, feeling how comfortable it would be to have a home here, re-Sourcing, having money, having fulfilling work. Having the experience of belonging only happens when you're comfortable in your body. If there's a part of your body that's squeaky or asks for oil, give it oil. Give it the molten gold energy flowing in the top of your head and let your shoulders relax. Bring in this wonderful golden energy. Fill your ears with it. Fill your eyes with the molten gold if you don't like what your vision is doing. Connect with your gums and whatever else you want to support. Experience that you are the one that gives life to you!

This is where religion and the way of spiritual truth differ. Of course, you can ask God to help you. And yet, if you ask God to help you and do not help yourself, then you and God are separate. If you talk to God and help yourself, you are unified. Ask for information and guidance on the rest, and it becomes a Sourcing because you are the Source and you contain the Source. You speak to the Source, and you incorporate what the Source is. It's consolidation and the sense of feeling the union flowing from and to simultaneously. This is the secret of this model. Feel that. It's a completion.

When you want something you do not have, when you feel uncomfortable, there's not a completion because you haven't received. There hasn't been the validation to unify the experience. What we're suggesting is that it's "from and to" at the same moment, which completes the circle. You can do a lasso with it by bringing the energy of those points closer together. You experience that one supports the other so that you have a domino effect or an acceleration curve.

YOU ARE A CONTINUUM

You are bringing the time element and the continuum of union closer and closer together so that the experience of where it comes from and where it's going is the same. There's an acceleration powered by the result, which is powering the whole circle. Each of you is being powered by your comfortability—what it's like to be home in the body, home on the Earth, with the creatures, with your own design, and in oneness with all people. Being powered by your comfortability is to be co-creating as Gods and Goddesses and to feel the framing of this so that you open the dynamic to your own threshold of absoluteness.

It becomes a pendulum that moves in multi-dimensions. This is a way that you can focus for manifesting money, land, resources, health and memory. It's a way of manifesting your destiny, maintaining comfortability, and sharing resources with the universe. In many ways what you empower is the result of your total consciousness rather than an idea that you want this or that. When you do this experience from and to, and back and forth, so that you're going around the bottom and up to the top and around, the above and below become the same unified field.

What it changes are beliefs, limitations, thought processes and fear structures. Yet you haven't paid attention to any of those things because what's getting the oil is the comfort.

Expansion and validation and union get the oil. Everything else falls away and you don't pay any attention to it because it doesn't matter. When it doesn't matter, it doesn't have form anymore, so it's not associated with principles and experiences and habits that you learned as you were growing up. Because it doesn't matter, it has no energy, no form, no substance. The only thing that is being substantiated is the critical mass of the unified field that's created when you flip the below into the above and fill in the gaps, which creates the momentum, which keeps you going.

It becomes a continuum and you jump in just like you waited for the rope to turn when you were little. It's turning and turning and at that moment when you know you can step in there and the rope will go around you and contain you, you just jump in. The feeling of the physical body when that happens is that you have leaped from your normal conditioning to your natural state of being.

You will have found your way home, and you also will be present here and living in all dimensions comfortably. This process is one that is available to everyone without exception. You do not need to understand all the points before you begin. Many times people will stop doing something before they start because they're not sure how it's going to come out. So just jump in and feel it.

BEING FULLY PRESENT

If you are not present in the body, you will get mixed results. Make the commitment to be present in the body fully, or you will do what many people do when they meditate and use it as a way to leave. That is fine, and yet may not be your intention. It's about clarity, making choices, doing things fully instead of halfly, and understanding that if you do something halfly, that's the result you're going to get. There's no judgment; it is just a fact. If you do something starting out at 50 percent, you can expect to magnify the 50 percent. If you start out at 100 percent, you can expect to magnify the 100 percent.

Begin observing your patterns now, looking at where you're comfortable and where you're uncomfortable. Make a decision about that, stating, "I'm now choosing to be comfortable. I now move in a direction to sustain my presence fully, by choice." That adds up to, "I am responsive to everything that I create. If I am unresponsive, then my creative capacity diminishes. It doesn't have anything to do with anybody else. It has to do with me and my commitment to being."

When people say you create your own reality, it's about how present you are. If you're not present, something else is making decisions for you, and you are, in a sense, absent from that experience. Whatever's going on, if you're not comfortable with it, you weren't present when the decision was made.

Being fully present means being fully alive, a feeling that everything that has been ordained in your life has been chosen by you consciously. This means that you were fully present during that decision. You asked about it and you clarified it, whether it's with God, the Goddess, the Source, or whoever you may be in relationship with.

What's interesting about full presence is that you're the only one who can give it! It means a commitment to it. It doesn't necessarily mean that you think about it all the time or you're always pouring gold in the top of your head. It means that you make a commitment and are present to when you're non-present so that you can make that choice. It isn't to worry about. It's to commit to, and that's very different.

Chapter 6

Receiving Brings Us Back to Heart

Reception is being in a place where organically, etherically, and foundationally you are able to receive. To build a new foundation in a natural way in the world requires receiving and re-Sourcing from energy and from sources that are extraterrestrial, that is, outside the terrestrial body of Earth itself.

This means opening to be a conduit for the fields of energy which support the Earth and foundation creation, and yet are not of the Earth inherently. It is the experience of being open cellularly to have the energy of that which you wish to receive available for absorption. It is important to understand the way this works so that you can more easily facilitate the experience.

Reception is traditionally seen as feminine because it means holding a container and supporting the intention for union, and yet not doing anything about it, actively. It doesn't mean that you go out and build something. It means that you wait for that which is supportive to come into being. It is preparation and sustaining rather than activation.

As you see yourselves in total recall, information and energy come to you through your receptive modes—through seeing, feeling, and knowing that which is out of this realm—clairvoyance, clairsentience, and clairaudience. Your propensity to receive is completely balanced with how much you get.

Your ability to allow becomes sustainable. That means that you're not controlling it; you're not deciding about it. You're lying in wait for it to re-Source itself. That implies passivity, and yet it is not, because passivity would lie in wait with its antennae closed because there was noninvolvement. In our definition, passivity means noninvolvement. So you are not being passive, you are being receptive. That is a very important distinction, because lying in wait and allowing involves a state of excitation. As you're lying there waiting and are open to receive, all of your antennae are up. All of your conduits are available to run energy, and you're in communion with or communication with that which you are receiving from. So it means union again. It means merging again. "Allowing" in this instance means sustainable communication and orientation.

OSMOSIS—BEING SUNLIGHT ON WATER: AN EXERCISE

Prepare your body and psyche for the process of receiving this total recall. Open all the cells of your body as if they are pores in the skin. Imagine that the cell wall opens out and allows this exchange osmotically.

Open your field so that you don't have form anymore, you don't have edges. As you open, let go. You are becoming an oscillating field that looks like sunlight on water. As it moves out, breathe back in. When you breathe back in, imagine that all the cells of your body can receive total recall, that all the cells of your body are sparked, lying in wait to sustainably receive the energy and information that is available to you.

You actually energize your system from this very easy exercise. A consciousness is born about what's happening. You know what you're receiving because it has a velocity to it. It has an energy field. All these pieces provide you with an opportunity to receive the essence of your divinity.

Being in total recall is a divine gift that is your birthright. It is the place at which all things are understood. Understanding has to do with relationship so that all things relate one with the other sustainably.

It will also be a process which allows people to love each other in new ways, to sustain energy fields in new ways, and to provide for creation to be as important as manifestation. The model that is normal puts much more emphasis and value on what is created, what is done, and what is produced, than on what's received. That's how most people think about creation. Unless it produces something it has no value.

We have a society that has value placed on buildings, and on process, and not on heart, not on the things that are hard to measure, like love and sustainability. So it's easy to comprehend that because of its orientation, technology has moved us away from the heart. Receiving brings us back to heart. Receiving also provides an essential ingredient for consciousness because when one is receptive, one is open. The field is open. When the field is open, there are no barriers. There is no, "Well, I'm this, and then I die and I'm that," or, "I did that yesterday and I can't undo it," or, "I need to do this job because I can't survive if I don't."

Being open means that you are boundless and limitless, and each opportunity comes from the Source instead of from logic and mind. When you are open it means that you are re-Sourced. So if you lie around all day open and receive, you are energized. Your mode of operation will change from task orientation to creation. Everything you do fulfills you. Being receptive and open sustains the whole.

Because we are now co-creating a new model of fulfillment where all are fulfilled at once or none are fulfilled, it allows for new ways to create and new ways to synthesize consciousness. There is no restriction because you are re-Sourcing from everywhere.

This new model is synthesized through critical mass—the combination of all energies flowing toward the same point of realization simultaneously. Each soul may be in a different part of this flowing, of this wave, and yet the movement of the wave carries all forward at the same time.

Choosing to be open and receive greases the holographic wheel and spins your piece into the total equation so that more is created and more is viable. Your piece stimulates union, so more people meet more people and it's all a system. As you open and receive, the system grows.

Instead of lying awake all night and thinking that you've got something that's really important, and then talking to others about it and having them tell you it doesn't mean anything, when you lie awake all night and tell people something, it moves the whole model toward completion.

Each valuable piece you receive has a place to be put because the reception is authentic. Every time you open a window to the truth, the truth provides something to gratify the consciousness of the whole.

In other words, it's not ahead of its time anymore. We are all midwives of this new consciousness. The difference in terms of being receptive in the old model of the normal and being receptive in the new model of the natural, is that what one receives fits into the process of creation. It's rewarded, acclaimed, accorded, validated, and affirmed, not because your ego needs it, which is the old model, but because it is in symmetry with creation.

The exciting thing is that each of you participates by putting in a piece when it's needed, and it moves the whole into resolution, completion, and fulfillment. Adding your piece can also move creation to a new place which supports more creation and more sustainability.

As a child you wanted acknowledgment. If somebody had just acknowledged that you fell down and hurt yourself, or you did something very beautiful, or that you had the courage to laugh at something that hurt. If only someone had acknowledged that you are fundamentally a good person. If everyone who was a good person had been acknowledged for being a good person, there would be a lot more good people. If you could just watch and wait for someone to do a really good thing, and then say, "That's wonderful!" then people would be children from ages 0-99 or 199. If you were just there to say at that right moment, "Oh, yes, it was a good thing you did," acknowledging it would create more of those actions on the planet.

As you experience the receptivity of this exercise—opening all your cells and pores and letting yourself out, and then breathing in and receiving from all dimensions—you are acknowledged by those dimensions, and that acknowledgment seeds you. It turns you on. It plugs you in. It opens guidance points for you to orient with your truth, which provides a way for you to fulfill your destiny. This is the way creating will work from now on. It won't be that you do something and then people say, "Yep, that has real value. Now I wonder how you could do that and make money," or, "I wonder how we could get somebody to buy that from you so that you could produce more and make more money, or get more fame or success," or, "I wonder how we could duplicate this so that we could sell lots of copies."

The old, or normal, model says that whatever someone does that has value has to be marketable and to convince other people of its worth. The new model is sustainable. "All I want to do is contribute it. All I want to do is give it back to God, give it to the whole, give it to the experience of oneness." When it's given back to the beginning, it magnifies its outcome and multiplies the result.

This is why so many people are so enamored of service. When you do service you are contributing it, not necessarily valuing it. Service is the experience of absolute giving without expecting return. When one receives absolutely, without worrying about what one gets, it is service in the opposite side. It's receiving as service, rather than receiving as something that has to mean something so that you can have something as a result.

The way this works, the way it's natural, is that it was yours to begin with. It will always be yours and it's your divine right to have it, whatever it is—information, understanding, guidance, energy, resources, whatever. Everything that you now receive belongs to you already. You give everything that you are into the design. Then the design brings you back to receiving what you need to make it work. Sustainability happens when one is in absolute receptive mode because then one is receiving one's own essence and making it available to this dimension.

It's balance. Nobody can count anymore who did what for whom how many times. The tit-for-tat system that is normal becomes unnatural. You cannot give anything because it already belongs to whomever you're giving it to. You cannot really, in an essential sense, receive anything because you've already given it somewhere else, so you're just getting it back. It's balance in motion. You're receiving truth. The foundation of all receptivity is truth. The divinity of your essence as an individual is known and you are the same as the place you are receiving from. The truth is that it's all one.

Receiving is living oneness with no conditions upon it. Being in the oneness of truth means that there is no separation between any dimension with which one is communicating. We can make God and humanity synonymous, make them the same even though there seems to be divergence. If they are diverging, we can bring them together.

If there were a balance in each person's life between what they receive and what they give, oneness would not be a question on this planet. Violence would not be happening. There would not be the dissolution of all the things that are dissolving. What is making the models dissolve is that there is not enough or there is too much. The reception and the giving are out of balance.

Everybody knows everything is out of balance. Nobody knows what to do about it. Start receiving. The more you receive, the more you give. The more you give, the more there will be balance between what is being received and given. The more balance there is, the more there will be for the people that need it so that there is not fear of survival, the need for conquest, the need for power, the need for fame, the need for success. The balance will be felt. Opening to receive is a primary part of this time because it upsets the apple cart of the old model.

OPENING TO RECEIVE: AN EXERCISE

Structure receiving time into your daily schedule. If you can take one day a week and lie in bed and receive, that would be the optimal; one day a week where you just lie there and open your cells and let your physical form dissolve. Absorb like a sponge. Energy comes into the body, revitalizes you, hooks you up, and orients all your physical systems to receive. Every time you hook yourself up, you'll find that it's time well spent. Your circuits will be deep. Your thinking will be clear. Your heart will be open. Your soul will be present. All the systems of your body will be flowing as if there is one drum beat of order and truth—and light will flood your system.

There are many levels that want to communicate with you. In the receptive mode this is possible because it fosters a capacity to telepathically create connection with the invisible—and a lot is invisible. Orient your consciousness to support you from the sources in the universe that bring light, creation, and the sustainable. Those areas of consciousness, awareness, and practice are what you need to build strong bodies, clear intentions, and purposeful, fulfilling lives. Instead of going to school, reading books, or whatever it is, you say, "I'm going to a non-human level. I'm going to go to a level outside this density and vibration." It can be a hierarchical level, a celestial level, an angelic level, the God level or the Source, the Creation, the Goddess, the lineage, whatever you think of it as. It can be anything that you want it to be. You are moving out of density.

You're going to hear the angels talking in your ear, see them manifesting in front of your face, know why you met that certain person, and understand synchronicity and coincidence. The angels show you the design of the future and help you live it. They put the pieces together so that you take the next step.

You have etheric societies of guides on all dimensional levels that are here to support you. Talk to that guidance and find out who they are, what they're telling you about where you come from, rather than asking somebody human for that information. Make the links and bring the energy into your body. Honor the invisible and the inaudible, that which nobody else can hear. Honor the subtle, those knowings that come to you, the faces you see that aren't there in form. Open to see gnomes and fairies. Ask, receive. Belong to the universe of spirit, call forth and recall your intention and receive it in truth.

It's important to do this with non-expectation. This is because if you want to see a person or an object or something that looks like this, and has this kind of eyes, and is this color and this size, you're already defining it. Go there instead in a receptive mode. It's about being, more than it is about deciding what you think they're going to tell you, and what you're supposed to be communicating with, and what you've already had communication with. This is about a high level of intention that's pure. Go into reception with this affirmation: "I choose balance. I want to see as much with my non-physical eyes as I've seen with my physical eyes. I want to hear as much with my non-physical ears as I've ever heard with my physical ears. I want my heart to love that which I've never seen as much as I love what I have seen." Another way of saying it is, "What awaits me? As I open and explore the universe, what is there for me?" What is there is excitement. Excitement!

In each moment you have the opportunity to open to that which is, and yet in many instances has never been recorded or oriented in language before. You're going to get solutions, and acknowledgment will come to you from those around you. This is because you are providing miracles and magic.

You're going to speak with beings about such things as saving the planet—beings of truth that understand that there is order to all this. It isn't total disorder. This is about order—sustainable life. There's no panic in it. There's no "this is a lost cause" in it. You are talking to beings of integrity that consciously hold a position in the universe and are ready to share that position with those of you who approach this in the model of balance—that what you receive you will give. There are many, many beings all over the dimensional universe and in intergalactic spaces that want very much to get information into this place of Earth. And it comes from you and through you, into the world and back again, in the twinkling of an eye.

That's what sustainability means, and that's how receiving in this space of knowing works. Everyone, everything, every point of consciousness is the same. So we're back to the theme of oneness. We're back to the theme that there is no separation. You may not be able to distinguish at times who speaks to you, or whether they have a name, or if they want to give you that name, or if it's important. Whatever you receive will be your next point of application. Enter it with a blank mind, a blank screen, aware that you don't know anything about anything in your logical experience in proportion to what is. As you open to receive, you are linking into your greater psyche where you have a balanced position within the whole universe.

What comes for you will be whatever is regarded by the whole as the next point of your fulfillment. What is ordered and what greases the wheel of the hologram will be born. When you go into that space, it is with no expectation of result. It is with intention of service. Receiving is an honorable point at which you are served, and that service is then full circle. You are served and then you serve, and you are served again, and then you serve. It means you're useful, viable, important, dedicated, valuable, sustained, acknowledged, upheld, and nurtured. Approach it from the pure intention to serve the whole.

So lie there on your day off and receive. It will be like all your days are on because you will have a viable charge to work from. Every minute will be the experience of fitting your piece where it belongs into the whole. That is your yearning in fulfillment. It is the solace of knowing that you're in the right place for the right reason at the right time. As you go forward, you'll experience that everything is a means for expression, for joy, and for union. This is an absolute model of union, so it's perfect, it fits all the criteria. It's a way for you to get what you need in a way that serves everybody. That's what balance is about. In a linear model that's almost impossible. In a circular model, it is self-sustaining, self-perpetuating, and self-fulfilling.

It is feminine because it allows and because it does not control. All the facets of the system can support one another, which makes it co-creative. You are more than you were before, and all you give up is the form of the way in which you live it. What it gives you is the sense that your piece has more value than can be estimated, and so it provides you with the feeling of absolute peace. You are where you belong, and the system is working, and you're the reason why. And that's true for everybody. That's the beauty of the system.

Chapter 7

Guidance From All Worlds

As your soul comes toward the experience of life in this dimension, you attract to you energies from all dimensions, which will assist you in completing your task or design on Earth. Called guides, spiritual helpers, or the society of spirits, these dimensional energies live in the firmament and have attenuation to Earth—they attune their frequency to the experience of your particular destiny.

Your guardians come into being through your life and are connected to the world through your auric fields and through the soul's intention to vibrate at a certain rate of speed. Much of what you've chosen in terms of your design, your intention, and the experience you would like to fulfill in this dimension is supported by other dimensions that accompany you, which are invisible.

When you come into the body there are many other levels also committed to the same process that you're committed to. They establish themselves from different levels to bring together a multifaceted, multidisciplinary approach, so that you're not really alone, even though you might think you are. These guardian levels are affiliated with the intention of your life and come to serve the world as what might be called "adjuncts" to what you're doing individually. Many times when you get a thought and it seems to come from some part of you that is new or faintly familiar, these messages are being sent to you from these levels that accompany you.

You may get suggestions in your awareness, or see new pictures, or feel called to do something that seems out of context with your identity. They support you with a suggestion-box approach, so that your life has more options or available assets. Many times, as you develop relationship with your guardians, you'll receive suggestions and ideas that intensify your consciousness and help you serve what you chose to do before you came into this lifetime.

Your astral guides bring skills and connection to you from different lifetimes such as Lemurian, Mayan, Atlantean, Egyptian, Greek, or Roman. These are times when society pursued knowledge and developed skills which brought all dimensions into contact, literally fostering a sharing of the infinite, dimensional spaces of the firmaments between the Earth and her people. You may find that you are drawn into a quest for remembering and acknowledging your other points of reality, or lifetimes, to bring forth the knowledge you carry.

Particularly now, in this time when all the ages are manifesting together, the synthesis of this information is highly recommended. The pieces you fit together will help explain your yearnings and preferences in all areas of your human experience. They will fill in the blanks of your psyche to assist in understanding where you come from and what your easiest path will be. You can work with your guidance directly to synthesize your innate memory and knowledge and bring it into conscious awakening.

As you open to your spiritual and astral guidance, not only will you experience the reception of information and direction, you'll also find that tremendous input comes to you, helping you to respond to your senses rather than your logic.

As you listen to this guidance more and more, the voices get stronger within, as ideas or patterns emerging in your life. You will find these voices, thoughts, suggestions, and leanings move you away from your habitual, patterned life and conscious thought, into reception, remembering, and re-cognizing.

They encourage you to develop a relationship with the invisible. To do so requires an inner hearing, an inner responding, and a commitment to change your usual way of perceiving. For example, perhaps you are typing away at the computer, where you always put in an eight-hour day. You have committed to remember your path and develop your innate wisdom, and suddenly you have to get up from the computer. A voice inside you is saying, "Go for a walk."

So you start out and then get another subtle nudge which instructs you to sit under a tree that you are approaching. So you listen and sit down under the tree. The subtle nudge comes again with the instruction that you're going to become part of that tree. When you listen and respond to the inaudible voice or the inner awareness, you are given a gift, perhaps instruction, or a request to do something that will sharpen your skills or put ideas and energy into the experience of life for you. You may receive answers, or put together bits and pieces of information so that you understand a dynamic you have been searching for. You may receive a message from the rock or the tree or an element of nature—the fields of order. As you listen to the guidance, you have access to levels of reality that you've not yet consciously tapped.

You might have an astral guide named "Great Stone Man" from the American Indian, or "Alexander," the Greek teacher, or "Helena" from the Temple of Joy. Born with you into the astral as you are born into the physical, they come to help you with their particular knowings, writing, physical strength, or speaking with animals and dimensional beings. They may help you in ways such as doing ritual, contacting the great spirits, talking to the directions, or developing skills and doing tasks from the physical level.

These abilities are held in the psychic informational level in the astral experience. Astral guides have shapes, form, and names. You can address this level and call it out by saying, "I ask that my astral guidance be more present in my life. I ask that I experience the rhythms, cycles, and skills that I have maintained in other times or that want to be maintained through me in this time because I am now listening to those levels and committing to be a part of those levels."

As you create that dynamic you find that you are calling together all your forces. You can talk to the astral level and ask questions about your diet or health, things that you should be or could be eating to assist you, questions about the weather, or travel. These are wonderful questions for your astral guidance. You can ask their names, what their specific intention is and what their skills are, and how they can bring those skills to you. You can ask what the marriage of the intention and skills would bring out in you so that you find your missing pieces.

As these levels work with you, they are calling forth your plan and your blueprint because they are here to make the passage easier, to fill in the blanks, and to put the puzzle pieces into order. You'll feel something happening in your consciousness to provide a reality for you all the time, as if you can hear the heartbeat of the astrals, very present, and very close to this dimension.

The spiritual is more subtle than the astral. From all "time and space," aspects are called together to unify and come into this space with you so that the overall design of the hologram is seen in terms of spiritual relevance. You are shown what the impact of your future is going to be, or are assisted to see the design and put the pieces together to take steps for humanity.

The spiritual level is very connected to the outcome, to the overall design, and to the formula that you chose before you came into the body. Spirit is here to assist you in organizing all your capacities and living them, whereas the astral is specifically oriented to providing you with the more mundane process, skills, capacities, and tasks. These reference systems "fill out" your consciousness. It's as if when you are born a whole hierarchy is born with you. Whatever is to be actualized is coming with you. The levels open this commitment within their dimension, also.

Entities or spirits can come to you bringing knowledge, order, truth, the holographic design, the framework of what we call pre-knowledge, or the accordance of creation. Those people who are here to work with creation, and with the promise of archetypically creating designs here, usually have connections to guardianships in the Hierarchy (where we're speaking to you from). These beings of light many times have not been in the physical body. They accompany the journey so that the hierarchical consciousness can be contained in the experience of life, brought forward into this dominion, and married together.

Remember that when your guardians choose you, it is based solely on vibration. It's not based completely on what you've done before, or what you're going to do; it is a mixture. Many times you foster the guardianship so that you can have support and guidance. As you create a level of your own distinction—fostering your own informational data base about who you are and what you're doing and how that's structuring—the guardianship communicates, deepening its response.

This moves you toward more and more of a commitment to expressing that which has been held for you in the continuum, and which is now ready to be born in form. The guardians, through their intention and ability, give you information and suggest and express through you, communicating their dominion or dimension, and you are a conduit for that. That's why many times we will speak as if you are the expressive nature of our eyes, our ears, our hearts, our hands, and so forth. We suggest and sometimes charge you with the commitment to act as if you are our particular embodiment on the Earth plane, because we are unable to be there and do what you have chosen to do. There is a commitment by the light forces that they will not incarnate as such and will steadfastly hold a frame or container around your reality. As you live it and support it, you are framing it, almost as if your presence makes it possible for the light to be not only available, but actual.

Ultimately it is your commitment to the experience of life and your choice to help the design unfold that supports the universe, and vice versa. Your intent can affect creation itself. So it's a viable exchange system. The guardianship that comes and fosters the reality with you is very easily called back to this etheric dimension so that you are a conduit for the expression of that commitment on Earth.

You are making available the union of consciousness on this plane. Whatever you're doing and whatever you're relating to are often supported by the guardianship so that you're doing it not only for yourself, but for these other levels as well.

Many of you are here to call together the forces of light within your life. Your guardianship will show you that your experience is here and there simultaneously.

Sometimes astral guides communicate to lead you toward experiences and places which elicit memory and knowing. Sometimes you'll experience an urgency that you might question from your conscious mind and yet cannot be denied.

Perhaps you have to live on the ocean, or in the mountains, or fly airplanes, or deep sea dive, or work with children, or flower gardens, or read books, or write poems, or draw pictures, or cook food, or grow plants, have animals around, or communicate through hobbies. Many times these experiences come to you from the dimensions and call you to experience, unconsciously, something that you've always known was part of you. Sometimes the longings that draw you are to bring development of skills and abilities you have known and mastered in other lifetimes. Sometimes it is the natural development of your psychic abilities and inner awareness of different dimensions that brings you to the realization that you are "plugged in" somewhere.

You receive gifts and have assistance in nature, in creation, in maintaining order, or there's a foundation in you that's trying hard to substantiate new realities here. And you may ask yourself, "Where are they coming from? Why am I linked to the future rather than the past? Why am I interested in models about health rather than models about economy? Why am I looking for ways to make the world a safer place for the children, even if I don't have children, or don't like children?" Many times the commitments come to you from someplace else. You may not have been taught about these things, and yet they are a part of your reality, you seek them out, and you create a context through which they might work.

As you develop these areas of awareness, you may begin to receive assistance from the angelic realm. Angelic levels help with taking the next step through coincidence and synchronicity. The angels are here to help you live the design more fully. They put into your experience what you might miss otherwise. This is wonderfully intricate because they look at your design and see the person you need to meet next, what needs most to happen, the foundation that's going to provide the most interesting and most viable means for your growth and support, and then the magic begins to happen!

As you work with the angelic, pray to them and speak with them, you understand that everything in your life is being created from an intention that was made before you came. Yet you need sign posts and road maps, street signs, and posters with big red letters to help you understand, "What am I doing? Where am I going, and why?"

The angelic is that next-step finder. The angels coordinate people, places and facts to assist you. For example, they help you to choose books to read (many times a book will fall off the shelf in front of your feet and when you pick it up, it falls open to just the page and paragraph to help you with a current question, concern or need). Greatly acknowledging the presence of the angels, in gratitude, will elicit more direct communication and guidance to magically bring your design closer to your experience.

Information and guidance from the spiritual dimension are also available from your society of spirits. The spiritual society is comprised of light beings committed to your personal process. These beings are beams of light in your awareness, which change as you grow. They have affiliation with light, creation, and aspects of the greater universe. They link you etherically to the dimension of light beings who serve your consciousness. As your vibration shifts, these spiritual energies change dynamics. Your society of spirits is that which surrounds you most prominently all the time. They can be hierarchical or not, depending upon your intention and what your work is in the world.

You can look at what level of guidance you communicate with and how this relationship to the interdimensional serves you. You can see what is working in your life, what you want to make more comfortable, and what areas you'd like to put together differently.

Perhaps you are grounding and connecting to the Earth and to your skills, aware of what is available to you. Perhaps you'd like to receive some guidance about your experience here and how it will be lived. What is it that you've come to do? What are your next steps? What's your connection to those souls who surround you? What can you experience from the overall viewpoint which can see more than you can see? As you go to bed at night and when you awaken in the morning, you can call in your spiritual society and receive specific information about what your design says and how it can be accorded in this reality.

You can receive guidance on whatever level of the design you would like to work with. The astral level can give you information about the physical body, and the spiritual level works to attune that energy frequency so that it comes more deeply into the cells. If you're working with compassion, or the Absolute, freedom, forgiveness, union, or intention and affirmation, you'll want to include a spiritual dimension because those more universal concepts are part of the design and part of what is being resolved in the human experience. So the resolution process has to do with a spiritual connection or the spiritual design. The practical experience of learning and committing to unify with levels of the invisible on Earth connects you with devas, gnomes, and spirits more astrally, helping you develop skills of sensing, receiving, and visioning.

When you come down the tunnel and approach the canal of your mother just before birth, you absorb the frequencies of those parts of you, or parts of the universe that want to be expressed through you. Sometimes at that point, it is possible to connect with the thought-form energy of one or more of aspects of your total reality, or what we call simultaneous points of reality. These points of reality have lived before or are living in the future or in an alternate reality. Instead of thinking of just past lives, these points represent all of your reality throughout time. These points can be with you during your Earth journey as part of your energy field.

There can be from one to twelve thought forms with you, and at certain times during your life these thought forms will be triggered, giving you information and assisting you energetically to unify with that particular archetypical process, personality, or alternative identity. It is a gifting space, as it were.

If you have chosen to have thought forms accompany you in this lifetime, as you go through transformational experiences of initiation, particularly challenging times of physical danger, near death experience, extreme loss, etc., you are calling together these important pieces of information.

You may appear different after these experiences. Your vibration will be different, or perhaps you will have a different way of holding your body, or your face will change. You may have observed this in other people, and said, "That must have been a really powerful experience for them." Many times when you go into initiation, you change the frequency enough to embody another of your thought forms. You can actually carry them with you as an Indian life or Egyptian or Atlantean or future life.

People who do psychic readings can see these thought forms lined up behind you or around you. As your vibration attunes itself, the thought forms unify with you and are no longer distinct.

When you open up to all of these energies and thought forms, many memories come together. Parts of you are realigned and re-evaluated, because when you begin to take on these thought forms you expand your vibration and grow. You have more charisma, more energy, and more intention because you know more than you knew before. You are able to exist in more than one place at one time.

These thought forms receive information and understanding from many levels simultaneously, and as you experience those levels, you're also more committed to your responsiveness in the universe.

CONNECTING WITH YOUR GUIDANCE: AN EXERCISE

You can find your astral guidance in nature and your spiritual guidance in the realm of meditation. One way to work with the spiritual dimension is to close your eyes and feel your own vibration. Then imagine that you could take your vibration as if it were a pillar of light or a candle flame, and expand it out in every direction. As you expand that vibration, you touch dimensional levels of reality. Feel or see these levels, touch them. As you go out, they will become more palpable to you.

These levels of energy are as responsive to you as you are to them. If you create a commitment to connect in this way, then you can receive the vibration and information which help you take short-cuts in your evolution to see the design from a viewpoint you don't normally see. If you do not know how to work with the spiritual level, if you are taught to pray to a God above you that doesn't have intricate relationship with you, then you're not taught how these infinite levels respond to you and how they belong to you and are committed to your growth, expansion, and experience.

If you go once a day or so into that experience of sitting with your little flame in the center of your body, and then move that out, very, very slowly and gently to the sides of your body, you'll feel that you rub edges or touch the boundaries of those other parts of yourself that have a vibrational seam with you. There's a little seam between dimensions, and when you feel that seam, you say, "I'm moving into another paradigm. I'm moving into another nuance of response." You begin to listen more clearly, receive more fully, and you understand more dimensionally. This is because as the flame goes up the center, and you experience the truth of what you've come to honor, a foundation is built that is organizing that intention with you.

In doing this, you create the capacity to stay in communication all the time. You also begin get your own information.

You now can understand how these levels work, what they mean, and what they're doing. You feel more confident about your choices and the designs that are there for you. Your capabilities feel as if they've increased because you feel spirit as an inherent guidance system.

Having a name other than the spiritual society for the spiritual dimension is unnecessary because this level is light. It attunes with you more and more as you take your light out and experience that there are patterns and pathways around you. You find your own corridors of consciousness, and patterns in your life start to make sense. The power of this is important because it aligns you with the intention that you came to experience and shows you how to live it.

Acknowledging, according and validating are of phenomenal importance. Having a spiritual energetic pact with the consciousness of light that's ordained to assist you is a gift of the highest order. You feel that the intention of your life and the intention of your foundation are being called together so that you are able to respond. Whereas before you were trying to live your life, now you can respond to all of your dimensions.

It is time for you to honor that your commitment to being is specific, and that your level of reality is specific. You can get answers which apply 100% to wherever you are, and you can start doing that right now. The spiritual society is one entry point for calling forth your own knowing. To go to your own spiritual society, close your eyes and suggest that the answers are going to be there with you and that you're going to call them out.

The intention is that you begin it, and say "yes" to receiving, and that you are ready to explore those realities and how that level of consciousness is going to affect your experience. This is about always knowing where to go, where you are, why you're here, and what's going to transpire. Be in the awareness space. Sharpen your skills. Instead of sitting there saying, "Well, I don't really know," say, "I go to my awareness and spiritual guidance and ask for information to assist me."

If you're here from a hierarchical level, if your lineage is created from being an original soul, this means that you inherently have full memory that can be tapped at any moment. You have a direction which deals with the totality of humanity. You are not just here for personal experience. You can live your personal life but feel you must affect the outcome of the total paradigm of life, always looking at the bigger picture.

People who have this memory have the closest connection to the Monad—the creative force in the universe. And yet, even then, it is what they remember about the steadfast point of evolution, the Absolute, that is important. In evolution, souls who have moved further away from the original point do not have the same strength of memory. That's why original souls come to this planet to start with. They choose to seed the memory so that those who have either lost or diminished their memory can experience the memory again. They can be honored by one who brings pure intent.

Many of you will meet or be connected with original souls. Original souls draw people to them. They have an ability to make things happen, to see things other people don't see, and to be there first. They have an ability to contact consciousness and make it work for them. Sometimes they appear magical or miraculous. Many times they are teachers or people who share perceptions of different dimensions or invisible levels.

Original souls direct their life from the Hierarchy. They may have astral guidance and use their spiritual society as everyone else does, and yet their primary directive comes from the seeding place. These people are the first wave. They are out there seeding the world, creating the connections and the unification points that are necessary.

The people who come to be with them are the "army of consciousness." They are the ones who make sure things happen. They are the stable pieces in the puzzle which link the worlds together. Those who come to work more with the practical have the experience of living in the energy dynamic of consciousness. They put the practical pieces together, and have tapped the resources of the Earth, nature and humanity, and want to see those reaped, expanded, and proliferated. All of these levels work together.

That's why it's not better to be anybody other than yourself. As each of these pieces becomes available to you and you put them together, things start clearing up. There's much less jealousy and envy once people realize that they are as important as anyone else and that their piece of the puzzle will help the whole thing prosper. All the levels are necessary.

It behooves you to learn, "Who am I? What did I connect with? What are my guidance points? How does that differ from other people? What is it that I can understand and work with? How can I live who I am to the highest degree of my capacity? I'll stop wasting time working with things that I'm not really sure about, don't understand, and am not interested in. Let me develop that which is going to fully serve my own experience."

When you come down the birth tunnel you have all the paradigms set in place. Whenever you decide to awaken those levels, they are there. There's no need for you to do anything to make them come forward because they are part of you already. The more you develop all the parts of you, the more open, expanded, and wise you are.

The guidance begins assembling when you intend that it be so. These guidance points are pretty much silent until you ask for them to be verbal. They are available, and yet because of the free-will system it's important for you to ask for what you want.

Ask for who you want to talk to, ask for what you want to know. Go to levels where those awareness points are angelic, or have wings, or have consciousness of light, and say, "I want to know what we plan to do together. I want to know what skills you can help me with. I'm open to experiencing and perceiving from awareness much more deeply. I'm ready to acknowledge that I have lots of help and am going to use that help so that it is no longer out of the realm of my possibility to do magic, miracles, and whatever is in my design and pattern to accomplish."

If you're in a really difficult place and don't know what to do, many times there will be some event, situation, or process that brings you out of it or sheds light on it. Someone will cross your path at just that moment or speak to you in a certain way, or you'll see a sign of what's possible. The commitment is there even when you don't ask, and the signs are there if you choose to see them. The support is always there.

As you synthesize all levels, you become a very beautiful picture because there are no blanks in your aura, in your connection, or in your consciousness. It is rich and sustaining. The fundamental purpose of aligning with all these levels of guidance is to be who you really are, to open up to that full potential. It is also to use all of the dimensions that are coming together in union for yourself. As you do so, you stand as a guide for others.

The more unified your field is and the more the commitment is made to be with all of your parts, the more congruent, present, and powerful you will be in terms of living your spiritual force, your zeal, and your commitment to be what you chose before you came.

The levels of guidance respond significantly to you because they respond to gratitude, particularly the angelic realm. The more you initiate gratitude and communicate with them and are thankful, the more they will respond. The more you receive and respond to these levels, the more deeply the relationship develops so that you have a sense of belonging to all these levels simultaneously.

All these dimensions, as they communicate with you, foster a reality inside and outside that's consistent. No matter who you are with or what's going on, you have the sense of being an absolute being, receiving attention, information, and knowing that they all work to serve you. You are of more service to humanity at the same time. The circular process of serving and being served continues so that the more the service of consciousness affords you with a level of integration, the more that integration is available to the planet. And, of course, that's the design.

As these invisible levels come together for you, you'll have the vision, the skills, and the perspective that includes all dynamics—a synthesis. You have chosen this synthesis because you have chosen to be fully alive, living your full potential, in and with full awareness.

Remember! You chose to come, and you were chosen as a vehicle for the expression of all dimensions, so according your place in the unfolding makes it real and brings you fully into being.

Chapter 8

Accessing Your Akashic Record
Your Vibration is Your Library Card

We would like to tell you all that, as speckles of light and consciousness, you have come here from important processes of information, knowledge and wisdom. Your lights have come together from the integrity of what we call the records, and you are here to live and ordain these records into reality. These records are called Akashic. They are where the storage unit of consciousness is located, where all the pieces of the plan, the design have been articulated. They are available for your perusal at any time.

Your present vibration is the most important link because your vibration is what reflects the truth of what you have embodied and incorporated. That's why we say that you can have total recall. Total recall is the place where your foundation is laid in the structure of consciousness.

This time that you are living in is very important because it is the time of resolution. All the pieces that you've been carrying, and everything that you've learned and worked through and understood, can be used. This is why we call this time the Coming Together of the Ages.

Each of you has the capacity to synthesize everything that's on your record. You have the ability to frame those experiences differently than when you lived them before, which means that you can alter their vibration now. Creation can be manifested through intention because you can take those paradigms that you've already done and redo them. You can do them from a different vantage point, a different perceptual base, a different level of understanding, and from a different vibrational force field of unity if you choose to. You can bring together dynamics and coordinates that haven't touched before to enhance your assets and make them more available. You can organize your consciousness in any way you want without limit. You can design whatever outcome you want.

This means that you can take the karma that you have with someone and shift it. You can take what you would like to have done in a certain instance and make it happen. It's not that you decide, "I'm going to make up with Uncle Joe and go back to the time when I was five years old and dumped a bucket of water on his head. I won't dump that bucket of water on his head when I was five years old. I'll just walk by him and not do anything to him so that he'll like me. I'll change that karma now."

What we're talking about is your vibration. If you go into alternative realities, into parallel places, into the experiences of knowing your dimensional connection to someone else's soul, and reorder that union or connection vibrationally, you change your vibration. You are fostering resolution in your own circuits, clearing that experience, which opens you to dynamics which you may not have had before.

This gives you an opportunity to decide that you want to live from your total vibration so that you can get your design and manifest it into your life without delay. When you do that intending, and when you live from the vibration of your field as it would be aggregated in truth, your vibration of emotion and mind is clear, your body and spirit are unified, and you're grounding and saying, "Yes, this is who I am. I make the intention. Let it be." Then those circuits all get clear. Taking the bucket of water and dumping it over Uncle Joe ceases to have happened. Not because you go up to Uncle Joe and say, "Will you please forget that?" or you think about it and pray hard that he'll have a lapse of memory, or that you can somehow erase it off your karmic sheet.

You go into the experience of being absolutely pure and clear, with that pure intent, and as you experience your vibration, it is resolved. It is resolved through the circuits of the body and through the frequency it carries. That's why you start getting along with people, and things start moving easily. There are no more of edges, and life becomes much easier, because you are in the place where your potential and your actual are the same.

If your circuits are clear, through intention and grounding, and you open out, what you've designed begins to take hold. Your actual record, which is what your potential says, and your actual frequency, which is the now of your vibration, can be linked. These aspects come into unity for you.

If you take it as the gift, hold it, nurture it, sustain it, empower it, intention it, ground it through, drink it through, feel it in fluid and immerse yourself, you actualize the union of the two dimensions which are most profoundly available to humanity in terms of contribution and design.

The Akashic record comes into this dimension when you request to connect with your record. In the vibrational energy you're receiving from your record, you have access to more places in your psyche than you've ever had. You have the ability to read your record as if it were a forecast of information that says, "This happened yesterday, and that happened five years ago, or 50 million years ago. This is where I am now, and this is what's coming in the future." You see all of that simultaneously.

When you experience your own frequency, everything you've experienced that impacts this lifetime (which we call hinge-lives) will come back to you. When you say, "I'm in this vibration, I understand what that experience was about, I learned this, I contributed that," it is immediately sent into resolution, and your frequency accelerates. You can change the story line of your karma now, even though what you might be changing could have happened five or ten thousand years ago. Because of the simultaneity of reality, you can affect anything.

In the Akashic field is the Swing Between Worlds, an inter-dimensional space which shows you everything—all time, all truth, all dimensions. When you choose to come into a lifetime, there is opportunity to reflect not only upon what your capacity or occupation will be, but also where your opportunity will be fulfilled in terms of service and contribution to the whole.

As you go from the Swing Between Worlds and are born into your life, you are assisted at the critical moment when you need most to remember what you chose to do in the Swing. You are assisted to bring together those pieces that would serve the opportunity for you to remember and to orient vibrationally to that which provides the highest degree of unification and success in society. You're bringing all those points into a solution, into the fluids of the substance, where they can be lived.

Looking at it in the perspective of your whole lifetime, you will see that what happens to you, almost across the board, is a reorientation. Something very deep gets reoriented. The reorientation is to bring symmetry and balance to the levels, to ordain your consciousness so that you understand you have been called on and awakened. Something has transpired which allows you to know your importance to the design. There is a collaborative effort to assist you in whatever part in that design you have to play. The millions of pieces are woven into a pattern so that when they're presented, the right bells go off.

SHAPE-SHIFTING REALITY

We talk a lot about changing your reality, and that you are responsive to—able to respond to—creating that reality. In certain instances you can decide what reality you want people to remember about you, decide how you want to be understood by others, and realize that because you can create your own reality, whatever you intend, is.

For example, perhaps you give a lecture on Sunday morning, and when you are finished with the lecture you think, "I left this part out, or I stumbled over that word, or I didn't like the way I said this, or my facial expressions at this particular time might have been inappropriate with what I was saying, or I'd like to refresh the memory of the people about something that I briefly mentioned but was really important." Let's say you finished the lecture an hour ago. You're thinking, "I wish I'd done this." Do it again in your head and send it back into the lecture framework. In other words, imagine that you're standing there again and talking to the group. The group is hearing what you wanted to say. Set it like gelatin in a mold. "This is the way I want it to be remembered." If you do that within a twenty-four hour period, the people will remember it as if it had happened during the actual lecture.

You can use your consciousness to direct energy so that you establish the kind of relationship with your being and your abilities that reflects your intention to be known and understood. Regardless of what time it is, and how time is moving forward or backward, you can insert whatever you want into that time. If you have a conversation with someone and don't like the way it went, go back in and say, "This is who I really am. This is what it was really about. I just want you to remember that this part of my essence is also present, even though it might have been played down, or it might be different than you experienced it. I might not have given myself permission to be who I really am, and I want to send that essence to you. I want you to receive it." As long as you do it within a twenty-four hour period, it will be incorporated.

You're learning in terms of vibration and intention, that you can shape-shift your reality. You can move wherever you want and decide how you want the vibration to be received by others. You can decide where you want your focus to be and how you want your energy to be received. You can change your mind and create it differently. This is because when you learn, you do something at a different level than you did it before. You learned as you gave that speech, so after you did the learning you said, "If I'd done this, it would have jelled better," so you go back and do it that way. You can only do something at any one moment based on the knowledge of that moment.

If you have the ability to look retrospectively at something, why not have the capacity to enhance it so that it reflects more truth? It only works to support truth. It doesn't work to support falsehood. You can't go back and say, "I'm going to take that out even though it's true, because now that I've said it, that means I have to do what I said." That would not work. But if you're adding more value, adding more truth to it, then the consciousness is going to reflect a higher level of learning and growth. That's systems theory.

You have opportunities to adjust the realities of your present situation within twenty-four hours. You can also connect with your record, use your own library card, get out your own experience, and begin to look through it at those experiences you're working at in your life. You can get more information.

We say often that this is the time of resolution. For it to be the time of resolution, you need to know what to let go of in order to move to a place of union. This means that the Akashic records are more and more accessible to you so that you know the how and the why of your design.

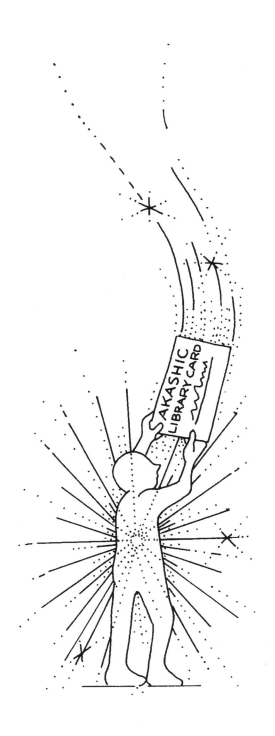

THE AKASHIC RECORDS

The Akashic records can be accessed in front of you, in the same place that the hologram is located—at twelve o'clock, about two to three feet above your third eye area. No matter what direction you're facing, the Akashic records and the hologram are always in front of you at that twelve o'clock point.

You have opportunities individually and collectively, to go to the record, use your library card and find out everything about a person, about a part of your personality, about lifetimes you had, whatever. When you go into the Akashic record and use your library card, you have to present identification. Your identification is your vibration, so you must present your vibration to the Akashic records. You cannot present your brain, your mind, your thought, your yearning, or your emotion. You must present your vibration.

GOING TO THE AKASHIC RECORDS: AN EXERCISE

In a quiet and supportive environment, close your eyes and breathe deeply, clearing your mind and relaxing your body. Ask to go to the records. In your mind's eye feel, sense, or see yourself walking up to and knocking on the door to the Akashic library in the sky. Say, "Knock, knock, this is my vibration. I choose to know everything about _____, _____, _____." When you say that, doorways open for you. There is a panoramic view of the universe. You see the scrolls and books which record everything. There are myriads of file folders and index cards. But rather than giving you the scroll or the book, they only give you back the actual energetic experience of who you are in reference to what you ask about.

It is like a research project because you're not going to get all of it at the same time, and you can understand why. You get what you ask for. You can go back as many times as you want, develop the theme, work it out, and ask about anything that you want to ask about, once you've given your vibration. You can learn about cultures that have effectively dealt with some of the phenomena that would now be helpful for your society—Lemuria, Atlantis, the Mayan cultures, Roman or Egyptian cultures. If you want to understand and learn, you can ask about certain subjects.

When you present your vibration, you get back what your vibration would resonate with in terms of that experience. You're presented with your next step because that's really why you're going there. As you're presented with your next step, you find out why you asked that question. Whatever question you're asking, the answer was calling you to it. What you need to finish off this round is what it gives you, to answer the question in your head.

All of this is happening etherically and energetically. You are finding out where you are, where your psyche is, and what's important—what's valuable for you to invest in, open out to, and ordain in your life. These awarenesses are given to you so that you have the opportunity to explore your own divinity through time and space. It's going to be the wildest trip you ever take because it's like exploring all the outer space themes that you've ever seen on the science fiction channel.

It opens out to a dimension that is familiar, ancient, futuristic, at times dogmatic and at times creative. At times it's sustaining and at times releasing. Every time you go and present your vibration as your library card, you receive a blip of consciousness. What you get is what you need. Going to the record is authentic and valuable because immediately you start getting it.

In the chapter that talks about pure intent, you will read about how to look at your back to see who you are and what you're missing, the part of you that you cannot see, the part that eludes you. This is the human struggle. What am I not getting? It pertains to denial and repression, because the psyche believes that if it knew everything it would be ashamed, embarrassed, possibly incarcerated because of the consciousness that evolved through humanity's journey. Many of the things that occurred were, if seen out of context, creating large amounts of separation.

When you go to the Akashic records you get the "why." Information, images, and the feeling of being there is panoramic. It's huge and all around you. You can feel the motion of it because it's your being unfolding. "Why did I do it that way? Why did it happen at all? Why were we together? Why are we apart? Why?" It's like the questions that children are always asking. Nothing seems as if it is in context because so much information is missing. You have the divine right to know everything that you can know, at any moment, because it is your life, your process, your universe.

Through eons of time there has been amnesia. Huge chunks of information are no longer available to humanity. It's not good or bad, and yet it requires you to unify your consciousness without all the pieces present. And that's challenging.

So, take a daily, weekly, monthly, yearly trip to the Akashic records—whatever strikes your fancy—present your vibration, and say, "I am here for the purpose of remembering why." That's all you need to do.

The part of you that is asking the question, that is wanting information on XYZ will ask the question, and then the librarian will go and find the next step for you. The knowledge will come in and diffuse throughout your body. You're just going to sit and receive and feel the experience of the why and the clarification happening all around you.

What does that do? It alters your vibration. The next time you go back you won't get that step because it has already been ingrained in your consciousness. Your vibration will be enhanced by it so that when you go back, you get the next step. On a cellular basis, when you get that charge, that ray of consciousness is sent to you. It will accelerate your vibration to the next level. Every time you go back you go to get the step that's going to take you further.

Knowing why is very important because if you know why from a design level, everything gets clear. That's where forgiveness comes in, resolution, understanding, balance. You no longer have a charge on what didn't work. You have a charge on why it happened and what's been resolved, and how you've gone on from there. It's a great way to resolve relationship, particularly long-term ones that you've been doing for thousands of years, those patterns you've lived with people which aren't yet clear. Why are you still doing the same pattern? What didn't you learn?

It's also effective for questions about health: "I realize that every single lifetime I have this or that, or this happens to me, or I always pick parents who are sick, or parents who do this or that or the other thing. Why do I do that?" This level of understanding opens you to the design, assisting you to recognize that there's no blame, no real right or wrong.

This is about recognizing how creation designs a framework that starts off in union, ends up in dichotomy and polarity, and then results in the optimal resolution of oneness. What you're working with in this time is to understand everything as quickly as possible. When you do this process and show up with your vibration, you get accorded by the Absolute space that contains and holds steady the wisdom of the universe.

You're getting information and accelerating your circuitry. You're getting a beautiful level of validation from the universe. It's going to shift you from whatever consciousness level you're on to the deepest consciousness level available for you at that time. It's going to support that next step for you so that you become familiar enough with it to say, "This feels like exactly what I needed to find out," even though it might take you deeper into the experience than you had anticipated. It's okay because it's made to order.

As you make the time to explore your totality, very interesting things begin to happen. One of those things is that, after a while, you get free access to the Akashic records. This means that when you show your vibration enough, it's like going by a gatekeeper who can identify you, knows your vehicle, what make and year you are, and everything else. Whoosh! You can just whisk by. "If you'd like to go into the top secret files, go right ahead. It's okay, you have clearance. You've been here enough times."

That starts to happen after a bit. This will vary with each of you depending on many circumstances—your history or herstory, your karma, the amount of times you've been to the records, how deeply you live your vibration on the planet, how you understand and implement your design, and so forth. Mostly it depends on pure intent. If you have absolute pure intent, the Akashic records are open to you without limitation. It's a big deal, for it was not always so. It means that you now have access from that pureness of intent to what needs to be made known to humanity.

At the moment you make the decision to begin, you are on a circular frame that brings you everything you need. As you have access to the information, you can learn how it was all constructed, how everything is made, what it's about, what its function is.

This is a very exciting time for humanity because just having pureness of intent opens up all the secrets of the universe to you. Up to this point, the knowledge and wisdom have not been created on Earth in a way that could be assimilated because it might have been synthesized dogmatically into a linear way of thinking.

Now that we have the opportunity to keep truth as truth, and there are enough people on the planet who know how to do that—how to hold pure vibration through pure intent—there's an opportunity for as many of you as choose to, to explore not only your record, but the record of how it came about and what it is moving toward. Go into the hologram of the large design. Look at it, see your part, see the part of everybody around you, and see how things are going to happen.

It's bringing the future into the present and also looking at what you designed in the past. If you don't grasp the principles of how the past and the future can be the same point, and how you can be in now and in both of them, that's okay. Just know that if you have pure intent and sit in your vibration for a few seconds so that you feel it, then you can fly up to that circle at twelve o'clock in front of you, and say, "Knock, knock, knock. I'm here. This is my intention. I want to feel this now. I want to live this now. I'm tired of being blind and deaf and out of sacredness and out of kilter. I want to live the resonance of whatever is my next step."

FINDING YOURSELF

It's interesting to think about the fact that in your society you go to somebody else to find out what's going on with you. You do that from the time you're very tiny, whether it's to figure out whether you're doing something right or wrong, what you should eat or drink, what you should be saying, what you should not be saying, and on and on. Why do you go to somebody else for the answers?

You do not see the part of yourself that you're asking about because it's between your shoulder blades, in the back. That's the part you want to look at. That's where your wings attach. If you can't see that your wings are attached, you forget that you are a holy spirit. You forget that you're a divine essence of light, and you say, "Since I don't know very much about being a human being, even if I've been around the block a lot, I have to go to somebody to make sense of my life for me. I have to ask them what's going on because I certainly don't get it." And then you find out that they don't get it either, that they are also going to somebody else to find out what's going on in their life.

We're saying to you that it's time for that dogmatic structure of unknowing to stop and for each of you to take the bull by the horns. So you say, "I'm going to the Source to find out. I want the non-biased, impartial, nonjudgmental, absolute truth about who I am. Why wouldn't I go there? It isn't in any way shadowed by someone else's perception of me, what my mother told someone about me, or what my blood test told them about my body. This is about my essence. This is about what is really going on, and why. I've wanted to know why since I was two years old. Now I'm going to find out."

By making a clear intention to recognize your truth and experience it, you bring it into your consciousness. You are aware. You are in relationship with yourself for the first time in as long as you can remember. When you're in relationship with yourself, some important dynamics change. One is that you are able to be in relationship with someone else for the first time, truly, because you understand how to relate to yourself. You understand why you are the way you are. You don't have to make excuses or decide that something was left out when everybody else got what they needed. There's nothing you're failing at. You're fully present, knowing why, understanding who you are.

Another dynamic that changes is that you have no guilt about anything. You have no separation about anything because you're getting it all, you're understanding why, and you don't need to separate anymore. No matter what's going on around you, you're able to see it clearly, you're able to understand. "This is happening for a reason. I can find out why. I don't have to react to it, I don't have to get depressed by it. I don't have to be saddened by it. I can just go up to the record and say, 'Let me see what's really going on here.'"

You see reality on such a level that illusion dissipates. There's nothing to worry about. Everything comes together. Consciousness shows itself to you so that you feel as if you are on the inside track of creation.

After a bit of time there are no more questions because you are living in the answers. You're feeling support. You understand how the universe works and what its intention is for you. Not only is that profound and meaningful, but it also brings a great deal of solace to you because the peace that is making its way into the pattern of your life is because everything is resolved. There aren't any more questions. At that moment you are a creator.

Chapter 9

Unifying Your Energy Fields

When you are looking for a relationship, a place to settle down, a job that is amenable, and friends who share your interests, this is based on how many of your circuits are compatible with the fields that you encounter. Your compatibility with anything has to do with the amount of frequency you have in common. If something comes together and feels like it's matching, it's because you're vibrating at the same rate of speed. You're creating a consistent wave frame and not hitting against each other's waves.

An example of hitting against another's wave is the concept of people having chips on their shoulders. When people learn, there are certain areas of density in the body which reflect that learning. The shoulders are one of the most prominent areas. When people walk around in a room full of people, their shoulders "hit" each other. In other words, they don't feel compatible with the other person. This is an opportunity for you to be teachers for each other.

UNDERSTANDING YOUR FIELD OF ENERGY

Understanding your field of energy is one of your most valuable assets because energy is everything. When you discern your field of energy and know what it's doing, you can master your life, captain your ship. You experience order and truth. Honoring, opening, receiving, and aligning your circuits is very important. By grounding them and experiencing your own mastery, you feel equilibrium. All of that makes up a wave frame—that is, how you think, what you do, how much you respond to telepathy and mental intuition, the experience of receiving, the experience of communicating, connecting, and grounding. These are the determining points which reflect the total field of energy.

If you are not grounding, your energy is usually perceived from your waist up. If you're grounding and not receiving, it is usually from your waist down. If you think a lot and do not speak, there will be energy flows which come into the head and have no place to go, if you're not expressing them. If you're using the center of zeal at the back of the neck—which unleashes your spiritual force—you will find that tension is eased in your shoulders, and creation moves through your body.

The channels at the top of your head come into the center of zeal and are transformed into expression, which means that they are spoken, breathed into the body, or used by the arms, fingers, and hands through writing, drawing, sculpting, or painting. If you dance and move that energy of the zeal through the body, it grounds into the feet and you will procreate and co-create more easily. The objective of this particular process is to be consciously aware of your energy patterns, how they foster growth and expansion, or keep you constricted in the body—keep you held back.

The wave frame is always touching something else. For example, your etheric field of energy goes out in a twelve foot circle around you all the time. When you sit in a room with other people, you experience your spiritual level connected to theirs. That's why, when you walk into a situation like a bar or someplace where there are mixed energies, you might want to leave. The energies mix and match with each other and sometimes cause confusion because of cross purposes or underlying currents such as expectations, judgments, etc. The field of energy will be incongruent.

When you walk into a situation where a group is praying, the energy will very likely be congruent. People pray together and meditate together, or experience alpha together because the easiest way to pick up a wave and feel harmonious is to be in the spiritual energy of people who are together in a way that is non-mental. When you have spiritual and mental aspects mixed together— for example, a group with a spiritual intention that holding a meeting to make a decision about something, and you walk into the room. You may feel the energies as vibrationally incompatible. The energy could become compatible through holding hands and praying, meditating, grounding, or being quiet for a minute.

Once you refine the circuits, any level of incompatibility or incongruence will give you a strong readout. As you practice unifying your circuits, you also learn to discern what the circuits are telling you. In other words, as you refine the circuits, it gets easier to maintain them.

It gets much easier to choose ahead of time where you want to be and who you want to be with. You can go through the experience energetically and decide if it is for your highest good. You can actually make a short-cut in areas like relationship and choices for work. You can align what the outcome looks like it might be with your frequency and your calling and see how it feels. Does it resonate in the field of your own wave? If it doesn't, you know ahead of time that it is not for you. Your awareness of your vibrational situation can give you valuable precognitive experience before you initiate physical action. That is to say that much of the processing you will do will be ethereal, visual, sensate, and much less physical.

YOUR RAINBOW BODY

The physical organism is a multi-faceted energetic system which responds and communicates through vibration. It is possible to access your present state of balance by viewing the energetic system of your body and sensing where the energy is most predominant or most absent. This can be accomplished through the use of vibration, sound, and music. For example, the human energy system is comprised of seven major wheels of energy, or chakras. The following is one system of chakra philosophy.

The Root Chakra

Drumbeats, cricket sounds, night sounds, the color red, and the key of C are associated with the root chakra area. The place of red is the area of nature, passion, anger, physical responsiveness, the genital area of sexual interaction, and pro-creation. Having a spiritual idea or creative energy manifests most directly when it is brought as energy down through the energy centers and unified at the base chakra or root area. The root is your gateway to doing anything in the physical.

The Spleen Chakra

The sound of flutes and wind instruments, the color orange, and the key of D are associated with the spleen chakra. This is the center of assimilation, what goes in and what comes out, on

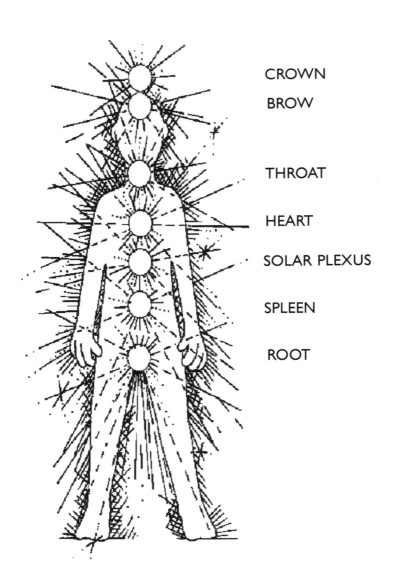

CROWN

BROW

THROAT

HEART

SOLAR PLEXUS

SPLEEN

ROOT

all levels. The spleen is the center of balance and purification. The wave frame of the spleen is associated with people who are socially active and helpful. Social workers are an example. Sometimes those centered only in the spleen are afraid they won't have enough (food, money, job, relationship, acknowledgment, etc.). The spleen area is also associated with those looking to gain knowledge and produce results so they can balance their wisdom with their actions.

The Solar Plexus

In the center of the body, in the solar plexus center, the vibration is tuned to the key of E. The sound of the piano and harp activate this center, as does the color yellow. Here is where the mitochondria of the whole being are located—the power center for self-actualization and fulfilling the potential—the power to be who you are. All memory, conscious and unconscious, is stored in this plexus. Coordinating the sounds, the color, and the vibration stimulates innate memory and releases fears and constrictions about demonstrating one's power (self-actualization). The solar plexus is the lowest point in the sacred space and provides the foundation for living one's calling in the world.

The Soul Space

The soul is the center point of the sacred space and is sometimes called the Source chakra, although it is not traditionally associated with the seven major chakras. The soul area is under the xiphoid process where the ribs come together, is a luminescent pink color, and has a resonant field that is absolute union. Focusing attention here stimulates the emergence of order, concentricity, and the activation of the design or blueprint of your life's work.

The Heart Chakra

The heart chakra is the uppermost point of the sacred space and calls you to temper the vibration and sound of your being through love. It vibrates with the key of F. It responds to and emanates a green color and deals with practically anything green—healing, plants, money, etc. The heart is the meeting place of the above and the below and fosters a union between dimensions. The sound of the heart is bells.

The Throat Chakra

The throat chakra is associated with speech and expression. It vibrates to the key of G and the color of light blue. The throat is where the unconscious and the conscious mind are brought together. Questions associated with the throat are: "Do I speak all the time? Can I sit in silence with others? Do I always talk about ideas? Is there something that needs to be expressed? Am I always trying to bring what I don't know about myself from the inside, out? Can I be in a space with sound, perhaps music, and not necessarily need to express? Am I the opposite of that? Do I have lots and lots that I never express? Am I afraid to express from or speak about my zeal, my spiritual purpose? Am I always sitting in silence because this area doesn't feel powerful enough or real enough to me?" The throat center powers the communion between what you are and your expression of that in the world. The throat responds to the sound of the wind and the rushing of air, which opens and balances the throat area.

The Third Eye Chakra

The indigo of the brow chakra responds to the key of A and the sound of streams, showers, and rushing waters, which balances and stimulates this center of vision and knowing. This is the psychic center where all things exist throughout time and space. To open the third eye brings sight of the invisible and signals the etheric to ground truth into form. The third eye is connected with practical and cosmic understanding. The grounding process we so strongly recommend stimulates this center, providing understanding between the above and the below.

The Crown Chakra

The key of B and the sound of silence draw you into the cosmic consciousness of the crown chakra. This is the place of all color, ultraviolet, or no color; the place of all sound and no sound; the place of no-thing; union beyond words.

It is very important to discern, without judgment, "Where am I, and what's happening?" Go up the scale of your chakra system, starting at the root. Play or listen to music and other sounds that pertain to the chakras and open those centers that you realize are in some way dampened down. For you to be in a wave frame of a unified field, all of the centers need to be open at the same rate, zinging with energy.

Using music and sounds appropriate to a particular chakra, feel it vibrate and open. We recommend that you listen to Steven Halpern's *Spectrum Suite* because every key note is played in succession. If you listen to that particular recording, you can feel the centers opening up in your body.

As you go up the scale, up the rainbow in your body, up in sound from drumbeats to silence, what can you understand about yourself? What colors are you drawn to? What are you working through in this lifetime? What sounds, notes, and keys resonate with you? Where do you want to be? High in the mountains or in the desert? On the sea or under the sea?

Where do your ideas germinate? Are you creating a reality consistent with the force field of energy that's coming into your planet, or are you learning about it from other people? What kind of people are you drawn to? Ask yourself, "Am I drawn to people who read books so I can sit and talk about other people's ideas? Or am I drawn to people who are visioning on their own? Where am I in my own advancement and evolution? Where am I in my own body?" When you start to put the pieces of your vibration together, you can figure out, "Where do I come from? What am I learning? What's my purpose? How does it feel to be with certain kinds of people? Do I want to be with people I'm like, or do I want to be with people who work from different energy centers and align differently with their consciousness? What feels comfortable?"

ALIGNING YOUR ENERGY BODY: AN EXERCISE

Take some time and go through the different parts of your body. Listen to music that lends itself to a certain chakra or area of energy, and fill your body with light. Experience the flow of union throughout. After you've done that you'll know what to concentrate on. You can see how your actions and intentions create certain experiences; you will understand what irritates you or find those things that are your red flags. When a red flag happens, you can ask, "Where's my energy? What's my choice? What's my intention? How can I balance that and feel the flow of union through my being?"

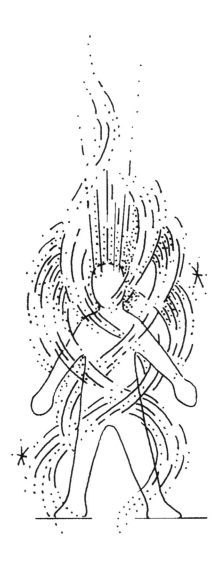

The objective is to feel that you are orchestrating this design so that all the pieces fit together.

As you think about your being, are you in your feet? Are you in your lower body? Are you in your upper body more of the time? Where does your energy pool or constrict, expand or flow? How might you arrange your field of energy so that the above and below in your body are consistent? Accessing your energy flow is the first step.

The second step is to open the top of your head, imagine that you are a wave frame of energy, and that you don't have a body. You're like sunlight oscillating on water. Imagine that from the top of your head to the bottoms of your feet you are moving the sunlight. Energy is flowing through you beautifully as if you're standing under a shower. When you do this exercise, the field of union shows you a movement of energy around a particular location. It might be your eyes, your ears, your third eye, your throat, your heart area, your left hip area, or your right knee.

All of your patterns and those things you analyze are indications of what's happening in your energetic field. So think about everything in terms of the field rather than in terms of personality, good or bad, or, "I'm spending too much time in my head. What does that mean to me? What am I avoiding?" Just focus on where in the energy field the pattern of energy does or does not flow. Where does it flow best and why? Observe, then use the energy of your predominant centers to support those areas which feel depleted or constricted.

If you take everything to the level of energy, it's much easier to understand and activate it so that it becomes balanced. That's the objective of reflexology, polarity and other therapies. Having the energy flow in the left and right side of the body equally, and having all the chakras open at the same rate of speed and oscillation allows for the physical, emotional, mental, and spiritual bodies to vibrate at the same rate of speed.

All of this is your pathway to mastery. It is the process that will allow union between peoples. The body is the foundation and home for all the processes we've talked about. It's where you carry and emanate your light, where you receive your experience and oscillate your frequency. When all parts of you are firmly connected, you are a system that supports itself.

BALANCING THE CHAKRAS: AN EXERCISE

Once you have brought the shower of light and energy in the top of your head and gently touched all the parts of your body, focus your attention on the root chakra. See the diagram for locations of the chakras, or energy wheels. Focusing on the root chakra, imagine a red rose bud in the center of the chakra. As you send energy and attention to that place, the red rose bud begins opening. This is a way to open the chakra easily at your own pace and to feel the energy being released into your whole system.

Remember the attributes of each chakra as you open it. You can create affirmations which will align your intention with your physical energy. Open the energy of the root in a counter-clockwise direction because you are gathering energy into the body here. When the rose bud opens fully, move the energy to the next center, the spleen, in a smooth visual motion like you are painting with a wide hand-movement. Here the rose bud is orange, and the motion of energy is sending out, so it is clockwise.

Every chakra has its own color and goes from counter-clockwise in the root to clockwise in the spleen to counter-clockwise in the solar plexus to clockwise in the heart, etc. The Source chakra is opened after the seven major chakras and so is not included in this diagram. It is not opened in a clockwise or counter-clockwise motion.

When you have opened the crown chakra you can open out to the infinite. This a wonderful time to travel to the Akashic records, or do Silver Chalice work, make intentions, or go into substance. You can then bring the energy of the infinite into the matrix in the center of the body and tap the soul space, ask for your blueprint to manifest, or spend time in the soul gathering the fullness of your essence.

We strongly recommend that you ground to complete your visualization or meditation. You can do this by bringing the shower of light into the top of your head. If you are meditating inside, you can go outdoors and stand on the earth, bringing the light through the crown chakra in the top of the head, down through the root center, and out the bottoms of the feet. This balances and closes the chakras so that you are open to both earth and spirit and thus maintain a congruent energy field in the world. This smooths your edges, balances your thought with knowing, and tempers any areas of expectation, belief, or fear.

When you come into contact with someone else, you will find that your wave frames are matching or not matching, or only a certain percentage is matching. This is how you decide whether or not you stay in a particular situation or relationship. If the wave frames don't match, you may find that you want to retreat or withdraw your field, regroup it, and approach that energy differently. You stay open and decide how you want to approach them. You do not have to send your wave frame in and keep it there if you're uncomfortable. Comfortability, as we have said, is a strong indication of how you can monitor your own level of resonance.

Many times you will go into a situation and be completely open and experience being with others who are only partially open, who have expectations of you, demand something of you, or whose realities are different from yours. Again, it isn't a judgment, it is comfortability. You say, "I do or do not want to participate 100% in what's happening here. I'm going to stay open and in a unified field, yet, as I approach new situations and go into new groups, I am comfortable with my own field. I choose to feel this comfort in reference to others."

An exercise to foster energetic integration is to pick a partner with the mutual intention that you will work together to understand your individual wave fields—to understand the way you resonate in the world. You want to know what feeds you from the world.

Of course we're all being fed from the substance of the infinite, and yet, in this exercise, you want to determine how your energy field relates to the experience of the physical—from people, to plants, to nature, to the sky, to underground mines, wells, aquifers, everything. What is your orientation with the Earth? In this exercise you're responding to the way your innateness manifests in your physical circuitry.

There are certain foods you like, certain colors, shades and resonances that are important for you, certain kinds of people that you gravitate toward, certain kinds of music and books. All of this can help you identify your wave frequency. Each of those items we've mentioned can be put together according to vibration so that you develop a picture of your responsiveness.

You and your partner decide that you're going to take your energy fields apart so that as you foster your own understanding you can reflect on it with someone else who has that understanding about themselves. Pick a neutral person to start with (it's much easier than picking someone you are already in relationship with), so that you have no axes to grind and nothing to expect—but rather to learn and discern how it works.

TRY THIS!

1. Begin with an intention to be freely present, open to your partner, and receptive to any awareness that surfaces.

2. Sit across from each other or stand, whichever feels the easiest for energy flow and observation. Hold hands or not, practice with eyes open or closed, have

silence and then feedback or dialogue, whatever unfolds. Part of the comfort you have with each other will determine which physical positions are most appropriate for you at each moment. If your comfort level changes, be ready to discern why that happened and what message it brings you or your partner.

Your objective is to witness for each other and to understand:

- how you each communicate without words;
- how you each receive communication energetically;
- what creates comfort and/or discomfort in you.

When you've balanced all your energy centers, say to your partner, "What are you feeling from me? How does my energy come across to you? Is there anything in it that feels incompatible for you? Are you receiving all of my centers equally? Am I opening my field so that you can receive me easily? Are you receiving me and realizing that there is no demand? Is there something being communicated that I'm not aware of?"

These questions ask for honest feedback about what's consistent and inconsistent in the field.

Opportunities may arise to practice with people. You might ask, "Can you sit down with me and do this exercise? I can explain it to you easily. I've always felt comfortable with you, but I don't know why." People will come together and say, "I want to be with you a lot, and there's so much compatibility. Where does that come from?" This is an opportunity to understand your process energetically and satiate your mind with the experience so that it is impressed by your essence and your consciousness. You can say, "We can do this energetically. My personality can take a back seat and we can work together as energy systems."

The way you approach other people and the way you feel generates resonance or dissonance. This is important, not only because people will like you or not like you, trust you or not trust you, accept you or not accept you, but also because if your field isn't resonant, you will not be emanating union, regardless of what you say you want to emanate.

You might say, "This is my intention." But only half the circuits are working on that intention. Then you realize, "Wait a minute, the whole bottom half of me is missing, I'd better go back to square one." And that's fine, except that you might have only one opportunity to make a first impression, like a job interview or first meeting. How do you want to represent yourself? If you are half missing, the results of that interview or interaction are going to be different. The question is, is that the result you want?

CONSTANCY AND THE UNIFIED FIELD

On this planet there is an influx of new energies and massive destructuring on all levels. It is very important for you to have something constant in this process. You are your own constant. With your constancy you can go into situations where you experience order and disorder in varying degrees and you know who you are, why you're there, and what to do. You know how the experience will unfold because you've already seen it through your vision. You know the purpose, the design. You're on that energy wave, serving and being served by the universe at the same time.

The wave of your destiny comes from the soul. When your major seven chakras are balanced, you can come into the soul in the center of the body, and say, "Here I am. Show me my calling." When there is balance in the physical body between the metaphysical and physical realms, through the chakras and the breath, you can feel your direction. Guidance will be there for your re-Sourcing. You want to return to the experience of oneness, to be at one with all things, and live union—that's the design. That's why you're here.

You do not have to wait until you fulfill the design to be in union. You do not have to wait for XYZ to happen before you know what it's like to be in a unified field. And it has absolutely nothing to do with somebody else. Creating, sustaining, and living in union is about you. When you live in union with you, then you live in union with others. The objective is for each of you to live union with yourself and then create a world where union is the basis.

The first thing is the individual intention. The collective intention is to get it all together and re-Source it, cooperate, and feel it as unified. It's really very easy because it's up to you. It's not up to your husband or wife, your uncle, aunt, mother, father, child, minister, or teacher. It's not up to anybody else. It's just up to you.

We suggest that you balance your energy field once or twice a day and then find someone to reflect with. Keep records by writing it down. "This is how it was when I balanced my chakras, and this is what my pattern seems to be when I'm with this person. This is what they're picking up. When I ground, it changes. This is what happens when I drink lots of lemon water. This is what happens if I have good rest and feel joyful. This is how I might bring relaxation and joy into my experience so that when this happens, I can affect my energy by this thought or behavior or activity. I can drink water or ground or bring the shower of light through my energy field."

You are your own diagnostician. You may get reflection from the other person, then go into solitude, and say, "What do I do with this? How can I maintain the state of balance in my body and heart and all parts of me? I'm always getting instruction. What is my body telling me it wants to eat? What is my body telling me it wants to listen to? What is my psyche saying I need as surroundings? When have I been the happiest? What do I most long for? What am I most drawn to?" It's an opportunity to really scope yourself out and look in all your nooks and crannies.

This is not about what you believe. It's about messages you're picking up constantly. How could you listen more? What are your tendencies, yearnings, and inclinations? What is really going on inside you all the time that you either ignore or pay attention to? It's time to walk the talk.

When you are in the point of union, you experience being a wave frame of energy, and the field that you generate is concentricity, which means going out in concentric circles. Your field goes out from the sacred space and begins to magnify. First you understand how you interface with individuals. You go into situations and realize how to be comfortable. You can understand where others are and either merge energy with them or not, order your experience with them or not, by choice.

Once you've understood those parameters, you move to the next level, which is to remain a constantly flowing field of unified fiber and resonance, choosing to unify on a personal basis with certain individuals. Yet the whole field around you is responsive to this unification that you're feeling, and all those levels go out and touch other levels. This is why the critical mass happens, because if you hold the level of union based on order and truth, you stimulate that in the people who are in that surrounding pattern or environment with you. They feel their own consciousness activated and sense you are giving them a mirror of their own capacity.

The ultimate goal is union on the planet, and the initial goal is union within yourself. As you feel each step of that union accelerating and working itself through you, becoming integrated into your life system, you'll find each of those levels easier to understand. This is because you have the nucleus vibrating at a rate of speed that has balance, and it moves in all directions, touching everything that is—that is concentricity.

When we talk about the regrouping sensation, that's when you're meeting new people or want to be in a relationship, and you're not sure about the person you're with. Or you're meeting someone new and have an opportunity to sense the differences in energy, not to judge or to protect yourself as much as to return to your vibration of union. You will interface with people who have varied levels of information about their own process. In a very intricate way you will be the first wave of individuals who create new superhuman consciousness.

It takes hours and hours of individual work to understand your own field of energy, to integrate all your aspects, to be comfortable with who you are, to walk into any situation and hold your own field close to your experience, and move it out as it is amenable for you to do that, and to feel in each moment that you can orchestrate that. That's mastery.

It isn't that you don't have compassion, love, warmth, or anything else. These things are always flowing from you. However, you do not give your unified field away. Because if someone else does not have a unified field and does not match you in that space, it will always end up being an incompatible process.

Union becomes a place where order and accordance are always flowing from you. Union is always expanding itself, always going out in all directions, and there is nothing that it requires. As you balance the innate system of your body from the metaphysical, you have all the fuel you need. You just move that union out. People around you respond to that. Union becomes an example of what's possible. The world reflects the truth you choose to create.

When you make choices to be with individuals who are in union, you will end up together in the potential destiny of the Earth, and you'll create a new world. Part of this is discernment. You are not judging someone or avoiding someone or choosing against someone. Everybody is going to make these choices.

You are an energy system—always remember that—you are an energy system, first and foremost. Being an energy system is natural. Looking at the chakra system to find out what is happening energetically is a way of viewing old symptoms. Since pain is caused by congestion of energy, you can evaluate or sense what centers are open and which are closed. You can ask yourself how your other centers affect what's going on in that particular center.

It's important to call a spade a spade. You're in or you're not. And if you're in, you're in all the way. There's no room for someone to be half in and half out. It won't work. The choices must be made and the actions must be taken ("must" meaning strongly recommended). Choose union, implement the circuits and the energy centers from conscious choice so that they support the level of integrity that you chose before you came. It's all about congruence. It's about you saying "yes" to what you know you are so that the outcome is the same vibration. You can start manifesting union today!

Sunlight on Water

Chapter 10

Relationship With Self/Union With Others

This is the time of seeding union into form. What is being ordained from this is the seeding for the new world and the new soul expression. A total reweaving is happening between all dimensions and dynamics here on Earth. You will see that reweaving most prominently in the area of human relationship. Honoring of the self from the soul is the basis for the new way of relating with others in "relationship."

Since the structure of relational reality is now dissipated in the etheric level, and because the political, educational, and familial structures no longer really exist anywhere in this or other dimensions, there is the unsettled feeling of knowing that what you want to do, what you know you can do, and what you have done, are three different energies. This is a time to weave together all those energies—past, present and future. Bringing together the past, present, and future when the normal is no longer palpable can happen most easily when there is a container for the known in which to place "new" dynamics.

THE STEW POT: AN EXERCISE

One way to establish a "place" to contain the unfolding dynamics is to imagine using a stainless steel container as the place to "hold" your present state of being, much like making a stew. The container makes you safe and is constructed to hold the frame so that it represents the past. That's what's going to be rigid. This may be challenging because the belief system might say that in order to have that past container exist, the old stew or memories will also exist, and the stew has to taste the same as the stew you made last week and have the same ingredients. But the structure has nothing to do with actual memory or making things the same. If you free the memory from its container, the memory can be a consciousness which adds new dimensions around and into the container, while at the same time, you might not have tasted the flavor of the stew yet that is part of what is yet to come.

For each person this is an alignment of the knowing from all spaces of time, that is, past, present, and future. Whatever has been known, aggregated, or put together from all dimensions can be solidified and put into the pot. You might put in where you have come from, where you are now, and where you want to go. Finding the similarities in those spaces helps you bring them together and weave them consciously into the psyche as the experience of self.

You can put into the pot your focus for the moment, your intention, what you want to live, resources from the universe, abundance, creation, love and harmony, peace and well-being, health, prosperity—all those pieces.

Because of this new seeding of consciousness, many people are available to the manifestation of their dreams now. They sense the destructuring as a pathway to something new and exciting, to living from the soul. Many things that have worked before will not work now. We're in a time of the procreative or co-creative, which means that the future has no structure, even though it has an energy frequency.

The ideal is to take this container of past experience and knowing what works—the foundation—and marry that with the upcoming process, synthesizing it so that you imprint it and weave the dynamics together. If you take both hands, the left hand represents the existing form, and the right hand represents the existing essence. The left hand is the structure—the stew pot, and the right hand is the essence—that which is being woven, the unknown. When you bring the hands together, they create the present.

The present is the space that is most unclear. The future seems somewhat clear to many people, yet they haven't structured it into the world. So for those of you who are in the critical time of choice, all your frames are being woven together so that they exist in a pattern that has the potential and actual in that same moment.

THE DOGMA OF RELATIONSHIP

In relationship we can take existing structure and know exactly what it is. If you do certain activities with certain people, you're in a certain relationship; if you do other activities with another person, you're in another kind of relationship; if you have another kind of experience with someone else, that's a different kind of relationship. Until this point humanity has kept all relationships separate. We use the word "calibration," saying that the heart calibrates itself vibrationally in a different way in each of these different sets of relationships as they have been standardized by the status quo, dogma, and law.

If you have done a certain action with someone, society supports movement toward certain commitments or actions. The dogma has been that you are going toward a permanent commitment if you have a sexual relationship with someone. Certain kinds of experiences are supported by society and are given energy from society. As soon as a person connects with someone, society supports certain ways in which the framework of that relationship "should" exist.

There is usually an underlying tension in relationship because you're either doing what is expected or not. As these new paradigms experience themselves, the tension becomes very taut because the old structure tries to hang on to what it believes is the norm and the sanctioned. If people move out of this sanctioned experience, society puts tremendous pressure upon them to conform. As the models are changing, because they need to change, those people who are change-agents, who come in to frame things differently, become uncomfortable with the calibration. Those people have to take a quantum leap.

As people learn about and choose a spiritual path, the calibration of being in a certain part of their heart at certain times with certain people no longer fits. It feels constricting, as if there is not room for full expression of the soul. The old model says, "Stay inside certain bounds." Then the soul says, "That's impossible! We don't have just one lifetime together. We don't have just one soul we can love. We don't have just one way of expressing love in and around the soul. We need a different model." So we have the tension between those two models. We're suggesting that you bring those models together.

Take what has worked in your life before and make that your container for your stew. Make that the pot, the structure. It might be honoring, it might be communication, it might be terms of endearment, ways of expressing closeness and intimacy that seem appropriate, it might be ways that certain levels of love are experienced and expressed.

Let's say, for example, with a teacher, you might not experience certain levels of intimacy. Yet the calibration in the heart would lead you to open out to that person in a way that would be very expressive and deep. If you take the new awareness and place it into the old space, you allow for the expression to be dynamic, innovative and unified.

The calibration no longer structures the relationship from a cellular basis. What has happened, as humankind has structured relationship, is that they have imparted to the cells an edict that says, when certain levels of relationship are lived, the cells only respond in a certain way. For example, when we have passion and love and deep longing for union, there is an energy surge that happens from the root chakra. It opens out to levels of creation that are dynamic and have no threshold of limitation. When the calibration says, "No, we can't have that kind of intimacy," a wave motion goes down and closes the root chakra and raises the vibration to another level of the chakra system so that there is a response from that level.

If you look at a relationship, and if you have a calibration that says, "There are no holds barred here. I can open out to any level of relationship with this person," the first thing that happens is that the creative energy is stimulated, and people feel more alive in the relationship. They feel more passion and experience more union from deep creational levels of the root. As the relationship progresses, different levels come into play, and sometimes, as a result of that, the passion is decreased. There is more heart, or more mind, or more connection in different ways. What has happened cellularly in the past is that an edict has gone into the body and said, "This is appropriate. This is inappropriate."

In the new space, the energy field remains open. The passion, creation, experience, expansion and relationship are all going to be the same caliber so that there is no limitation to the experience.

MODELS OF THE AQUARIAN AGE

The Piscean Age has said, "Stop the energy. Put it into definition and expectation." The Aquarian Age says, "Have it always open, and then see what's appropriate for you in that moment with someone else." The Piscean Age experience of "love," intimacy, or connection was unified through belief. In the new time, it's unified through personal expression. Creation and passion don't need to be expressed toward someone else. They are directed within the self. The difference is profound.

In Piscean society, people were only open at certain times. In the Aquarian time, people are open all the time. It's not going to be in relationship to someone, it's going to be from the commitment to be completely energized within one's own being. The difference is that the people of the new model are always alive. All the chakras are relating and working and merging and unifying. There is an ongoing explosion of the creative spark of the commitment to living, being, and expressing. And that allows the soul to emerge.

Another major difference is the level of vision. In the old paradigm, the vision had to do with the model. "We're going to get married, that's my picture. We're going to live together, that's my picture. We're going to have a child together, that's my picture. We're going to take our resources and combine them, and live together so that it's easier for us, it's safer for us," that kind of thing.

In the new model vision becomes total aliveness within one's being, total expressiveness within one's soul pattern. Then, whoever and whatever happens does not diminish that charge. It has to do with being in one's full capacity.

The difference in these models is more easily expressed in the human feminine space. This is because the human feminine space has more vision and more passion. It has more capacity as a general rule because it has not been allowed to contain its creation only through sex and structural belief. The feminine goes outside structural belief because it procreates life and because the system of the feminine takes the unknown and brings it into form. The masculine, or Piscean model, takes only the known and brings it into form. So the feminine, because it can create life itself, generally has an easier time moving into the new model.

Since the structure of the feminine is created through dynamics associated with safety, nurturance, procreation, co-creation, sustenance, manna, and protoplasm, they are more easily woven into the individual and collective feminine pattern. The feminine looks for ways to introduce the Aquarian principles of soul equality and soul expression into the existing model. The feminine is saying, "Let's redo the model. I don't want to cook and clean all the time, necessarily. I don't want to be cast in a role that was chosen twenty years ago. I want to find my own life system. How do I do that? And what, if anything, do I have to give up in order to create something new from within?" The feminine is tapping into future realities, so feminine energy is being restructured on the planet.

Some women may have difficulty with that space because they have a more structured or Piscean process, and they want to stay within the models that exist because they feel safer. So they may begin co-creating ideas and energy from the soul, yet compromise by staying in old patterns of relationship or security.

Some men also have that kind of structural process and are only able to leave the structural influence of the old model to be with "another woman," or to be with someone who is able to tap into that creative resource with or for them. That was the way men used to escape from the old structure. They went outside the monogamous bounds that were instituted from the structure. So each sex has found ways to cross over into the new dimension.

THE INTEGRITY OF THE NEW MODEL

The design for relationship and humanity in the future is that both sexes cross over from the old model, but they do it in a way of integrity. They honor the structure of their own being, and they do it without compromise. This is basically the difference between being in integrity or out of integrity because when one is in a structural relationship (Piscean), and crosses over in a non-integrous way, there is compromise. When one crosses over from a total sense of knowing and commitment to truth, there is no compromise. Honesty, integrity, and validity are born out of these experiences, which create new models and new ways of expression.

If you want to go forth and say, "My soul needs to express in this way," it's suggested that you clarify that expression. Open all your chakra systems and energy fields, and align with the truth. Then compromise is diminished, and the commitment to oneness and intimacy happens. This is the key: in the new time there is not a commitment to a person, there's a commitment to the process of deepening intimacy with the self through connection with others, in whatever way that unfolds.

RELATIONSHIP WITH THE SELF

These basic differences in paradigm are what the tension is about in the structural system. Weaving the vision of the truth and the expression of the soul into the moment requires a commitment to non-compromise, commitment to full expression in each person, and the commitment to being in relationship only with the self, with no one else. That means that no matter who you're with, or what you're doing, integrity will be maintained. If the commitment is to relationship outside of the self, then there is a marriage that comes together out of need rather than out of wisdom. Marriage with the self means marriage between the masculine and the feminine within each person. That's the kind of marriage that will work in this new time.

We're looking at a separation from the existing paradigm and the movement into a totally new paradigm. That separation in paradigms is creating the conflict we now experience in relationships. That is what creates the need to leave, the need to expand, the need to procreate or co-create differently. It does not need to be a separation. It just needs to be a weaving—each person becomes clear about where they are in the process of unfolding newness. They don't think of themselves as having failed at relationship; they think of themselves as needing to enter a new relationship with themselves.

This is going to be the new basis of society. As this unfolds it becomes very powerful, because if one says to oneself, "I am now only in relationship with myself," it immediately frees everyone else with whom you are in relationship to be in relationship with themselves. The words, "I don't want to be with you. I don't want to be in relationship. I don't want to have this. I don't..." do not need to be said. Because if one just says, "I need to be in relationship with myself," then the pressure is taken off the participants in a relationship. If one says, "I need to blend my own masculine and feminine. I am making the commitment to be in an honoring space of vision with my own capacity, and to open up my own passion for life, my own experience of oneness," there is the opportunity to develop that kind of internal space in each person.

This seems to be the most dedicated way to serve the changing evolutionary experience, individual needs and capacities, and whatever existing parameters are in effect in relationship. If that statement is made about relating to the self, all the frames shift immediately, and they are no longer responsible for providing happiness. They are no longer responsible for making things good, right, or better. A space opens and says, "I am now responsible for myself. I am responsible to my own knowing. I am responsible to my own vision of what will work for me." Then a person in relationship can come together with the partner and say, "This is where I am now." You have a place to start meeting.

You have a ground that is accomplished, and if you're in relationship with someone who doesn't want to work with themselves—doesn't want to honor the whole space where they are—very naturally there will be a gravitation for them toward someone who is still in that same frame. And there will be a gravitation for the initial person who has claimed their experience of self to find someone else who is also claiming that experience.

The loss and abandonment issues, the betrayal issues, and the many dynamics which have woven into the human experience cease to exist. This happens when one says, "I have to be, first, and primarily, in a relationship with myself." Then there's no longer a way that the frame can be divided against itself. When people are in wholeness with themselves, no one can divide them anymore.

This takes the blaming, rituals, and experiences that have been in the outer framework and dissipates them. If each person makes this commitment and combines individual knowing about that choice with the collective etheric model for the new dimension, the future becomes the present with them immediately. If they resist that, they're going to be in resistance against all dissolution of existing models. They get caught in an abyss of eternal desire for something which is no longer valid.

What we need to remember is that when one clings to an old model, it's because the new model is not yet as viable or palpable. It is only by people such as you going forward and saying, "I'm ready for the new model," that there will be enough inherent energy in that model to support a critical mass which will assist in the transformation of the old into the new. It's very important for people who have an awareness of this process to live it fully.

This does not mean that any new way of being replaces the old way of being in a structured sense, for example, non-monogamy, or non-commitment: "This frees me up to do anything I want." That is out of integrity. It doesn't mean that you throw the baby out with the bath water, that you get rid of everybody in your life who wants to be a certain way. It means that by claiming the self, you learn how to stay in a dedicated space of ritual with your own being. It means that everything you're living makes sense because it honors everyone at the same time.

It honors you and it honors the other person. It frees them from responsibility to make you happy, to have sex with you, to marry you, to give you children, or to in some way be present for you—supporting you financially, emotionally, or in any other way. It says, "I'm going to do all this for myself. I'm going to live this in a way that makes sense to me. Every moment, from this time forward, my own honoring is my primary focus. If I honor myself, it means I put myself together. I hold myself together. I sustain my field in integrity. I live in a fullness that makes me awaken all the time to my own capacities and potentials."

You are creating a reality so that the other person can respond to you from that set of circumstances. It's very important that each individual understands that until they can make that commitment, they are going to be in a relationship that's nonproductive, that doesn't go anywhere, that doesn't have any vision or potential. Because anyone who is in co-dependence with someone, needing them to do something to sustain their viability, is not working with interdependence—not working with systems theory where growth is essential to participation.

GROWTH AND EXPANSION

Growth doesn't mean pain. Growth means expansion into a full capacity of experience and expression, and changes relationship from co-dependence to co-creation. There are no promises. "I promise you I won't do this or that." In the new model you don't say, "You're uncomfortable with this, so now I see what we have to do." Those ways of relationship suppress individual and personal expression.

There are literal ties between people called Aka chords. In the Hawaiian Kahuna philosophy, Aka chords maintain the status quo and separate one from growth. People who are ready to foundation a new reality dissolve the Aka chords by choosing their own volition and proliferation. They live their own passion.

You don't need to worry about those chords and try to make them different. It's more important to focus on the fullest expression of your own field of energy, rather than focusing on yourself as a person, a body, a mind, a heart, or an emotion. It is important to take together all the ways of being and say, "I'm a field of energy. That means I open, I expand, I bring in light." It's like photosynthesis. You bring in the capabilities and release what you don't need. When people focus on what's wrong, what they need to change, what doesn't work, and where they are feeling pain, it aligns them with only those fields of energy. Nothing seems to work. There's a stuckness.

When people align themselves with an intention and experience only those things that are part of that expression, then what is not expressed is no longer valid. It is no longer sustained in the field of energy. There's a sense of being on target and creation emerges.

They are in a space of acceleration. Anyone who is humping along, going two steps forward and one step back, experiences an extremely high amount of inertia because this is the time for movement, growth, and expansion.

Support will come to create new levels of reality. For example, in relationship, if one says, "I'm going toward this experience of accelerated growth where I am unified with myself," the body, mind, emotion, and spirit come in and say, "I'll support that for you." The way free will works is that whatever the intention is in terms of vision, idea, knowing, calibration, or whatever, the energy field will support that. If one says, "I'm open," then the chakras open. If one says, "I'm hurt," then the chakras close.

If one says, "I'm tired of my marriage. I want to have an affair," immediately the cells of the body begin to open and send out this magnetic wave that says, "I'm ready" for that kind of experience, and those associated chakras open up. The heart chakra may not open up at all because it feels a division. A commitment has already been made, and yet there's a decision from another part of the mind to do another kind of activity. There's a separation in the energy. Only certain things are possible because the whole being is not called on to express the passion of the self. It's called on to experience only a certain thing with a certain person, which basically shuts down the field of energy. This creates both acceleration and depletion and may be experienced emotionally as exhilaration and depression. One goes into a situation feeling a lot of passion and then feels sadness and loss. Anytime there is variation in the field like that, there's incongruence. Something is out of order.

There is another difference between the Piscean and the Aquarian Age. In the Piscean Age it was normal for there to be happiness in one or two areas of life and unhappiness in another area. Let's say someone had a vocation they loved, but they would have an unsatisfactory marriage, or they would have health problems, or they would love what they were doing but not make enough money to cover their rent. That's the Piscean limitation process. You can have some of it, but you can't have all of it.

In the new experience, the acceleration of being at one with the self and totally in alignment with your consciousness says, "Here I am, and I have it all." The only way to have it all is to be in union with the total self. That's exactly what the experience of the future is about. In a sense, we are moving from the need to concentrate on relationship to the need to concentrate on the full expression of the essence of being, individually. So families, structures, and relationships are no longer important in the same way. That has been translated by individuals who have fear about the change into the dissolution of family, the dissolution of the structure of marriage, and the dissolution of integrity. That is not at all how it is intended. When one has absolute integrity with self, one will have absolute integrity with everyone else that one relates with.

If the focus is on keeping integrity within the self, then the structures that serve the self and the full expression of being are honored and expanded. Those that don't are diminished. There will be certain marriages that proliferate in this new model, and certain ones that don't. The proliferative marriages will be woven with integrity into individual integration, union and expression.

Union with oneself becomes the passion of being alive. As one feels this passion for life, the emotional co-dependence where one needs something in order to feel safe in relationships is reduced and ultimately eliminated. There will be a division between the people who can understand the new model and integrate it and the people who can't. This isn't good or bad. It's just that any time you shift paradigms, when there's not a weaving, people think that somebody has chosen something that doesn't work for them. And that's fine because it's free will.

What can work in weaving the old and new is, "I'm in a relationship. I now choose to be shifting the focus of the relationship to myself. I would like to shift a bit, and yet honor the commitment I already made. I want to weave the pieces that feel most congruent and hold them steady—creating a new structure between us—so that whatever we agree on supports each of us supporting ourselves individually." Then the relationship begins to coalesce. The focus for change is always on what works, not on what doesn't. As you weave, you strengthen the fibers of your fabric.

When one decides, "I'm committed to intimacy with myself, with my life, with a tree, with a dog, with my food," then everything serves you. If it doesn't serve you, you're not intimate with it! If that's the commitment, then when you're relating to someone with whom you are in relationship, it will be framed differently. There will be no focus on the person providing an intimate experience because the intimacy will be experienced with the self.

Weaving becomes the key. As soon as one partner says, "That doesn't work for me," the other partner says, "What does work for you?" Instead of being afraid of bringing up the differences and looking at them, everything gets brought out, but it gets brought out in the sense of what does work for me. If somebody says, "That doesn't work," you say, "What does work?" And if they say "I don't know," then you say, "Maybe it's time for you to do some unifying with yourself, and I'll do the same thing. Let's come back together when we're clearer about what does work for us." So you don't have discussions with people anymore in this new paradigm about what's wrong.

No energy in the new paradigm is given to the squeaky wheel. The energy is only given to what moves, expands and opens out. It is a very different way, because most people say, "Let's sit down and slog it out and come to resolution." Put things back into fluid where they are woven and move and synthesize. Working from paradigms that are opposite to this will not create union. If you go into the self and say, "Well, where's the union in me?" then you come back to the person unified, and then you have a chance of unifying together.

To get together to reconcile something, or make something different, or to create a new way of being works only when one is ready to dissolve the old model in the self. If one is unready to dissolve the old model internally, one cannot expect to dissolve it when more than one person is present. There may also be attachment to what the person believes is the way they need it to be.

If the belief system ordains that before the couple can come together and reunify, one of the partners has to compromise or give in to what the other person is attached to, then it is the old kind of weaving. This keeps things the same and tries to make everybody happy. The step which the individual needs to take to be responsible for the self has not yet been taken. The way of commitment in the future is that each person honors the self first. In that honoring, people unify the self and deepen the intimacy with their own life. Then they come together with someone who has made that same commitment. If that is not the commitment, whether it's spoken or not, there will need to be time spent apart and/or the need to work on the individual and create that commitment.

When you spend some time apart, you're re-doing the foundation. The more time you are apart, the more time you have to honor yourselves and come to that space where the honoring means something in terms of your expression of intimacy together.

As that unfolds, you have a totally new basis for being in a relating space. One of you can take the initiative to be the model for that experience. For most of you, that's what will happen. One or another of the parties will take the initiative to set up the new framework of honoring, and then the other person will either make that commitment also, or they won't.

The sense of loss is dramatically diminished when one takes the self as being the most important intimate space, and agrees to that. If the other person doesn't, there is really no sense of loss. This is because what's appreciated by the initial person, who has made that commitment for self-initiation, is that this is not the ideal place for that kind of framework to be experienced. There's a sense of relief, "Now I don't have to do this anymore." You know you have made it into that space when the other person says, "I don't think I can do this," and you say, "Okay, I get it, and it's fine, and if and when you can, come and see me, and we can relate whatever way our individual knowing supports us in the future."

There are no dead ends, no divorces of the old type, where you imagine that you don't love each other anymore. The timing is what is important, and without certain levels of affirmation, it's not going to move into the direction one would wish anyway. So the sense of, "This is my one love, this is the one I have to sustain to make myself happy, this is what has provided me with support and with the safeguard of security," no longer has any viability because the self is so strong that there's not a confusion between what the person believes, what the person is trying to live, and what the other person believes and is trying to live, which really makes a quagmire.

What is happening now is that people are being brought up short in relationship. They are no longer able to relate in the old ways. There's a lot of back-pedaling, trying to bring back the things that used to work. And of course they're not working. So it's thrusting individuals, particularly those with a spiritual intention and commitment and connection to the soul, to take this new step to provide a whole new container for the self to relate from. And because this is so dynamic and so necessary, there's also a wave of this new "frame" happening on the planet that supports large numbers of integrous changes in people's experience.

UNDERSTANDING YOUR RELATIONSHIPS: AN EXERCISE

Three basic concepts provide a basis for learning how to stay in the self and be clear about what will call forth the connection of intimacy.

CALIBRATION: how open is your heart in each of your relationships

BELIEF SYSTEM: what you think you have to believe or have to be in relationships

ENERGY FIELD: where the cellular level responds in the body without conscious direction

Look at the kinds of relationships you have in your life. Ask yourself, "Who do I actually have relationships with?" Categorize certain areas of your life into family, friends, etc. first, or begin by listing the people and then seeing where you want to put them according to how you perceive it. However you choose to do it, list each person, i.e., "I have Susan, and Susan is my friend; and I have Paul, and Paul is my husband; I have Samuel, and Samuel is my son; I have John, and he's my great uncle; I have this one and she is a teacher; I have this one, and he's my grocer; and I have this one, and she is my neighbor."

After you have listed the people with whom you are in relationship, then access the calibration with each person. Questions you might ask are, "How much of my heart is open with each of these people? What part of my heart is open? What kind of deliberation do I do with this person? Is there an emotional attachment? Is there a sexual attachment? Is there any attachment? Maybe this is my child's physician. I have an attachment to this physician because this person kept my child alive. What kind of emotional bond do I have with this person?" It's very literal. You say, "What is the bond? Does this person create stability, security, love, affection, passion? What?" Go through so that you're very clear about how your heart has been taught to respond to certain individuals and group situations.

Then go into the belief system. Say to yourself, "What do I believe is an appropriate behavior or relationship with each person?" Write down your responses. Then go back into the calibration, which is unconscious and automatic. The belief system is what makes the calibration what it is. The belief system is also what you think is happening.

When you do these exercises, you find that a lot of times you're giving off energy that your belief system doesn't feel is appropriate and that you don't think is a part of your calibration, but the other person is receiving. When that happens you have triangles and experiences where you feel disillusioned, misunderstood, or betrayed. One is never really betrayed by another. One is only betrayed by the sense that the three levels that we're talking about—the calibration, the belief, and the energy field— are functioning from different levels, giving different messages, and experiencing connection in different ways.

The next level of focus is the energy field. When you think about the people and the situations that you wrote about in the calibration, you go back and look at, "What do I believe about this person—what do I believe is effective, ineffective, appropriate, inappropriate, right, wrong?" Then you go to the energy field and say, "How does my energy field really respond with this person? Let me see it as it really is." So you go into each person and feel your field of energy and say, "All right, what part of my body comes alive when I think about this person? What part of my body closes down? What part of my body is more expressive? How do I feel? Am I warm? cold? expanded? diminished? What's happening?" Then make columns and put each person's name at the top, giving them three different read-outs. See if all of these levels work together or if they don't. How are they compatible and/or incompatible?"

The objective is to have the calibration be totally open all the time so that the love is never categorized, diminished or expanded for just one person, group or situation. Have the belief system clear so that there is always love, and appropriate expression of love depending upon what the union and weaving of those three levels says. When these two points are open, this opens your energy field always, consistently, to the passion with self. That is the foundation for this new time and experience.

When each person goes through and asks, "What is my belief system about being with a certain person? What have I made appropriate? What do I wish I was doing?" A lot of times in the belief system there is a very strong dichotomy, "I think this is appropriate, but this is what I want." When that happens inside the belief, there can be a very strong experience of discomfort, guilt, and the feeling that something is unclear, or as if you're betraying something or someone, even if you haven't acted. This happens frequently on the subtle body levels.

There may be varying degrees of incompatibility in certain areas. If a person has trouble trusting, there may be a high degree of incompatibility in the love center, in the calibration in the heart, in trusting and being open. If someone has an unbalanced root center, there may be a high degree of incompatibility in how they feel about certain people and what they feel is appropriate, and what their body energy is doing. This is a good way of seeing where the fields of energy receive their information. What is the response? What is the desired response? Each person can clarify what works for them and what they would like to see happen.

Our objective in giving you this information is to assist you to clarify your process, to feel very clear with your responses, and to know yourself and the way your energy works so that when you go out into the world, synthesis happens. That synthesis provides a high level of functioning so that the energy field is consistently opening out into the world. And that's the difference, also, between being married to yourself and being married to someone else. Because if you are married to yourself, you're always on, you're always open and expressing. Then you can make distinct choices about marrying your field of energy of wholeness with someone else's.

You're not at the mercy of one of your chakras, or one of your beliefs, or one of your calibrations. It gives autonomy to your being which is extremely valuable and honors itself. There is such a high degree of functioning that you feel masterful and live in the world without fear of being taken advantage of, of being raped, disillusioned, or abandoned. All those fears dissipate when the being is fully alive and these three levels are in balance. That's why it's so important.

This exercise may take up to three weeks to do. It is invaluable because it will help you clarify what's going on. And it's not to be judged. Very important! It is to be honored as a signal from your being that there is a readiness to be consolidated, to make the commitment for integrity and intimacy. To know yourself intimately gives you a capacity to choose response rather than to react. That is mastery also, to choose your response.

THE VALUE OF SYNTHESIS

What is important is synthesis. Many people are conflicted because of the structures that have been imposed upon them—the tension that's being held in the dynamic. Many people think that they're doing the right thing and that everything is fine. Actually, they're being held in tension with the models of expectancy outside themselves and don't know it. Many times they don't know what they want. They don't know who they are, and they don't know what's possible. So these insights would be valuable for each person. Even people who think, "I'm monogamous. I don't have to do this exercise or change the dynamics in my relationship. I have everything cut and dried. I know exactly what's going on. I don't have those kinds of feelings. I'm not ready for this kind of relationship, or connection to myself. I don't think I need it. I have a good relationship with my family, my husband, or my significant other, and I don't have to do this," are deluding themselves and eluding the experience of the truth. Because the models are changing etherically, this is affecting relationships on all levels.

It is valuable to look at the energetic messages given and received during childhood, particularly the triangular situations which develop in incestual relationships, or if there are marked discrepancies in the exercise suggested above. Doing this kind of responsive informational indexing from the levels will assist people who are dealing with these life situations to understand the dynamics involved and to know how those situations were created energetically.

What parts of the energy system were open to others that you had interactions with and feel were uncomfortable or unpleasant? What was really going on in your field at that time? What was your physical response? Were you conscious of this response, or responding from a perspective of your calibration only, or only your belief system, or as sometimes happens, only the energy field. Many people go every moment with what their energy field tells them to do, and are out of touch with the original space of intention for that particular situation—the experience of what is right or what is wrong for them.

They may find that they go the other way around. They're always responding to whatever root chakra instinct they have or whatever heart chakra instinct they have. These are the people who fall in love with everybody, the people who have sex with everybody, or the people who never have sex, or never have love. There can be any range of this, from complete closing to complete opening, and all of that can be going on at the same time. You experience an imbalance between these levels in you and/or in someone you're relating with.

When someone has woven their levels together, they have an integrous body of light and consciousness. They are able to make the choices that are going to serve everyone in the situation, which makes it a win-win. How that's lived comes from an integrous bonding together of the calibration, the emotion, belief, and the physical body and energy system. The dynamics of light, when they enter the system of humanity, clear out the circuits so there is only an absolute space of oneness with everything. This happens in societies which are based upon soul expression.

The connection with souls can be extremely deep and sometimes, extremely dramatic. For example, even when individuals are in a relationship with someone, they may come together with a new soul and feel that they have found or desire to find the deepest level of intimacy with this new soul. Their soul has been so long suppressed in their experience of life, that when they begin to birth their soul, they are open to so many dimensional energies, that there is sometimes confusion with commitment, with love, with loss, with passion, and with many parts of human interaction.

There are many times when they develop or initiate a momentary sense of finding their soul through someone else. When these soul experiences happen, however they do—and they seem to be sometimes very dramatic and out of context with one's "life"—the person taps into their initial soul dimensional frequency, so they feel as if they've never been as understood before. They've never had someone who could touch them as deeply.

This experience occurs because as the soul gets activated, there is such passion in the soul that it is transferred to the other person. The new person linked into the existing experience of that person from the soul level. That new person catalyzes the individual developing on their own—which is the inner passion of union with self. Sometimes people will leave relationships, saying, "This is my soul mate. This is somebody I've got to be with because I feel that this person understands me." And then it gets worked through, and the soul passion energy gets added to the sum total of the person's expressive capacity, and then all of a sudden the light bulb goes on and the first person realizes, "This wasn't about the second person, it was about me. It was about my finding a part of myself that this person was vibrationally able to connect with and therefore bring out in me."

Some people will feel that they have found the relationship they want when all they have done is tripped over somebody, or brought somebody into their design at the place where their soul is able to express. If they come into the soul expression on their own and feel it from their own integrity, then they can integrate these people into their lives so that they don't cause a lot of dramatic disintegration on other levels. It's often because the initial person has not done their own work, has not experienced their own capacity, that these other people are able to come in and turn everything upside down. It's because they need to make a shift, and they've not chosen to do it internally. They have chosen to do it externally, which creates a tremendous amount of pathos. They leave their life in order to experience the soul.

HONOR AND INTEGRITY

Another option which creates integrity is to choose to experience the catalyst from one's own response-ability to the self. Then instead of feeling that things have been destroyed or upturned, one feels they have the capacity to honor their own experience and hold that in the light. It has integrity. The person can say, "This is something I am honoring within myself, and if another person is honoring it within themselves we can come together. But I won't come together with this person because they're honoring a part of me that I haven't honored."

That's a distinction we want to make. None of it is right or wrong. Sometimes looking outside the self creates a lot of waves. A roto-rooter effect goes through the life and upturns everything. Some people need to learn that way, and they can choose that, but it isn't the only choice.

If you choose to make the experience integrous, then when you meet people, you validate each other, mirror each other, and go into a step of growth together. You do it in a way that is a natural unfolding of the design rather than an insertion that feels out of order. That's the difference. When one is in a state of completion with the self and meets another person, it's as if the person is enfolded into the process that's already going on. Nothing has to happen from it.

There is no resentment or challenge or rebellion, which sometimes happens otherwise. It becomes integrated into the whole picture. Let's say, for example, there's a couple, and they're each working on their own level of mastery, and they've experienced the integrity of themselves. A new person comes along and is added to the equation, but a triangle is not formed. The difference in the future design and the past design is that when mastery is not attained on the individual level, triangles form. If there is mastery, circles form. That difference is profound. It means that one can move into community and into expansion and not necessarily into separation.

When we work from mastery, we work toward union. If we're working from the egoic space, or the separate space of, "This person came in and has more to give me than you do, or they're understanding me better than you ever have, or I think we'd have better sex," separation is created. That's the old model. It's not right or wrong, it's just being phased out.

If people want to work with the capacity of truth, they work with, "What's the overall design intending for all of us? Where are we going with this? How can we fit this together?" Each individual honors the self, so they don't need a relationship to honor them, which means that it's possible for expression of these connections in different ways than used to be possible.

There is not a dishonoring in order to honor. There's not a choice like, "I'm choosing somebody else instead of you," which is also dishonoring, and says, "The commitment I made to you, I'm now negating. I'm throwing it out like the baby and the bath water, to have this new thing." I'm saying, instead, "I honor myself, I honor you who have been with me, and now I honor this new person. As the three of us honor ourselves and each other, we'll create something new from this."

Without this space of couples forming circles instead of triangles, adding new people so that they are families of a new type, the new community of cooperation will have a harder time existing. It's very important to experience all these levels so that we accelerate the models of group union, interaction, and creation as quickly as possible.

If you do the exercises of calibration, belief system, and energetic body, you see where your glitches are—where you hold the energy, where you expand the energy. These are the same places where you hold energy when you are a couple or when you're in a family or group situation. To the experience of relationship we add the capacity to know everything at one time about ourselves and practice knowing about ourselves with another significant person. Then we practice opening that to more people. Sometimes, if there is a challenge, a group can assist in the process of honoring. It needs, however, to be honoring of the self first, and then honoring of everyone who is added on later.

Then the honoring becomes more important than having sex, being married, having a relationship, or being safe. When you get a group of people together who honor themselves, they can say, "We agree on this, but we don't agree on the other." They then say, "Let's go with what we agree with right now. Let's expand that agreement and unify through that, and make it strong and clear. We're going to honor what we honor.

It's very important now to give energy only to what you want to create. As the model changes and integrates and weaves together, you'll find that everything that the group does is honoring everything within the group. There has been a natural resolution of those things that were in some way disagreed upon in the beginning.

Part of the honoring is, "I'm not doing this to get my way. I'm not doing this so that everybody will agree." It's that the honoring of the self and the group (whether it's three people or thirty people) is the choice. As we evolve in honor, the actions people wanted to take that were uncomfortable for the larger number, are worked out automatically. The energy fields begin to balance and there's no longer one person's lust, need, ego, process, intention, whatever.

Moving from the egoic to the cosmic consciousness, we ask, "What's the best thing for the whole system?" This is the difference between getting one's way and getting one's needs filled, to contributing. This is where the foundation of life becomes critical. This is where communities develop from a different model than before—the difference being that now we talk about what's happening and honor all people. It becomes a model for the new kind of relational quality of interaction rather than being a new model of relationship.

Relationship in the old way will eventually phase itself out. It is too modular, too confined, too separate. We're moving toward group consciousness, group expression. It doesn't mean that we're moving toward group sex. When honoring is the primary focus, the experience of life will be that we have sex with ourselves, (raise our creative energy through our root), we have love with ourselves. We create together in a way that supports a long, real and lasting sense of union because no one needs anyone or anything else in the old way.

You create energy fields that open out and expand and experience new models so that the energy of the being gets balanced completely within the sense of the self. The consciousness of creating and co-creating is what's focused on, rather than saving a particular relationship or a particular model.

What we want to safeguard and effectively create are solutions for the world. How can we work better together? How can we share resources more appropriately? How can we be in cooperation with each other on an ongoing basis, no matter what we used to believe or think?

These processes are more important than getting individual needs met. This will create a very interesting paradigm in society. The forward movers and thinkers and masters will be in large world-wide communities with others who make these solutions, and other people will still be trying to figure out what they're here to do. There will be a sense of dichotomy, and that's why, for people who already think and know that they want to be the masters of consciousness, it's time for this shift to move the consciousness into this whole picture as quickly as possible. Be whole with the self as the microcosm, and then see where that piece fits into the larger macrocosm.

Relationship will not exist in the same way. People who have a primary honoring will honor each other so much energetically that everyone will know they are in partnership without the paper, the ring, the legal process to define it, and without society to make expectations or dogma about it. The honoring of a partnership will be completely energetic. It will be something everyone understands and ordains, and something that is a space which creates a foundation for larger honoring. People in relationship have a choice now because they can be the foundation for the new world, if they choose to do it from a new honoring.

This way of relationship is an expansion. It's appropriate to the time because instead of divorce, you can go into a new level of partnership that has no name and no condition and has absolute honoring. It's a very beautiful time and a very beautiful awakening.

Chapter 11

The Heart of the One

This message about keys to living sustainably in community was received by the Heaven on Earth community in Vermont in 1994.

You have each come here for a specific purpose. The purpose of your lives together is to enrich and enliven each day, each moment, and each cell so that you cannot tell yourselves apart from each other. That is why the distinctions between you are obvious—why you are forging your own personalities. If the distinctions are apparent, felt, and fielded, then they can be integrated. If they are hidden, they cannot be integrated. When something is clear, precise, and pristine, it can be clarified.

You have each come here to honor the self and live that in community. In honoring the self, you do not need to hide anything or go off by yourself if you need to express something.

When you are in spiritual community, you are creating a pathway to yourself. If you go outside yourself to forge a pathway, it will be less successful. If you forge the inner path, the outer path opens automatically. That is the secret. You begin with a nickel-size circle of consciousness. Then your consciousness grows to the size of a quarter, a fifty-cent piece, then a dollar piece. The circles get bigger and bigger and forge even bigger circles, one after the other, as your consciousness moves out into the world.

When your intentions are clear, they are recorded in frequency in the hearts of all of the people who know you. Your job is to hold the space within, clarify it, hold it, clarify it, and hold it again.

The heart is the center point, the threshold between the above and the below. When you come together with others, do so in a circle of silence where there are no words. Only when you come to the place where it is difficult to speak is the heart engaged.

When you want to speak, to think, to be right, and to be heard, you are not in the heart, for there are no words in the heart. If you make a statement and ask someone to agree, to understand, to compromise, or even look in your heart and see if you are pure, it is not the heart. However, if you forge this place of the heart, everyone around you will come to stand with you in the circle that you create. They will join you only if you are in the heart. This is the key.

This isn't about loving. It is not that you are not loving. It's just that when you are not in your heart, you are someplace else. It isn't good or bad, it's just a fact. The heart will take you home to the place of being. If you understand that you are here to create a whole new dimensional experience, then you can be excited and invested all the time in feeling the heart.

It doesn't matter who holds back, who comes first, who seems interested, who is against, who is for. If you focus on these things, then you are like you were before you came to this community. It is as you were when you were born and your mothers imprinted in you six generations of thoughts, ideas, and beliefs. If you are in the heart, you don't have disunion. You don't think about who is for, who is against, if it will work or won't work. This is subtle but important. If you think, "It might not work, we might need to do something that is different," then you are not in the heart.

It is not about deciding with your mind. For example, you want to create a relationship with nature, the wetlands, the herons, the fox, and the wolf. Think only about being in the heart, for if you are there, the animals will come to you. If you are in the human experience of valuing and weighing things that people have said to you, it will not work because it is not of the new model. It is of the old.

It does not mean that you forget to honor, that you do not learn, do not grow and understand things, or that you do not experience new awareness. It is just that you do so from the heart, which has the frequency to bring life together. It isn't about who's planting what and who's doing what to whom, it's about being in the heart. You are tired physically sometimes because you are not in your hearts. When you don't come together with others in your cells, it makes you tired. When you do come together, your bodies are stronger physically and spiritually.

You don't think about someone else understanding you or caring about you. The frequency is such that there is much to be shared, and you do not need to express it logically. Your oneness is complete because your frequencies match. The honoring is accorded. It is singular and collective simultaneously.

This process will lead you to resolution. The head will lead you nowhere. If you try to make a logical decision about something, you will be held away from it for a time because it was not originally considered from the heart. It's not that heart was not interwoven in the question or decision. It's just that it came from ideas rather than from frequency. Be in frequency first, and experience seeing and knowing second. Then what is to come will be made known to you.

CIRCLES OF THE HEART

We would recommend that you practice making circles of the heart. When you go onto the land, for example, feel the experience of the heart together. Have joy and laughter, sharing and community. These are wonderful things. The heart will seal this so that your differences are not really differences and your opinions are simply opinions. Your processes will not separate you.

When you are in the heart, the animals will come, and people will observe this. You don't have to convince them that you will do the land and animals no harm. Instead, you show them that you are drawing the wilderness to humans, pulling together that which has been held apart, because the heart is so great that it knows no separation. You don't have to prove or defend, and everyone sees this.

Humans push things around like bulls instead of using metaphysical energy to power it all, to take the weight out of things. Metaphysical energy can guide the direction of the forces that you elicit from your will.

If you understand that this is a process, you can enjoy the moment you are in without waiting for the process to be complete. You see the pieces coming together where people show up and things get accomplished without effort. If it's hard, then something is out of whack, so the hardness of something is an indication of how far you are from heart.

Instead of thinking, "It will take a while to make this relationship, build this building, or get this plan," (all those things that are normal to think about) say, "No, I cannot think about it. My heart must show me the direction and order in which things will happen." When you find yourself thinking about what to do next, go to the heart. If you do not understand or cannot make a decision, go to the heart. The more people who go to their heart at one time, the faster this will happen.

You have the intention to do this, but you're out of practice in how it happens. It's like knowing that you need the music to play the notes. The music is the heart, and if you go to the heart, the notes will be played.

Another important experience is to be in connection with the Earth while you're in the heart. Do ritual outside as often as possible so that your feet anchor your experience. Feel the Earth sending frequencies through her methods, which are deep and core-like, with many ley lines and vortices moving through her. Use every capacity you have to send messages from the heart. Send them to the wind, to the Earth. Hug the trees, touch the animals. This is not about the proximity of something to you, but your proximity to your heart, the group heart, the group soul.

It's very important for you to vision, to see what will come, to write it down. Imagine that you are with others in the heart. Establish the foundation. Then feel where you are going. Maybe you will be taken in a visualization to see what you will create, or feel what will be in your future, or who is there with you. If it comes from the heart, write it down. That will sharpen your vision and your clarity, and you will see how the pieces will fit together.

CREATING FROM HEART

The experience of being in heart is rare in your society, and it is more rare to create from heart. Substantiating reality from heart is even more rare.

The heart is the place where the design is available to you. It is where you can access that which is inherent in you, the piece of the microcosm that you bring to support the foundation of the hologram of oneness.

Talking about things that are not working or those things that detract is giving attention, or grease, to the squeaky wheel. You want to assist the wheel to turn faster, to be brighter and clearer and move you along the way more quickly. You say, "I don't have to pay attention to this. All I need to pay attention to is similarities, congruence, and where it makes sense to come together—not the things that would keep us apart."

If it feels like it's taking time, it's because until the foundation is established, you will not be given the "go ahead." Without the foundation, the universe will not support it.

When you come together and align with heart, the world will begin to change. That is the only thing that people will listen to. We repeat, it is not about love, it's about the vibration of being in oneness without words.

As each of you experiences this space, it grows. It doesn't just grow humanly; it grows on all frequencies. You have a share of the consciousness of critical mass to use as fuel for establishing this process on the Earth. Do not think about boundaries, fields, lots, trees and shrubs because it doesn't matter. If you're not establishing the foundation of heart, nothing will matter anyway.

When you acknowledge that there is no separation between anything, the foundation for miracles is set. It is like a magnet, like riding a wave. You want to stay in the experience because if you have a human reaction (get off the wave by analyzing it), then you are not credible.

MANIFESTING AND INTENTION

If you want to manifest, make an intention. Have your body vibrate at the same rate of speed as your intention. Then reach into the future and bring in that which awaits you. Circle it together with the intention and vibration, and when the three are one, you will manifest the result.

Every day, when you get up, practice. First remember the union you feel when you are comfortable in a group. Feel it in your body. Where does it settle in your body? What is the vibration like? Stay in the vibration and feel it pooling around you. As you breathe, it expands. You do not say, "I want to have oneness with the heart, or the sky, or the night, or the moon". You say, "My intention is to be always in heart, with no sound, no thought. Nothing is more important than being in heart."

Then your body will start being in heart, which means that the vibrations of all your systems will be attuned. That's very important because you want superhuman experiences. You want to work longer hours, feel less tired, accomplish miracles and mountains of things in no time at all and still feel as if you don't need rest. And that isn't will. It isn't thought. It's substance flowing through the body in such a way that it nourishes the intention and the vibration and manifests that. Sometimes you'll find it in the same moment that you intend it.

You will learn—must learn—how to do things outside of time. You want it to be quick, and it needs to be quick. You've touched it many times. It is your intention to draw into this time everything that you have experienced as power, commitment, and truth.

If someone is opinionated or has many thoughts in the head and is speaking these thoughts, just weave them in. It's important that all of that be released, mediated, balanced, and unified in the place where there is no sound.

Silence brings together all dimensions simultaneously. What you're bringing together in the dimensions is focused down here. It is communicated and all aspects of life reply. It's important that you hold the space and include everyone who you know wants to be here. Differences don't matter. If someone wants to be here on some level, include them in the way that is appropriate for them, and the numbers and energy will grow.

If you need to submit a proposal or agenda and you don't know what to do, don't do anything except go into heart. Then the pieces will come together. If you're going to trust the universe, you must trust the universe completely or none of this will work. It's not about abilities or capabilities. It's about the intention in your heart to make this work.

BEING IN SYNCHRONY WITH LIFE

Peace is the feeling you have when you're in the place of no sound. Your muscles relax, your thoughts still, your heart opens, your body rests, and you don't need anything. That's the feminine, that's safety, that's the place where you are nurtured and where you belong. This is what you've come to create: a place where everyone belongs. If you take the steps involved, you will find that everything flows beautifully from it.

For example, when you introduce energy into form, when you move your body, when you dance and sing, think, type at the computer, answer the phone, or move wood, there is a rhythm to doing those things in synchrony with life. If one goes out to do a task and does the task without the balance of the rhythm of life within and without, the ebb and the flow are disrupted. It just becomes something that gets done.

It is not something that is co-created because the rhythm and the cycle of the being is not in synchrony with the rhythm and the cycle of the universe. Therefore, what the land is saying to you is, "Please accord that we have the same rhythm and cycle, ebb and flow. If we align together, we can help each other establish the experience of order in this place."

The thing about tasks is that if ebb and flow are balanced, work is not hard. You're not pushing against something; you are flowing with it. Many times you do from the mind and the will instead of from the heart. Before you pick up the log, feel the log. Feel the air around you. Feel the muscles of your body. Get a meaningful relationship with heart in everything you do, from driving the car, to petting the dog, to eating food. This is what the honoring is about.

When you do tasks, visualize your energy moving in a figure eight. Then feel any substance that you're working with in the same way. If you move forward, do so by balancing the sides until the order of balance is inherent in every step you take and becomes natural.

QUESTION:

HOW DO WE KNOW WHEN WE'RE IN HEART?

It is when your frequencies are attuned together and you stop being separate people. It is when your energy starts to flow in such a way that you have no needs, no cares, nothing bothers you, and your being settles in. You feel more whole. Nothing is clamoring in the mind to be thought about and activated. The heart of the group becomes a louder voice. It's not that you do not have thoughts, but the energy acquiesces to the greater commitment to diminish self and respond to the needs of the whole.

You're all here because you understand that your wholeness as a group is what wants to express. You're tired of trying to express by yourself. You're tired of believing that expressing by yourself is what you have to do to be seen, to belong, and to be loved. You know that hasn't worked. You're saying, "Let's see what we can create together, what we can birth."

Being in heart is different from most life experiences. It isn't being in romantic love, because there's no outer draw to do anything with the feeling. It's a sense of coming in, of resting, and expanding.

It's all things at one time. And it brings peace. You may each feel it differently. You may have different adjectives for describing it, but the easiest thing is just to hold hands and feel the love, however you may determine it in your mind. Practice that, expand that, and the cellular vibration will become its own resolution. You're not trying any longer. You're accepting that it's here, and you're here, and you can begin. It's simple. That's why you don't want to think about what you're supposed to be doing. Intending to be in heart is important in and of itself. When you are in heart, doorways open so you can see things, know things, and participate in things.

We would recommend that you work with your communication and connection. Take the incentive. Know that you know, know that everything is available. Take yourself seriously. You are not playing at some kind of deeply evocative thought. You are creating an inevitable and absolutely necessary model of consciousness. Pay attention. Listen and respond.

Remember that you have tremendous assistance. Ask for what you need. Ask clearly and specifically. It is not that we don't know what you need. It's that you need to ask for it to receive it. That's the way it is written.

Write. Pool your journals periodically. See how they are similar and dissimilar. Share what you are experiencing, what you know, what you gather and receive. Take it all very seriously without worrying about it. Taking yourself seriously just means that you know that it's important.

Many times the sound of the voice takes away from the experience of the frequency. Know that we are with you in this frequency always. It is each of your choices to be in this frequency with us. This is the space that we call Heaven on Earth.

Chapter 12

The Silver Chalice of Justice

The Silver Chalice is the space in consciousness which represents universal justice and balance. Going to the Silver Chalice is an exercise in non-separation. It is the practice of aligning yourself with the true reason your reality happens as you experience it and a way of knowing the truth about your relationships to others. It's a way of ascertaining your true connection to someone, foundationing your consciousness with them, and seeing where and how it fits together.

The Silver Chalice is recommended when one has a dispute, conflict or disagreement with someone that they would like to settle in the universal sense. This requires the balance point of understanding that no one is at fault, that no one is wrong in the situation, and that inherently, the human design was fashioned on balance. If you look at the Chalice, you can see that two sides are balanced in the center. The perspective of humanity has moved away from seeing the balance to seeing and aligning (much of the time) with only one of the two aspects on either side of the balance point. So the Silver Chalice is the recommended "resolution constant" for allowing both sides to contribute to the balance, even if they appear to be polarized, particularly with legal disputes.

Putting all the aspects of a situation and all the players in the situation into the Silver Chalice is a way of bringing balance into effect. Patience and temperance, with the highest good for all concerned as the intent, is the purpose of using the Chalice. The universal concept is that since the beginning, there has been an unrolling of energy that comes from the Source. As it expresses, it finds itself in different situations and frameworks, and as these levels unfold through free will, learning takes place. Folds of this energy are rolling over others and calling out others and are dispersing the energy differently than perhaps it was intended.

As it comes down a particular channel of reality, as chosen by each individual, it sometimes will connect with and reveal itself through different kinds of situations.

If one stands in a fixed position, the perspective might be: "You were supposed to come first and not last, and now that I'm first it means that I have do this, and I thought you were going to do it." As the lineage, heredity, and karma unfold, sometimes the relationships between dynamics shift according to the unrolling of the force field, or the flow of the energy through form. As you live your life you will have experiences in which you could say, "From my perspective, I thought it would be different. I wanted it to be different. I went into this with good intention. I paid my money and I didn't get my floor done, or I didn't get my house sided, or the roof fell in after one huge rain storm. Now I have to take this person to court and create relationships with other people, lawyers, arbitrators and mediators. I have to bring all these people into this situation that I didn't want to bring in, and listen to their perspective, and all I wanted was to have it very straightforward."

These situations are getting more complicated all the time. On some level they create mistrust between people. The dynamics keep changing so that nobody knows exactly what's going on and somebody else has the authority and the power to decide what's going on in your life.

This is interesting when you think about the way some cultures experience reality. In some cultures, if you have a car accident with someone, you get out from the car and embrace each other. You believe that this is the universe telling you that it is time for you to meet, and you don't worry about the damage to the car. You get on with developing a friendship.

In your life you are dispensing with properties, relationships, old forms, and structures that you may have felt were legitimate, and now you realize may not be. You ask, "What do I do with authority? Where do I place my interest and energy? What is supportive of me in this moment? How do I most fully compare the consciousness that I am choosing to live and the consciousness that I'm participating in? Is there relevance between those two things? Am I being consistent between what I know I am and how I live my life? Is it reflective of the truth of my essence? If I went up to the Akashic records, used my vibration as a library card, and from that perspective looked down at my life, would it be consistent? Can I say I do everything with that same vibration?" The answer is, "probably not," and that's fine. The most important thing is to go up there, look down at yourself, and ask these questions.

The Silver Chalice is a way of putting together those positions, probabilities, possibilities, and parallel realities. This includes the experience you're having right now, whatever it might be, particularly issues which involve litigation or an authority figure. It might be a traffic ticket, going before a judge for something, a litigation, or a dispute you had with someone who still owes you money or who hasn't repaid a service to you in a sense of balance. If you look in the closet, you may find that something there doesn't seem completely in balance. The Silver Chalice is an excellent way to work these things out.

JUSTICE VS. INJUSTICE

You might say, "Every soul in this situation is as important as my soul. Everything that has happened has no meaning other than as it pertains to balance. I am not out to make a certain amount of money, to claim this property, do this other thing. I am out to understand that balance is what is important and that nothing else is going to be served except balance. That's not my good, somebody else's good, or the good of this or that. It is about the good of the whole." As balance happens, the conflicts in your life, the injustices and seemingly unfair situations begin to design themselves so that your creation no longer involves injustice.

You're changing the paradigm where injustice was the way justice got served. In the old model you had to have the question before you got the answer. Somebody acted out to raise the question so that the rest of humanity would say, "That isn't fair. We ought to legislate that out of existence."

The new system of order and justice has been taken from the "fields of order" in nature, the core of order in the center of the Earth, and from the order that is based in the hierarchy from which we speak. It has been handed to humanity. That's where there's a sticky wicket because humanity does not usually dole out justice since it doesn't have the perspective to see what justice is.

People don't get the "why?" information because they haven't gone to the Akashic records and asked, "Why did that person do that?" When you do go to the records, you see where they got jostled over there and what they did over here. In normal circumstances, you can only see where they come out. You don't see their journey. That's why there are character witnesses in courts. They are trying to establish reasons for why people do what they do. Something is going on in the life system that influences and supports certain activities and outcomes. They want to give the whole picture, except that it's the whole picture of only a confined time of 30, 40, 50, or 60 years, not 60,000 years, or six millennia, or the consciousness of the complete Earth time.

When you put something in the Silver Chalice, what you are saying is, "I don't know what I did to them, and I don't know what they did to me. All I care about is that justice be done as it needs to be served for the good of the whole." You give up your claim, so to speak. You decide that nothing is as important as the reality of truth.

Because the Chalice is your justice system, you give up control over what happens. You just put it in. Then you are able to receive exactly what you need from wherever you need it. This is the basis of the Model of Cooperation (See Appendix).

When you cooperate with the universe, the universe feeds you. You might think, "I need to get $30,000 from that person." You could pursue them for that $30,000 and, in so doing, give up the right to receive the $30,000 you deserve from someplace else. When you let go of the need to have things be linear ("I'll do this for you, and you do this for me.") and you exchange that for a system that says, "I'll open myself to receive it from wherever it's available," that will be the experience of justice.

As you live that way more and more, everything in your situation balances out. There is not the necessity to pursue things which are unpleasant to you and which don't reap the results you intend.

You are a different drummer, consciously working from a different paradigm that serves everyone at once. This brings people away from the old types of seeking justice and into a new space of representing and experiencing justice. The Silver Chalice balances it all with infinite knowledge that is usually not available in the human experience. That consistent point of reality becomes a cornerstone in your society.

The new society will be based on less law, less thought about what is right and wrong, and more capacity for justice to be handed out by the universe—which means that the Akashic records begin to come into play. You understand how and why it is that someone is doing certain behaviors. It's no longer upsetting to you or disagreeable to you because you can understand that this is their process. This is where they come from, this is what's important to them.

JUST RELATIONSHIPS

As you come into relationship with people from this point on, you can use the Chalice as a way of responding to them. In your dream and meditation state you can say the affirmation about the Chalice and you'll begin to get information about those relationships. You will understand what is being resolved. You will take an equal stand in each situation. When you relate to someone, you relate to everything that is valuable about that person and their journey. So you have fuller, richer, deeper spaces of intimacy. The part of them that you don't trust for some reason, that you cannot define, becomes clear. You say, "They did this, so it gives me this feeling. I understand that it happened thousands of years ago, or will happen thousands of years in the future. Now I understand my hesitancy." You have total awareness of each other. You're able to understand your responses without judging them or separating from the people involved.

As you are honing in on the truth more and more, you'll find that there are a lot of people who get left behind, people who don't fit into the model, who are struggling to understand why they are doing what they are doing. They have no clue. They don't know that they were in another reality that set up processes in them that are now in constant conflict.

Many people choose to stop having relationships with others. They say, "I'm just going to live by myself and I'm not going to relate to anybody. I've had some really difficult experiences, and so I'll just live alone." So they end up alone and don't understand why. There is a feeling of guilt, ineffectiveness, and unworthiness—the sense that they did something wrong, that they're unlovable. You can rationalize until you're blue in the face, "That person did that to me, so that's why I'm doing this." If you feel alone, there are accompanying feelings of separation, whether you're separating from them or they are separating from you.

For example, when you want to collect a bill from someone, the normal experience of human beings is to separate from each other, to separate from the person that owes you the money, or the company that owes you the money, or the institution. You get mad at them and send them letters. What's interesting is that that person or institution is teaching you about union because if you separate from them because they owe you money, then you're living an inconsistent part of your reality.

It's very important to stay unified with everybody, regardless of the situation. Place all the parameters, as many times as you need to, into the Silver Chalice and ask for justice for the highest good of all concerned. Levels of information, wisdom, and knowledge will be revealed. Union requires of all of us that we unify regardless of the situation and regardless of what appears to have happened.

REALITY AND ILLUSION

When we talk about illusion and reality, it's a very important distinction, because people think about reality as being that which they can prove is true and illusion as being something that is false. The way we talk about it is that illusion is anything that is out of union, and reality is everything that is in union.

It has less to do with truth and more to do with union, because truth is subjective many times. Anything that creates separation is an illusion. Anything that truly brings union is reality.

We're speaking about walking your talk, about looking at all the dynamics in your life and saying, "No matter how they were created, it is important that I take responsibility for living only in a unified space. Anything else that separates me on any level, regardless of how right I think I am about a situation, can be released into the Chalice."

As we provide a responsiveness to ourselves, we come together with truth as it is seen from total reality. That is why you're going to the Akashic records. You want to see absolute truth. You're not interested in nuts and bolts and pieces as much as you're interested in the why.

As you create the context of seeing yourself as one who serves infinite justice, you will receive infinite justice. And you don't receive it until you serve it. If you are coming from infinite truth, your psyche, your mind, your emotion, your body, your spirit, your soul, your karma, and your design—are working together in your life.

If for some reason there is a discordance going on, whether it is with somebody else that you need to put in the Chalice or with a part of yourself that you might want to put in the Chalice, you're asked to serve infinite truth.

It's not just about what you do with you because the veils are so thin that whatever you do with you is sending loud messages to the world. A lot of chaos is going on because so many messages are being sent to the world.

That's why sometimes it's confusing. "Who's telling the truth? What should I believe? Should I worry about this or not? Should I spend lots of energy and time preparing for it, even though it doesn't feel like something I need to worry about?" Where does the balance come in? Where do you live in safety? What will support what you want to create? How do you take all the information that's coming in and weed through it to separate the wheat from the chaff? And what in each person is the truth? These questions are going to get stronger. They are not going to become less important—they are going to become more important.

As changes occur physically on the Earth, in the psyches of people, and in human structures, these questions are going to be imperative to answer. The Silver Chalice is a vehicle where you can put all the information, all the questions. You stick all those parameters into the Silver Chalice and say, "I ask for balance."

This is a place where you can sort out the levels that you're working with now. As the destruction of old frameworks supports the creation of new ones, chaotic energy is appearing. You're going to have constant readouts about that chaos—what it feels like and how people are going through it—the fear, the grief, the pain, and the struggle. All of this will come into your awareness. Stay steady and constant. Honor it all and put the dilemmas in which you find yourself into the Chalice.

Your perception and awareness will increase. Your development will be on all levels simultaneously. This is about reality unifying itself so that the illusion falls apart. Anything that's been connected to illusion, or has been in any way separating, is going to make a statement as it leaves. If you put the Chalice into effectiveness, you can balance any information that comes in to you, any energy, any relationship, any process. Instead of paying attention to the details that don't seem to come together for you, or that raise as many questions as they answer, if you put them into the Chalice, you begin to see how it is going to come out.

HOW THE CHALICE SERVES THE DESIGN

The Silver Chalice has several broader and more diverse applications. After you work through the conflictual nature of human reality, you can go to a whole different level of perception with the Chalice where you work with global and universal frameworks. Use the Chalice to balance and measure earthly things which on some levels would be disturbing. Put them into the whole instead of looking at them from a linear framework.

Working with the Akashic records and the Silver Chalice simultaneously is a way of taking information, putting it into the Chalice, experiencing the balance, and taking that balance into the world. You can go into situations you've never been in before and aren't sure how to handle, where discernment, balance and solace are needed, and create new models.

You are creating a system where you use the justice of the universe instead of human justice. When universal justice is in effect rather than human justice, you will have the most capability on this planet for healing. You will have the experience of being in Heaven on Earth. When that universal paradigm becomes a viable means to settle disputes, to organize relationships, and to understand cooperative measures and partnerships, you will ordain new realities on the planet.

It is important to understand justice from the perspective of the Silver Chalice and how it is lived out in world situations. Part of the reason why accessing balance from the Chalice will occur, is because it's going to be important to document things. Some of you reading this material may feel called to go to the Akashic records, look at what's going on in the world, put that into the Chalice, and say, "Show me what the justice is in this. This race is killing that race, and this race is looting that one, and this person is prosecuting that one, and this person is killing that one, and this person is raping that one, and this person is stealing from that one. I came up to the Akashic records, and I believe I understand why these things are happening. But I get down here and I can't sort it out because it seems so chaotic and out of order." You then take the situations, put them in the Chalice, and say, "I want to know the 'why' of these experiences."

As people move through these levels of reality—up and down from physical, emotional, mental, to the Akashic, and up and down between the levels of the physical and the Chalice—you will make trails. Individuals who access that information, who go back and forth constantly, will make pathways for others to follow. Just imagine what the world would be like if everybody made that journey once a day to figure out why, the activities of the world cease to be chaotic.

Much of what you can do about violence, hatred, and separation, is to make your own path of peace. You will find that everything you experience becomes consistent with that place of order. Instead of relationship with whatever is going on in the news, whatever is being fed to you by who is deciding what it is you're supposed to hear, you say, "I don't want that anymore. I want to go to a place where I know the truth of what I'm hearing and seeing and feeling and the total picture makes sense. It makes sense in terms of the fact that there is a design, and the design has as its fulfillment the resolution of human dichotomy and the experience of union in all levels and dimensions."

If you work with the Chalice diligently, you will resolve karmic and legal processes easily because you clean up your act on every level. It's about honoring that your commitment to being is real, and that has to be on every level. It isn't just, "I meditate once a day for an hour, or two, so that's my work." The work is 24 hours a day from now on. It doesn't stop. The only rest you're going to get is being in spirit.

It's going to be like an incessant rain on a tin roof, "I'm hearing it again, I'm hearing it again." It's about changing illusion. Because illusion has infiltrated every crack of your consciousness, it will be let go from every crack of your consciousness. This is about being. It's about who you are in every micro-second of your consciousness.

Other dimensions, lifetimes, and points of reality are affecting what's happening to you now. If you wake up irritable with somebody in the morning and you weren't irritable when you went to bed, something happened during the night to make you irritable. You might have gone to another dimensional space with them, and worked out something or not worked out something, and then awakened and said, "Something has happened. What is it? Let me find out because that's part of my beingness. I want to be with whatever is going on." Listen to your messages, feel them, think about them. Put everything in the Chalice that's pending for you. Know that everything is going to be fine in the sense that it's all going to come out in balance.

The more astutely you receive these messages, the more you realize that you can't separate yourself from everybody else. You don't have an ego in the same way anymore. Your personality is undergoing change because you're becoming a ray of light. You're becoming that consciousness of vibration that is able to live from the substance and be completely, universally oriented. Ultimately, everything that you require to live comes to you from the invisible.

THE CHALICE FOSTERS HONOR

You can be a Chalice yourself as a way of being. You can honor that in every moment, what you are called to look at about receiving, or giving, or substance, is organizing a reference in your consciousness.

If you use this system, you will bypass your present legal system. You won't need it because you'll come into affirmation with the consciousness of the people. You'll make agreements energetically before you make them physically, and everything will come out in balance.

You won't need to have understandings with people that are written down to the last "t" and the last dot on the page. Your word will be your bond. You will need no other framework except the intentional resonance between two people which honors what you've created, be it small or large.

People will go back to honoring their word. They will go back to stating what they need. They won't worry about having enough so that they try to cheat other people. They will have the sense that they're clear and steadfast and constant, able to live by their word. And the word is very important. It's coming again to the time of trust and the time when people can cooperate. As long as you have legal systems such as they are now, where people cannot speak to each other and make resolution, there will continue to be a sense that everyone is in competition, that everyone is out for oneself. The experience of being in a frame where everything is available and you can see order and justice come out of it, is very exciting. You can understand that the value of your consciousness is absolute, and you can affect everything by that consciousness. Everything starts making sense.

Because of the number of decisions that need to be made, it is very important for you to have a method of sorting things out for yourself that you can trust, that you can work with. Notice that we are not talking about your soul's calling or your beingness in terms of what you designed for yourself. We're talking about what you do with the world, with people, situations, ideas, and information. When you hear about what's anticipated and who's doing what to whom, what do you do? You can put it in the fluids and immerse it, and yet you're a human being, and you have relationship with other people and with your world.

To take this to the level of consciousness that has to do with infinite balance gives you a perspective that will be honored by everyone. No matter who's involved in the situation, if they feel that you're out to actualize the balance for them also, they will start cooperating with you to create resolution. This is a model that could be used for litigation, for mediation, or to support responsiveness in others. It becomes a personal tool that will guide you.

You will have an alternative legal process where groups make decisions in ways that are so easy that you'll wonder why you haven't created them earlier. Those of you who use the Silver Chalice will gravitate more towards working in community-based, co-creative consciousness because you will not have the kinds of issues that now face humanity. That's because you'll transpose those issues from looking at the dichotomy to experiencing union and balance. When you transpose them, you also create new models. Just hold the Chalice and ask it to show you. Wait for the result rather than trying to use all the methods you were taught or conditioned to experience.

THE NUTS AND BOLTS OF THE CHALICE

This gives you a way of looking into the future, of creating new systems, because you can put all of the components of an idea into the Chalice and say, "I want to create a community, and I have ten people who have signed up. I want to create a business, and I have a partner and this amount of money and resources." Or you can say, "I want to marry this person who has five children and ten cousins, and so what would my life be like?" You can take every situation, stick it into the Silver Chalice and get a projection on it. So you can say, "Okay. It looks like we're going to need about five thousand more dollars."

You can power the present with the future, utilize the energy of the universe, go into substance, and manifest through having the points symmetrical and vibrationally consonant. You can do many things for which you have skills. If you put it in the Chalice, it gives you a way of determining what the outcome in balance would be. This means that you can see, in a nuts and bolts fashion, what you might add to this to make it more effective, to make it last longer, to include more resources or people.

This can save lots of time and energy because any time you can use the vehicle of vision and the experience of energy to get an answer instead of using physical resources or moving from one place to another to check something out, it's easier. You can do anything with your awareness that you can do with your physicality, and more. So save yourself time and energy. You can also do that for somebody else by putting them into the equation and asking, "Will it work for them to proceed in this way?"

You live from absolute reality, which means that you can see the ways in which union will occur for the highest good all the time. You act as mediator between spirit and form because that's what the Silver Chalice is. The Silver Chalice is the framework through which mediation happens between dimensions.

You are now interdimensional beings. Once you have used your library card of vibration to access the Akashic, you're an interdisciplinary, interdimensional being in action.

The Silver Chalice is a gift that comes to the world at a time when many systems are failing. So we take it a few steps up, aggregate from more levels, and bring in more resources because we do not ever solve a problem at the level where it was born. We bring in other levels and dimensions to assist us to more fully live the consciousness we have ordained. This is a calling. This is an honoring. We don't have do it mentally, emotionally, or legally.

The balance in our system doesn't come from meditating once a day or once a week anymore, but from finding out, "What can I do for the whole? Where can I go in my consciousness to find the answers, not just for me, but for everybody? How can we create models that work?

You've made that bond between Heaven and Earth, made that bond between the part of you that is in the Akashic record and the part of you that's in the world. The more symmetry you have between those dimensions and levels, the more there is an experience of feeling that sense of belonging—that you can marry levels together, that it can be sacred here.

Whatever's going on has a purpose. It's honoring and receiving. It's also knowing that you are important in this process because when you orchestrate all these parts, you, as that point of light, radiate more truth, more fullness, more awareness. Remember that as long as it's in balance in the Chalice, everyone wins, and everything comes into harmony.

Honor yourself and what you have to contribute. Plant your feet and get yourself going. What are you here to contribute? Live that contribution rather than waiting for an infinite number of variables that don't have any meaning and cause you to feel ineffective. Do it now! Live it now!

Ask yourself, "What's my balance point? What have I really done in this life? What could I have done? Let me hold these two things up and look at them in the mirror. Am I doing what I came here to do? Am I living it as fully as I can? Is there something else that's in that Chalice that I have not resolved, have overlooked, have hoped would work out? It's time for me to do it now."

When you take the bull by the horns, and really start living that way, other people match that intention with you. The sacredness of the message of how you are to create balance together is forged. Then whatever you've been through together has meaning, and if it doesn't have meaning, you're missing something. Again, it's fine if you want to miss it, and yet you'll keep missing it, and as you keep missing it, you'll create another situation where you miss it.

It means that you live intentionally. You live in the substance of the fluid of the universe. You always expect the universe to be there whenever you remember to ask for something or communicate. The universe expects no less of you. Be there, because it's up to you now. There's nobody else to be blamed because we now have the Chalice. It's a co-responsible, co-created situation, whatever it is.

This is very freeing and allows you to support truth because whatever it is that you're about, if it's not about truth, it doesn't matter. You're the only one who can pull yourself up by your boot-straps, because it's a free-will experience. So whatever you put into it, you're going to get out of it. The foundation of this is absolute and infinite truth, and if you link up with this system, you will live nothing less than that. And that is how it has been ordained.

Sunlight on Water

Chapter 13

Coming Home

We would like to talk with you about the experience of your choice to be here as light. You have come here to support experiences which you remember and yet have never seen or lived in form. You have the awareness born within you of how it looks and feels and how it's sensitized by your light. Yet the design of it, the plan, the memory of where it is going to fit in the future is not as present for you. Sometimes you may find that you have a yearning to go home, a yearning to return to where the design was first hatched and see the space again so you can remind yourself of it. This is so that you can carry it more distinctly with you so that you are not feeling as lost or as separate from the reason for your being here.

To provide some background here, you are part of a light force. You carry an impulse within you to restore order to the universe. To do that you are conscious of instituting the Monad in the framework of the world because that's the choice for this free-will experiment. This is an experiment. The Monadal energy, as it split into the twelve initial points of reality, and those split into twelve, made 144. At that point in "time," there was what you would call a conference. At that conference it was determined that the space of this Earth would be inhabited by the experience of light in form with the ability to create whatever reality was ordained by each individual point of light.

The consciousness of God rests in the hands of the people. Because you are God, you can affect God. Until this time, that thought has been kept under wraps. As you think about it now, think about how you might affect every point of reality by your choices. Ultimately, the freedom that you experience is dynamically connected to the eventual resolution and the formula of the design of creation, which comes from all points simultaneously. In other words, you are here acting on behalf of your past self, your present self, and your future self.

You are here remembering an ideal, a space from which you were born, from which the free-will experiment was created. You are also here making decisions as if you didn't know any of this. You are also in the future reaping the results of the choices of the free-will experiment as it comes into resolution so that you are actually everywhere at one time, fostering all of this reality. You are in this body and you don't remember the design. So amnesia is rampant in the process.

As you think about that original design and being able to affect that design, if there's something you'd like to include in your present formula, some information, or some part of that experience of choice that you would like to recall, relive, and reorder, that is also possible. It's also possible to understand that you have the total capacity to create whatever it is that you desire. That means that the capacity you carry is equal to anything you've ever heard about or dreamed of.

It also means, for many of you who want to return home, that you can do that. You can experience it as a transcendence rather than a transition—rather than a death. You can experience it as a dream or meditation. You come back from that experience with the answers, the memories, and the charge of that impulse of energy. This is so that you are ready to do what you have come to do. Your life experience becomes literally changed by your volitional will.

Your consciousness remembers that you have come here to do something special. It isn't an egoic process that tells you that, it's a knowing. It's deep inside of you; it's not superficial. It's not about a person, a time period, an idea, or an experience. It's about your essential point of reality and where it's anchored.

If you want to, you can come home and experience what that anchoring means, where it comes from, and where it will resolve itself. Then your life experience becomes that knowing. Take the proverbial bull by the horns and say, "I want to know where my pieces will fit."

We recommend that you come home regularly, then project yourself into your present life and realize who you are in form. This is different from resonating and receiving, working with your light body, experiencing your energy fields, balancing your chakra system, and working to see the balance of those things which are already a part of your life. At some level when you work with these "physical" areas you function at a rate of speed which is consistent with your "normal" reality, like who's doing what to whom and why. Coming home is about your essential nature. It's about the spaces that are with you wherever you go and don't change.

It's the blinders coming off, the understanding which is necessary to dispel all the doubts and bring resolve into being. It's the part of your emotion that keeps longing for something to fulfill it but can't find it in the outer world. It's the part of you that mentally races back and forth and tries to decide what it is that's so important about being here and being a light worker. Sometimes you come up short and say, "I don't know what's so important about it. I think I just want to cash in my chips and go back because it is tedious and I don't understand what a lot of this means and how it will unfold. There are not that many designs in my thinking that I could imagine making models for the world— to not only survive but co-create, cooperate, and bring absolute resolution. Somebody's going to have to help me here with this one, because I don't quite get the game plan."

REMEMBERING YOUR MISSION

We recommend that a minimum of four times a month you come home for an evening and reorient yourself with the vibration of what it is to be in the space of light. You then function vibrationally and energetically as one who has a mission. The knowing is about your mission. You know you have a mission. You might even know some about what that mission is. Probably something is missing in your knowing about it, like when, where, and how the resources are going to come to you, and when it will be possible for you to relate more and more to who you are in that mission.

A lot of you carry your mission like a sword, like a book, a covering on your body, a hat, a pair of shoes, an automobile, or whatever. You use it at certain times and yet you don't embody it completely. It's as if you're waiting for something to show up to give you instructions about how to do that. If you don't know how your mission fits into the prospectus of what you're doing every day of your life, it's not only lonely, it's tiresome and frustrating.

We suggest that you come home to shed light on the parameters that you're dealing with so that the knowing and the mission start activating. This is so that you feel as if what you've come here to do is beginning to build inside you. It has to build inside you before it can build in the world. You feel as if you have a thousand angels carrying you through this process. A very deep space resonates and activates your whole framework of being so that you're not just someone who's landed on the planet without the instruction manual and you're not sure exactly what to do.

The other reason for coming home is because it's time to rewire your circuits, amplify your charge, and to put together, or aggregate, those pieces of your reality so that the foundation you're carrying is literal. You understand what you are here to do. What it's about is remembering. Remembering it all requires patience.

It's as if you're in the ocean. You know there are lifeboats and life-saving rings. Somebody's trying to throw you one. A current is sweeping you away from the ship, the lifeboats, and the rafts. You say, "What am I supposed to do? Where am I supposed to go?" Somebody yells, "Swim like hell!" Somebody else says, "Why don't you just float with the current, flow with the wave that will take you home?" Somebody else says, "Look around, use your eyes, use your senses, figure out where you are. Then you'll know where to swim." Another says, "Just float, let go completely, and become like a piece of cork on top of the water. Then they'll see you and come get you." There are probably fifty things that you could do, and at the same time, it's up to you to make that choice. How do you decide?

This is about remembering as much as you can, figuring it out from the level of knowing and memory, rather than trying to figure out what you should pay attention to and what's going to save your butt. Because if you're thinking about what you should do and where you're going to end up, you're probably not in memory, and you're definitely not in knowing. It's a very beautiful time for you, those four times a month, to throw up your hands and say, "Take me back, I want to go back. I don't want to make transition, I don't want to stand in front of a truck or anything like that. I want to let go of all of the parameters and things that I think about all the time."

So once a week you might say, "I don't want to do anything.

I just want to go home. I want to be a child. I want to be free of responsibility and the need to survive and the need to do anything. I just want to be in a place where I can remember and have my knowing surround me so that I am strengthened, rewarded, honored, affirmed, and feel the divinity of my nature. I want to really see who I am."

PHONE HOME: AN EXERCISE

To go home, go to bed at night, take a siesta in the afternoon, or meditate for a couple of hours, whatever feels best for you. Basically "tie" your body to the bed by anchoring your energy from the top of your head down to the bottoms of your feet. Say, "I want to stay here and be safe while I do my trip. I ask that all parts of my body, all my cells, and all of my molecular consciousness be ground into the Earth. I ask to be protected by all the angels of consciousness that come around me. I want to let go and transcend in these few hours, or in this night's sleep. I want to go home. I want to remember. I want to see what's real. I want to be renewed. I want to come back energized, refreshed and revitalized, with lots of things that I remember which are going to help me live my mission." This is about recovering your mission statement and mission energy. In other words, "Why did I say I'd do this?" You get it all into perspective.

Anchor your body to the bed energetically, gather all your sentinels and guardians, and breathe through your body all the way down to your feet. Make sure you're in your body before you leave. That's very important because your body will be in the same condition when you return, except that you'll be able to energize and charge it because it will be grounded. The circuits will be open to that last charge of energy and will be able to handle that charge. If you're not in the body when you leave, and you bring back all this energy, you might blow a few circuits, or at least make yourself feel as if the trip was not worthwhile. You want to foundation it, clear it, anchor it, and make sure that the energy you're calling to serve you is present as you make this experience of transcendence.

Get ready to go out through the top of your head by first going all the way down to the bottom of your feet, like a shower, like the oscillating current of sunlight on water. Fill your body, then reverse that mechanism. Take the energy and move it from your feet through the chakras, all the way up and out the top of the head. Ask to return to the space of your origination. Be sure to breathe deeply and rhythmically during the exercise.

You'll come through the time tunnel in reverse. You'll remember how you came in but be going in the opposite direction. There will be no pain, struggle, or problems with it. You go through that experience as if you're going through the tunnel and leaving the experience of the world, except that as you're going, you are watching, and you're not feeling anything. You're not feeling pain, you're not feeling separation, you're just aware of what the movement is telling you about your consciousness. You're moving into spaces where you ordain knowledge and remembrance.

This is important because unless at times you are absent from the density of your world, it's challenging to recognize who you are, that your knowing is real, and that your mission is going to take place. Maybe you know you have the ability to shape-shift, trans-locate, bi-locate, or assist other people to transform. Maybe you can take whole levels of consciousness and bring them into this reality. But when you think about it, you scratch your head and say, "Who, me? How can I do these things when I can't even pay my bills and don't know how to have someone really love me, and I'm afraid of this, or I'm not doing that?"

This is like a refresher course. It is a way of reacquainting yourself with your family of consciousness. You put together situations that seem to be very real for you in your dream state and do not necessarily support you in the physical space. You go through the tunnel and experience reliving, backwards, your journey into form. As you move through that tunnel in reverse, you begin to experience the reason for your choice.

You see the relationship between what you're doing in your life now (with your belief system and thought process) and remembering and re-living your lineage, the part of you that has come to do your mission. The experience calls you into being, saying, "Don't you remember this? This is why you forgot that, because you're supposed to remember it when this happens." You're getting details that will assist you to make sense out of your life and your reason for being here, which sometimes might be cloudy.

You might think sometimes that you're idealistic, or that you fantasize, or you're not sure that you can trust your own knowing. You might see yourself as a beautiful blue being under the sea, a mermaid, a beautiful green Goddess rising out of the trees, and flying into the ethers. Or you might see yourself dissolving as wind and carrying messages all over the world. You might see yourself as dynamically being connected to something other than yourself, but you don't remember what it is, and you're not sure how to get that information into the psyche so that you have the power to activate the charge.

This is a way of regrouping, of bringing in the stability to answer your questions, of looking at what keeps driving you. You wake up and say, "I've got to keep going." Why? "I don't know, I've just got to keep going." What are you going to do? "I don't know. I've just got to keep going." Stamina and strength forge you.

As you go toward the light again and regroup the pieces, your awareness starts to click, "Yes, this feels familiar. Thank goodness something feels familiar because I've been lost in amnesia for many years." There is an aching, a yearning to have this familiarity and to be full of grace and lay your burden down. All of you have moments when you lay your burden down, but then you pick it up again because your mission is unclear. As you retrace your steps, information comes. "That's why I picked these parents. This is what I learned. This is what gave me courage. This is what gave me strength. This is what gave me stamina. This is what gave me patience."

If you make the statement that you are returning home for your mission plan and want your statement clearly outlined in images, awarenesses, sensate feelings and knowings, and you don't want to come back until you have more knowing, then, with your free will, you claim the right to know. You are claiming the right to receive. That's valuable because in this time when destructuring of the belief systems is happening, if you go home and restructure yourself, you crystallize that intention. It's so crystal clear that you can go into the world and just start doing what you're here to do.

The foundation of this is very simple:

- Go to the place where the charge originated.
- Identify with the charge instead of your current reality.
- Shape-shift the energy.
- Bring the charge in the top of your head.
- Ground it in the same way you did before you left.

While you're in the ethers, sleeping, dreaming, meditating, visualizing, organizing, communicating, whatever you want to do, formulate your design from a place inside you at the same time that you're seeing it outside you.

In the ethereal levels that you travel through, it is important that you continue to modify that energy and keep going through all those levels of awareness until you say, "Wait a minute now, this is the most familiar place. This is where I think I come from. This is where I belong." You have your own path to take on this, so you're going toward the light. You experience that your intention is to actualize your mission and to reorient. Also, it is to go into the spaces where that knowledge is connected to the vision and the choice because the choice space is the Swing Between Worlds. So you're coming home.

You're going to sit in the Swing again and see where it is that your choices are destined to take you. Because once you see that, you can return to your physicality on the beam of light that you originally traveled.

And yet, since you've already been born, and since you've grounded into your body, and since the foundation is all the way through your circuits, you bring the memory all the way into your feet. It means you ground it in as if amnesia never happened! You know what the personality is, who you've lived with, who your lovers are or were, who your friends are, what your vocation is. You can go right back in your body with the full knowing that you had in the Swing Between Worlds before you came. But this time you're not going to forget it.

The more times you do this (you might want to do it four times a week or four times a day), the easier it will be to make the place of the formed body, where you have the circuitry and the anchoring, and the place of the awareness of consciousness, the same vibrational point. This is of course, the experience of living your mission. So the above and the below come together. The Absolute is living in form. You become God or Goddess.

ALL YOUR PIECES FIT

As you come together with the wave, the knowing, the mission, the consciousness, and the body—this is aggregation. Aggregation is the place where the pieces of the puzzle finally fit. This phenomenon is a rebirth. It comes into the experience of your life in such a way that it serves the design, makes you happy, relieves you of the burden of carrying something you're not sure you can manifest, and allows you to organize consciousness so that it shows you what it's about. You can acquiesce. You can relax and let go of struggle and trying and working harder. Just allow it.

There's this feeling of humor and joy and aliveness because you're receiving something that has so much value. For the first time in your life, you don't care about whether you're going to do it or not, because the knowing is stronger than anything else.

The mission you've come to live is organized in your consciousness. Even though it seems immaterial, invisible, inaudible, and unable to be tapped physically, it has already made the conduit so that it's in front of you showing you the way, not behind you, invisible, immaterial, it's in front of you, completely actualized. That's what happens when the circuitry turns on. You go forward and backward in the circuitry so that you get it coming and going. It translates itself differently when you're reborn. You already have the circuitry in place to live the mission because you put it in place by grounding your body before you left.

So you're coming down the "shoot the chute," and amnesia does not touch you anymore because you already know you're dense. You're coming back to density. So what? Big deal! It doesn't affect you anymore because you're working on your circuits. You're embodying light. You're going to make the circuits of your physical body equal to the circuits you had before you left the Swing Between Worlds. It's obvious to you what's going on.

Heaven on Earth means that there is a vibrational equivalency between dimensions that is fostered when you change dimensions. It's fostered as you experience going back and forth and back and forth. When you change dimensions, it doesn't change.

You're able to keep it consistent so that you can have both worlds. You can have all worlds. You can have fragments of whatever you want all the time. The dynamics are supportive of all dimensions, and you do not have to choose. You can go back and forth as many times as you want and have all those worlds with you, and you don't have to choose. The good news is that the foundation of your body is learning to hold your consciousness, and you can expand your consciousness as far as you want. As long as you're grounding the energy, as long as you're moving it through, opening your centers of energy, and learning to balance them, as long as you're experiencing the Silver Chalice and looking at all those pieces, it comes together, it's aggregating. It's a better life. It feels good.

LIVING IN RESOLUTION

You can apply this experience in many ways. For example, receiving forgiveness, losing guilt, having another go, receiving absolution, anything you want. This is about resolving, once and for all, those memories you carry that still bother you. For example, you can probably still remember the way your mother looked at you when you dropped that glass of milk on the floor. It will always be indelibly etched in your consciousness. Or what that second grader said to you about your hair, or your nose, or your face, or your teeth. It will always be there. You're walking around as a big person, wearing assurance on your face, and you're doing great, except that all those things are still inside the psyche.

You're going to go inside out and lose the pain and the hurt to attain the experience of your own divine mission. The only thing that erases those hurts is to experience that it was for some purpose that you now comprehend, and which really doesn't affect you any more. It's not because you buffed up your armor of self worth, it's because you recognize that your divine nature doesn't make mistakes. It doesn't matter if you dropped the milk and your mother was concerned because somebody could get cut by the glass, or that it was the last bit of milk in the carton, or that she had just washed the floor— something that had nothing to do with you. You understand that when you come back through the tunnel.

Your left and right brain can start communicating and activating so that you regenerate all the parts you started out with. You regenerate all that was lost through amnesia, or socialization, or behavior, or whatever you went through. Whatever you have done is going to be reversed. You have the opportunity to do this differently.

What happens as you reorient your psyche to your consciousness is that everything that doesn't matter falls away, and everything that you are emerges, which is what it's all about. No matter what was said to you or done to you, you are being moved through an oscillatory frequency that's turning everything inside out. You're accessing your memory of what's important and losing the memory of what's not important. The pain is being removed. Why? Because you're going into reality and losing illusion. You have a perfect scenario for resurrection—coming back from the dead, and you're alive. And you're bringing with you that which is your purpose, your potentiation, your mission.

BRINGING IN YOUR MISSION: AN EXERCISE

When you come back into the body, ground everything that you are into your body. Bring it in from the top of your head, down through your body, and send out through the bottom of your feet anything that remains of illusion. Transpose the cellular system so that anything that's in the body, lingering as memory in the cells, is taken out through the bottom of the feet so that you have a transfusion of light into form. This time the mission is replacing the forgetfulness, the absentmindedness, the I'm-out-to-lunch, the I'm-out-in-space syndrome, whatever it is.

LIVING YOUR MISSION

You're coming in. You're planting yourself in the form of the body, and this time you are here in a way that you've never been before. Now there's a reason to be here, it's real for you, it's clear for you, it has vision, strength, capacity, and most of all, it has information that supports your knowing. When you come into the body, the knowing says, "Thank goodness I'm not alone anymore. I'm hooked up. Everything that comes into being through me is going to be recognized as my own plan, my own design. I begin to organize my consciousness, I begin to put the framework together and structure it so that my life supports my essence."

You see through things that don't work anymore. You see through those areas of your experience where you know you've been wanting to make a change but haven't quite known what it was.

Now you say, "What is my consciousness supporting, and is it what I want it to support?" I give permission to reshape my life. I've reshaped my consciousness, and now I want to reshape my life." You will see through the illusion of your own mask first. You'll see what no longer serves you or fits you. Next you see through the masks of other people in society, or community, or societal biological family. If there are not masks, that's good—if there are, you see through them. And it's not going to hurt you this time. You're not going to say, "I made a mistake. I shouldn't be here." You find that you have a strength you didn't know you had to make those choices.

This happens only if you go home. That's just the way it is because if you live from this dimension you have attachment to it, most times, without a broader perspective. If you live it from the knowing that "this is my mission, or this is not my mission," then you're decisive about it and you're clear.

We talk about this in the chapter on relationship. When someone says, "I want to live from my full essence. I want to be in love with myself and have a relationship with myself," and the other person says, "I don't really think I want a relationship with myself," then the first person understands that there is no pain involved in this. The person needs to do something else. When you choose to be in a relationship with yourself, you will find someone else who is in relationship with themselves. It's easy to make that transition when it's time to do it because there is a great relief that there are no longer masks. Take illusion off. It's a deep and rich experience. Then you turn around and there's somebody there who wants to be real also. It's a beautiful transitional space to be in at that moment because the transition you're making is not that you're dying and your heart is dying—it's that you're really alive for the first time. You're not afraid to be alive by and with yourself. That's very important.

As the mask comes off people around you, you realize, "We're starting to live here. There's zing to this! We're alive in ways that the mission has always stated that I would be alive, yet I was looking around and nobody seemed to be doing it. So I was waiting." Your direction and calling are clear. The calling is the frame to the mission—what it looks like, what it feels like, how it fits. Now is the time. We would recommend that your first mission be to find your mission and that you design time into your week to do this.

You go home on a regular basis. You can always go home when you sleep—you can go to bed at night, close your eyes, and do the shower meditation. The energy comes in through the top of your head and out the bottoms of your feet, like a shower of water. Ground yourself strongly, tie yourself etherically to your bed if you want to, and feel the angels come around you, your guides, anything that makes you feel safe—your soul, light, whatever. Put crystals around you, and then breathe the light through the body. Ground it in one last time, and then breathe and go right out the top of your head and say, "I'd like to return home. When I awaken I want to come through the levels again, differently this time, because I want to bring my memory with me. I choose to remember." The most important sentence for a human being to say is, "I remember."

Remember. Reorient. Support yourself. Familiarize yourself with your own game plan. Go up to the Swing and say, "Look, I want to know what's going on here. I really want to understand this. I want to see my mission as clearly as you're able to show it to me." We will play it back for you so you can see the innocence with which you chose it, the divinity which surrounds it, the flame which calls it out and keeps it alive, and the integrity of your mission, which was important enough for you to come here in the first place!

Getting the pieces together, resolving all those nagging doubts, situating yourself in the universe so that you belong everywhere, this is what it's about. When you come back with your mission, through morphic resonance and the concept of the tuning fork, everybody else is clearer about their mission also. Resolution is easier. The pain that people carry gets resolved. If you don't have pain and you're walking around clear, you can imprint everybody that you meet with that same clarity, and they can start feeling as good as you feel.

Everything you do serves the whole. The clearer you are about your mission, the faster it will actualize—facilitating resolution, bringing oneness into form, making the sacred marriage between your above and your below, and the instrument you've come to live it through. So balancing this is imperative because many of you are at the end of your rope of suffering and at the beginning of the experience of complete and absolute resolution.

So come into resolution and let the struggling end now. Fill yourself with the solace of knowing that everything about you has a reason and a purpose, and you're experiencing what your purpose is. You're free to receive fulfillment and resolution. Everything makes sense. The pieces click together. The symmetry and beauty of the design come in and feed the substance that you're carrying, and you begin to flow. The fluids and dimensions match and marry through your experience. Nothing is missing. There's nothing you have to do because you've kicked the mission into its unfolding. You go down the "shoot the chute" again, but this time you know where you're going.

differently this time, because I want to bring my memory with me. I choose to remember." The most important sentence for a human being to say is, "I remember."

Remember. Reorient. Support yourself. Familiarize yourself

with your own game plan. Go up to the Swing and say, "Look, I want to know what's going on here. I really want to understand this. I want to see my mission as clearly as you're able to show it to me." We will play it back for you so you can see the innocence with which you chose it, the divinity which surrounds it, the flame which calls it out and keeps it alive, and the integrity of your mission, which was important enough for you to come here in the first place!

Getting the pieces together, resolving all those nagging doubts, situating yourself in the universe so that you belong everywhere, this is what it's about. When you come back with your mission, through morphic resonance and the concept of the tuning fork, everybody else is clearer about their mission also. Resolution is easier. The pain that people carry gets resolved. If you don't have pain and you're walking around clear, you can imprint everybody that you meet with that same clarity, and they can start feeling as good as you feel.

Everything you do serves the whole. The clearer you are about your mission, the faster it will actualize—facilitating resolution, bringing oneness into form, making the sacred marriage between your above and your below, and the instrument you've come to live it through. So balancing this is imperative because many of you are at the end of your rope of suffering and at the beginning of the experience of complete and absolute resolution.

So come into resolution and let the struggling end now. Fill yourself with the solace of knowing that everything about you has a reason and a purpose, and you're experiencing what your purpose is. You're free to receive fulfillment and resolution. Everything makes sense. The pieces click together. The symmetry and beauty of the design come in and feed the substance that you're carrying, and you begin to flow. The fluids and dimensions match and marry through your experience. Nothing is missing. There's nothing you have to do because you've kicked the mission into its unfolding. You go down the "shoot the chute" again, but this time you know where you're going.

Chapter 14

Hearing Without Words

You are moving into a time when there will be no language as you know it now, so your level of awareness will increase. Your potential will be expressed and experienced vibrationally and shared through waves of reality that you create together. Before long there will be no words to define consciousness.

As you approach this time, we suggest that you use fewer words, that you focus on what is important, and shine that out like a light. Foster the vibrational frequency that you intend to be. As much as possible, limit discussion, particularly of things which you don't understand, do not wish to manifest, or are afraid of. If this is your intention, you will substantiate that through the substance and the fluids. You will accelerate the vibration that you choose to manifest through and will magnetically attract what you are intending.

If you feel that you don't quite get what's going on, or you're striving for something and it doesn't seem to manifest, surrender it to the vibration of what you want to feel like and support. Bring that together as the charge inside your body and let the rest be. When you seek something, you are going outside your vibration to find it. So stay in your vibration and surrender to it.

This is about emotional reaction or response, mental thought or patterning, belief systems, and that which you think you want but don't know how to get. It is about what you want to express but don't know how. It's also about anything that isn't congruent. Allow it all to be dissolved so that what you are is the frequency of what you carry and nothing else. It's important to structure your reality so that it doesn't take from you. It only gives to you.

THE DESTRUCTURING PROCESS AND SYSTEMS THEORY

Destructuring is the massive energy of taking what is, disintegrating it, and returning it to the no-thing space. It's time to rise like the phoenix out of the ashes, and that takes energy, intention, and being on the wave of consciousness as it unfolds. It means having your vibration be consistent with that which you are.

As things fall apart around you, choose to excel, to expand, and to vibrate as a master. In doing this, you will be non-reactive to the destructuring and will support your integrity. As the foundation of human technology dissolves, societal structuring no longer will stand for anything. There will no longer be faith in government, religion, education, the health care system, marriage, or other institutions which seem to represent what is real. In the process, there will be grief, emotional response, reaction and loss.

You may try to deny those feelings, yet what will support the advancement of consciousness is focusing your intent on the desired outcome. This lifts this challenging time to a higher level of responsiveness, which releases energy.

As you choose to substance yourself from the procreative, co-creative, essential fluids of the universe, you are energized. As you are energized, you put out magnetic waves. You attract energy to you, which is helpful for manifestation, collaboration, cooperation, unification, and synthesis. As you emote the magnetic field, it returns to you and supports new growth.

Systems theory works here because its premise is that all life is intelligent. Everything that is being destructured understands on some level what's going on. It may not always be conscious, but it's always known. All life is co-creating the reality being experienced. Even though it looks like much is being lost, nothing is lost that has value, or that is consistent with truth, or that will support new life.

Everyone and everything is co-responsible for what's happening, so there is no blame. As structures decompose, there is co-responsiveness. In other words, even if something is falling apart, there is the opportunity to reorient it, to re-establish pieces that would serve new growth.

Systems theory works for the whole, for growth, the expansion of union, and integration through all dimensions. Growth will move the system toward light, more production, or more co-creation. The release of energy is prolific, abundant, and absolute. This is where all of you come into the picture, because the model of the hologram of oneness begins to discern its pieces. As each of you puts in your unique piece of that design, it all starts clicking together.

It's not about what you think you're supposed to do in the future or how it's going to look. It's about riding the wave of energy and holding the vibration for manifestation. This will magnetically attract to you the people, situations and resources that are necessary.

This is the new model of living. When the pieces become unified in the systems of life, then honoring, respecting, upholding, nurturing and unifying become the foundation of reality. What is natural becomes normal as the model changes. Make the choice to stay in the releasing of the energy. If you decide to watch the world destructuring, to pick up the pieces and put them back together, if you are moved to work with the old paradigm and try to patch it, you'll find that you could be overcome with grief, loss, abandonment, and separation.

You'll go through a period where you also will destructure. Vast emptiness may accompany the experience. It's not good or bad. Supporting life, helping with growth, healing abandonment, loss and grief, creating places of haven and resource for others, is working with the energy being released. It is much more prolific to support life rather than to support what is dying.

This does not preclude feeling, it's that feeling is accompanied by acceleration versus deceleration. It's accompanied by knowing rather than being in chaos or out of control. It supports integrity. Loyalty comes up strongly—loyalty to parents, friends, siblings, children, spouses, significant others, ideals, techniques, and to vast memories of evolution.

Many of you will be called by people who would not listen to you five minutes ago, or did not wish to participate in your activities ten minutes ago, or were in some way unaffected by your truth, because their mind controlled their response. You will be torn between going back and going forward. And we want to say to you, that if you go back, you release energy into the decomposition and assist in the decomposition. If you go forward, you assist in the rebuilding. It does not mean that certain people cannot come with you, it simply means that you choose to go forward instead of going back.

It may be that you will separate from someone because they will not come where you are going. You may have a telephone conversation and say, "This is where I am, and it's safe here. You may come." They have the choice, but you may have a parting of the ways. Your understanding about transition, death, loss and separation will be important at this time for there will be those who accompany you and those who do not.

What matters is your inner direction. This is true about where you're living, about where you feel is safe or unsafe. Consciousness supports your intention in every moment. If you choose one direction, there will be a certain outcome, and if you choose another direction, there will be another outcome. It becomes easier to go forward because you've made a commitment to the intention. You've recognized that this is where you belong, and this is who you are, and this is your choice. As it's fostered, others will come to be with you in that space, because you are re-working the design

The choices that you make must be made only from the vibration of what you want to create. This is the way the definition of truth will be assembled. It's the way your consciousness will be ordained. And it is a time of reckoning for you also, because even though your choices have been made, you will need to stay with them and affirm them over and over. Sometimes you will cling to each other and want to cling to the past, yet you will keep your feet in the motion for the future, knowing that you cannot go back.

Once your direction is set, proclaim it and rejoice in it. You are a way-shower. You live in consciousness and integrity and show the way to others.

It is not about faith. It's choosing to align with the vibration of what is being built. You are fostering relationship with that vibration so that it is absolute for you. As support for the truth of the future design of oneness grows, people will choose varied ways to reclaim their consciousness. This may happen on different levels and in different dimensions. They may be in a level of transition, or in an angelic space, in the astral level assisting on some particular point with whatever or whomever is remaining here, or with those whose choices take them from this planet. Varying dynamics are created. Because you are working with less words and more substance, you will be able to hear, know, see, and feel where these people are, what they're doing, why they're there, and why they chose to go there.

What you observe on the planet as transformation and transition is the foundation becoming unified. Developing telepathy and opening to being rather than thinking and "languaging" becomes a proficient stabilizing choice. This allows you to know what's going on, to be a part of human destiny. What is happening doesn't impact you in the same way that it impacts people who do not have connection with their presence in the way that you do.

There will be profound teachership during this process. Literally, every single second becomes packed with stimulus from all levels, all dimensions. It's not about trying to save the world; it's about creating an etheric potential destiny around the world. It's an alternative reality, a way of being in consciousness with light and truth and order and staying on the Earth at the same time.

The Earth that is belief-oriented and separation-oriented falls away. This is what many people see in their psychic projections about the energy changes on the planet. Many of you will be assisting to co-create unifications and energy fields so that there is a symmetry in the Earth's potential. The falling away of the levels that no longer serve will solidify this new etheric body of Earth.

The Earth is maintaining a level of integrity that is not available when there is destruction of natural resources and inherent separation and dishonoring of life. When you choose to walk in the light and co-create and cooperate with others, you share resources and make a foundation so that each of the pieces fits together and greases the hologram of oneness.

THE POTENTIAL FOR HEAVEN ON EARTH

There is the potential for all life to be exactly in balance in this new etheric potential of Earth, a potential for extinct species to return to this etheric potential Earth. Everything that you know about the integration of consciousness and the places through which the experience of oneness is already ordained, can be lived, literally, here as Heaven on Earth.

At the beginning of 1992 light workers began creating an etheric planet around the Earth; yes, we are going to "save" the planet; yes, we are going to create solutions; yes, we are going to work in systems theory; yes, there will be union of male and female on this planet; yes, there will be interspecies communication so that there's balance and acknowledgment of all forms of life; yes, there is repair of the substantial damage to the etheric level of the Earth's physical and emotional body, and her dynamic body. As each part of the system takes hold, integrates, and correlates, there is born a new dimension of reality.

You are probably very much aware that when you go forward and experience this recognition, that you're in a new Earth, in a new light body, and are in new kinds of relationships that vibrate at rates of speed that are not contained in the gravitational fields that you're now aware of. So it's obvious that something's going on here, and that it all is working for the good of the whole, and that it is moving away from structure. It's moving into inherentness, and as it does that, it provides new mechanisms for integration and for solution-based realities. They will be occurring at a time and space where there is aggregation of energy to support that advancement of consciousness.

When this happens the acceleration curve begins to move in such a dynamic fashion that there's no turning back, there is no sitting on the fence. There is no waiting for proof, there is just the opportunity for the advancement of this experience to be profoundly initiated in form. It means that you live from this dimension, and you create this dimension as the Earth's natural reality.

This is the formula for the next few years: orientating to nonverbal signals; receiving telepathic messages; ordaining your consciousness in the vibration of mastery; grounding and expanding the field as far as you can, so that your orientation becomes synthesized daily, and your presence is affirmed in this new dimension constantly. Where are you getting fed from? Substance. What does substance feed? Substance feeds the etheric. Where do you want to live? In the etheric body of the Earth's potential destiny.

As you make amendment to your constitution and accelerate your field and open your dynamic tension with truth, you change force fields. You literally change dimensions. That is why we are about the framing of a community that is based on those changing dimensions. That is why there will be many such communities on the planet, experiencing the profoundness of Heaven on Earth, because it is necessary. Choose to listen more with your body than with your ears, just as if your ears no longer worked. For those of you who have diminished hearing, that's why you are making choices to hear from the part of you that will be extinct, literally, in some time to come. Not tomorrow, but soon..

You are beginning to vibrate energetically, cellularly, in response to what other people are, rather than to what they are saying. Rather than watching what they are doing, you're beginning to hear them inside your being. The words that come to you from other people's lips are organized from their consciousness and provide you with a capacity to hear what the lips are saying from that organization rather than from the sound. You begin to feel their essential ingredients, their essential nature, instead of hearing the words, since the words are reflected always from the mental process.

You go right to the heart, to the soul, right to the place of the essence, or the essential, rather than spending time deflecting the words, or reflecting them back, or trying to figure out who's listening, or who's not listening, or who's really there and who's not really there. Practice being in the room and communicating in a silent sense, not that you have to be silent, not that you can't ask somebody something if you want to or have to, but in the sense that there doesn't need to be talking.

You can be together and feel the waves that are ordained between you as communication waves. When you walk into a store, or a room, office, family room, or your own bedroom, what is the field of communication? What is that wave that comes to meet you and greet you? Become much more aware of what that is, what it sounds like, what it feels like, what its purposeful communication is saying to you. Sharpen and hone those skills of mental telepathy and intuition. Your telepathic process is as clear as the physical acuteness of your five senses.

Eventually you do not need to be in the same room with someone to know what their wave of communication is saying to you. This is going to be very important, because there will be changes in the dynamic structure of the world. People won't know the conditions of others, or be able to pick up the telephone and have a discussion, because at certain times in the future, they'll be in separate physical locations. Or if you can talk to those significant others, you'll do so briefly, and then not be sure of the outcome, what the person will choose, whether they are on their way, or how they are faring on their journey, or where that might take them. This is a way to take that wave of communication and stay linked to them, as if you were on the telephone with them.

Ordaining this space within your own capacity by choice now, is very important. It also provides a relationship with your own sensate being. Of course it's wonderful to receive all this input and put the pieces together, and to see how people are doing, and to be in their vehicle with them as they are unfolding their journey. Yes, that's great, and yet what's really going on, is that you're sensitizing yourself. You're learning to no longer feel distant from those you love. You can feel them and open to them as they make their choices and decisions. You have an ability to affect the outcome, because you can put growth in there, and expansion, and etheric consciousness. You can perhaps give them some sound advice, or some very important boost of consciousness, or assist them in lifting their vibration in times and places where that might be necessary and strongly advised.

WAYS TO SENSE MORE FULLY

This is a dynamic of communication that becomes a wave of union that allows you to be in the wave of love and communication with those you care about all the time. It will be necessary for you to all have these skills finely tuned and honed.

Open your awareness—open the doorways, the gateways, the paths, osmotically, with all the cells of your body, by opening up your ears to that which is many light years away. Then experience, "I can hear what no one else can hear. I am in contact with that which does not have present tense, presence in the world. I'm hearing the natural rhythm of the universe. I'm hearing the breath of the Earth. I'm sustaining her rhythms and cycles because I can feel them in the bottoms of my feet. I can hear her creatures speaking to each other without words. I can hear the sounds of laughter of the devas and fairies and gnomes. I can experience the light of truth of the unified field of consciousness in the etheric realm of the Earth's destiny and her etheric potential. I can hear the singing that's going on as all of the psyches raise their vibration to experience subtlety, and begin expressing. I am aware of the levels that are being born into this dimension, that were never here before. I can hear the pre-knowledge, precognitive, pre-original space—the words that are beginning and becoming from the experience of that point— in this dimension. I can support that there is new integrity. Because I'm aware of it, I can represent it. And as I represent it, it becomes actual."

So listen, open out, stand firm and tall and stable on the Earth, open the bottoms of your feet, receive, acknowledge, expand, and choose. Stay in the framework of that foundation as much as possible, so that it's constantly giving you what you need to take the next step.

If you make the commitment to listen from your pores instead of your ears, to see with your eyes closed instead of open, to feel with the auric field instead of the fingertips, to sense and smell and receive from the levels of the invisible and the subtle, you will be born as a creature that has natural capacity to know, in each moment, without restriction or limitation. Perhaps more importantly, you will refine the skills of relating organism to organism without thought, belief, fear or separation.

Practice, first of all with yourself. What field is open? What field is closed? What am I doing? Then with each other, one by one, and then two by two, and then three by three, until what you feel is that resonance, and you can feed back to each other, "I sensed this, is this accurate? Send it to me again. Put it into perspective again." You establish realities without having to think about them

One of the ways to open the visual acuity is the grounding process. One of the ways to work with telepathy and intuition is to be aware, rather than to use the five senses. Close them off by your own choice, so that they don't close off organically. Then you can feel where you are in that spectrum of reception. It is the place of allowing, the place of being in connection with that which is most beautiful and most profound, and which calls the spaces together so that all of those dynamics begin to serve the whole again.

You are then made aware of that which you are to affect. The first step is to make the choice, "I want to have my awareness as finely tuned as possible. I really want to be available to my calling, so that I do not respond from emotion, from reaction to anticipated loss, disaster or separation. I'm a vehicle, and as a vehicle I am emotionally balanced and sensitive and yet I am clearly conscious of the fact that I am an instrument. I am not here to change reality as much as I am here to be a shower of the choices of what realities exist."

That's a very important distinction, and one which we recommend that you take to heart. The foundation of your consciousness, as it unfolds, provides a mechanism for the choices of your experience to manifest organically over and over again so that you're always on top of what's going on. You always know what's coming down, what's moving through, and what kind of affirmation is going to be best for you to hold in each moment. Sometimes it will be that you affirm order, and you will go into the center of the body to the order matrix. You breathe down into the soul and feel the fundamental order that you carry as a being of light, and beam that out concentrically in the spiral circles that happen when you drop the pebble into the pool—which is what you ordain when you go into the center of your being.

You send out the order wave in a concentric, consciously

spiraling clockwise motion, and say, "I make as much foundation of order as possible." Or you may be in a situation where you realize that what's needed is a field of energy that can assist in a transporting process, or a transmutation process, or transformation process. You may feel that what is needed is a supportive energy—the substance. You send that to someone and support them in substance so they feel safe, nurtured, expansive, or one with nature. In each instance, "This is what I'm being called to, this is what I'm aware of, this is what I'm going to serve through."

SERVING THE DESIGN WITH ABSOLUTE TRUST

Remember that when you serve, you are served. That's the way it works. You are in a communicative link with consciousness, and you know exactly what your course of action is—the actions and frameworks that will most inherently support the whole. If there's a distinction between the whole and a person, what do you choose? That's the sticky wicket. You can always ask for opportunity to digest that consciousness so that as it comes into you, you are shown only that which you are meant to affect, which takes personality and heredity and the familiar out of it, and puts you in contact with the expansiveness of your own soul.

These are going to be very important dynamics, and that's why we're talking about them. It might be easier not to talk about them and say, "We'll just see what happens and do the best we can as it comes down and shakes out. We'll foster it so that we're always on the edge of that wave of being in creation." That's true, that's accurate, that's consistent with the dynamics of your overall choices and yet your consciousness will also make you aware of things that are happening simultaneously, and you will choose that which your calling indicates is your highest point of resolution.

Always remember, it doesn't mean that the particular person you are aware of, who might on some level want to be assisted, or communicated with, or connected through, isn't going to receive help, isn't going to be okay. This is where your affirmation to be at one with the calling really serves the design. You know that in the process of the overall picture, if you do what you know you are intended to do, there will be resolution on all other levels, and everything will happen according to what's going to grease that hologram. It's not really as much faith as it is knowing: "This is how this will shake out."

It gives you permission to be the best that you are, to use your intention so that it fosters total recognition of this experience of union. You foster all these paradigms so that they all serve the whole and each other. That is a beautiful and very wise type of reckoning.

There will be less ability to discern by physical means, and more capacity to discern through etheric means, which defines itself in your reality as: the subtle gets the intention. The awareness, the fluidity, the invisible, get the focus. Everything that seems obvious, that's always been obvious, that's loud as a drum and continues to beat, and wants to be heard, and is squeaky, and wants attention, and wants to, on some level, be contained within or defined by the old paradigm, is ignored. This sets up some very interesting dynamics.

We still suggest that you ignore the squeaky wheel. Because what you ignore and do not give energy to will be re-solved somehow. It will come back into solution, and have to state its case differently. It will have to come up against its own parameters in a way that will define it for everyone and itself, and therefore give it the opportunity to transform.

If you are in there trying to change it or save it or make it easier, it will not transform because it won't need to. That's why many of you have made choices to move away from those who are constantly squeaky. Because it doesn't serve anything.

LIVING ESSENTIALLY WITH INTEGRITY

Habituation is another thing that will be destructured, so many of you will begin new habits and new ways of experiencing. Your foundation will be ordained from a different rhythm. This intention for transformation, for carrying the consciousness to a point where it can speak to you directly, is pure magic, it's symmetry, it's lovely. There is no miscommunication—it doesn't matter if Mercury is retrograde. It is synthesizing constantly this reality of truth that cannot be gainsaid.

The foundation always reflects and communicates itself

accurately as a part of the essential, which is expressed so there is no miscommunication or misunderstanding. There's an opportunity for honesty, clarity, resonance, harmony, and balance in ways that organize the system, so that the foundation literally provides its own resolution and affirmation. People can say, "Oh, I didn't really mean that," and you know the energy of their body meant it. You can get into discussions about it, and they can be adamant "No, I didn't mean that," and you know that it did mean exactly what you are feeling, because you can sense how they are organized inside, how their essence responds in those situations.

Each of you designs your capacity so that you feel the integrity. The beauty of having no words is that you hear what the capacity of creation is imbuing into you and from others to you, and so the levels start merging together—the Hierarchical level, the Source level, the Angelic level, the celestial level, the firmaments, the dimensions, the subtle bodies, all frameworks. They start foundationing over and over again in the same way that you used to hear and discern physical action and movement, and words, integrity and energy. Because you're really aware of these subtleties, all the windows and passages open for you to experience total communication with all realms.

When you are in substance, you receive communication from those levels because that's where those levels are sustained. The oneness becomes an inherently beautiful affirmation of truth. What you're about here is solidifying the fields of your energy so that they are equal and balanced and give you the optimal amount of information constantly. You feel as if on every level you are being sustained, on every level you are receiving, and on every level everything that needs to be available is available. Everything that you would wish to have at your fingertips, in terms of skills, capacities, or relationships with being, are available and present.

This means that as you hear from the being, you are more and more present as a being, and the normal ways of communicating fall away to the experience of what is natural. What is natural is that you know everything that's going on all the time, and there's no need to deny it, no need to replace it, no need to in some way change it. Dynamically, when you're in an honest place with total knowing, the truth of all beings is heard, sustained and created through. This establishes a natural order in your world.

That is how the new world relates. That is a very beautiful experience, a gift that you receive from each other, because it's the gift of your purest intent, your deepest integrity and your most absolute space of knowing. It's a gift you exchange as you receive, and there is accuracy to it, so it's quicker. This is because you're inherently connecting with the fundamental point of creation as one unit of being, regardless of how many you are, and this is where the absolute integrity of your union can best be lived.

Sunlight on Water

Chapter 15

The Flame of Pure Intent

Pureness of intent is the flame through which life is vitalized. When you live your essence and calling from inner truth, the pureness makes your life spontaneous, exciting, and essentially "yours." Pure intent cuts through fear and the thought forms of separation.

Now is the time of human reckoning, which is heightening the experience of separation and eliciting love vs. fear decisions. You can think of yourself in human terms with issues about survival and other considerations, or you can think of yourself as a pure form of energy that has come here to direct the force of light and pure intent into the world in order to break apart that which is mislabeled and misunderstood.

If you think about the way people choose their realities, you see that there are misconceptions about what the original space was like, which is where false gods come in and where people live separate from truth. Your purpose for being here is not necessarily to say what is real and unreal or to get involved in belief systems—rather, your potential is to be a level of conscious awareness where these things fall apart. Your pureness of intent is the clearest way for you to approach everything.

In making decisions about where to live, when and if you should move, what is important, how your fears operate, and what people say about things, hold the space and say, "I am of pure intent." When you think about these things as variables, pure intent assures that the variables become accurate. Then you are a truth finder, a truth initiator. You are able to boil everything down to the true space of knowing.

The knowing is born from the pureness. It's not that you search for the knowing, it's that the pureness engenders it. When you engender it, you hold the space. And when you hold the space, everything comes into order around that space. This is the primary way that the critical mass of union and the experience of oneness will be fostered on the planet. Everyone comes to that experience in the same vibrational field, which creates union. It is also magic, the capacity to communicate in ways that are not normally possible. With pureness of intent, a wave takes you forward and honors you. It fosters stamina, strength, and commitment to what you are. All parts of you are available and nothing is hidden from you, including where you're going or where you've been.

Pureness of intent acts like an eraser. It erases the covering on your consciousness, on your soul, and on your body. It lets you shine through. So you say to yourself with pure intent, "I choose to see who I am. I choose to see what I reflect, and what is initiated from within me. I choose to see the way it responds to the world around me, so that I can assist in bringing the light into form." That's why you're here. And yes, it's important to learn what you're afraid of and important to face your dragons. Pure intent guides you and gives you what you really are.

SHORT CUT TO SEEING YOUR WHOLENESS

Stand in front of the mirror and say, "I have pureness of intent. I want to see who I am." Now you can see clearly what's going on in the world. And that's what life is about. In the highest realms possible, it is vision, seeing what's there, making choices based on what is known, based on awareness.

You relate to your awareness truthfully. You hang up all your linen, dirty or clean, and say, "I have to look at it." You're not hiding anything. Nothing will leap out at you and say, "You forgot this," because the only thing that is really hidden is your own essence from yourself. You see yourself. If you are to lead in the truest sense of the word, you will also allow the unfolding of all designs parallel with your own. You won't impede anyone else, and you will support all life just as you support your own. In order to do this, you must be able to see who you are.

You watch yourself from every angle. This is the key, the little secret. Everybody else is looking at themselves square in the mirror, but you do more. Look at your sides. Look at your back. Look between your shoulder blades. What's there that you can't see if you just look over your shoulder? What does everybody else see but you're missing? Really look at yourself, but not with judgment, such as, "I don't like the way this looks or that bulges." Ask, "What is my essence? Where is it? Where does it come from?"

You become able to see the relationship of absolute truth in form. The form you see, the essence you are, the truth you bring, and your experience of being here are all the same vibration.

Now you can say, "I am congruent. The pureness of my intent makes me have less fear and experience no pain, struggle, or strife because my essence is so bright that it fills me up. I don't need a lot of things to fill me up. I fill myself up with my own essence."

The irony is that when you fill yourself up with your own essence, you attract whatever supports the fulfillment of your essence. It comes all around you and takes whatever form it needs to. So your perspective is very positive, very definite, very clear, very quick, and very much supported by the consciousness of humanity. This is because pureness of intent greases the wheels to get this consciousness moving. You are now creating a reality that is consistent with what you wanted to do when you were born. The congruence is between knowing your life's design and fulfilling it. That's power! And that's important, because when you know that you're doing what you came to do, there's no gap in your consciousness. You say, "I'm home. This is what I've been waiting for."

UNLEASHING YOUR SPIRITUAL FORCE

Your relationship with yourself is connected with your essence, your future, your past, the hologram of oneness, and the forces that will make it happen. These are unleashed by the center of zeal in the back of your neck. You want to feel open in that space because you're unleashing your spiritual force. The energy of your spiritual force moves down through your arms and torso and through your whole body. You're expressing, writing, dancing, and moving because unleashing the zeal fosters a reality that expands your consciousness.

The reason why many of you get so upset is because of some of the facts that you hear in certain settings. You're hearing about the illusion. You get upset because you don't want to support illusion.

As you support reality, the truth emerges. One way of doing that is through pureness of intent. The consciousness that you have brought to the world is dynamic and clear.

As you bring all the fields of order together within yourself and from yourself, everything begins to make sense. It's not about what you know or don't know. The clarity of who you are will cut through whatever you experience whenever you experience it. You don't have to determine ahead of time that you're supposed to know something. It's more that you're aware that illusion is there and you've always known it was there. You just weren't sure of the particulars. Now you respond to experiences in a stabilizing way through choice. You stabilize the pureness of intent, regardless of the situation. As you function continually in that way and foster the reality of truth for yourself, you see that everything that you have lived to this time makes sense and has had a purpose.

Part of what you're here to design into reality is that the consciousness you carry is an absolute consciousness, and why would you live anything less than that? If you choose to live anything less, you suffer from that choice. And it's not because you're bad or not doing the right thing. It's that if you have an immense consciousness and you're not using it, there's a sense of loss, abandonment, frustration, and invalidity—having less than the full worth.

You're really looking at your life system and saying, "I'm going to open my eyes, look at my back, turn around, spin around, and see it all." Invoke it, bring it out, and experience your level of awareness rising. The pureness of intent goes out and touches other people and you are supported, enhanced, accelerated and home free.

Then you are naturally a teacher. As you stand in the pureness of intent, in the light, people come around and you teach. What do you teach? Self-acceptance, self-initiation, self-awareness. You create the experience of honoring the absolute in everyone, and that comes out regardless of what you're thinking, doing or responding to. It just comes out. You begin to feel it consistently, as if you're feeding the whole Earth with that pureness. It has words, intonations, vibrational components, and it guides your way. What you're going to do, who you're going to be with, and where this is going to happen all comes from the pureness of that intent. It is very simple.

It is important for you to ground and to drink lots of lemon water. These will give you stability. You will feel aware, aligned, and connected to everything that is. You won't have questions, so as soon as something happens, you will know yes or no.

Your antennae are out, the light is on, and pureness of intent is with you. You're allowing the energy of zeal to carry you. It's like you're on your own motor boat, or you have your own channel or your own rail that's carrying you forward. You've got a schedule and you know where you're going.

PURENESS OF INTENT IS A MAGNET

Your life becomes much more focused. You do not have to try hard to think about what you're afraid of or what you need to forgive. The focus is on pureness of intent. It shines light. It paves your way. It's the current that carries you. This is different from a mental approach: "I think I ought to do this, but my intuition might say that, so I'd better balance my mind with what my feelings say." You don't do either because pureness of intent is the flame through which life is vitalized. It's deeper than intuition. It's an experience of being in knowing and following it home—not thinking, not trying, not analyzing. You don't have to worry about anything because the level at which you're living is an absolute level.

You may not believe you have the experience of the absolute, and that's fine. Just get out and do it, be with it, and you'll realize that none of the illusion makes any sense. It might give you a good going over, and it might get you to think about what you really believe, but you may not care to believe anything. You might say instead, "I'm not going to function on levels of fear, illusion, and constant questions. I'm going to function only through my pureness of intent."

When you function from that intent you actualize union because you are bringing together knowledge, truth, order and light. That's your back! You are moving your consciousness so that it makes a path for others to follow and you are able to see where you're going. And it isn't logical. It's absolute.

This way of being draws people from every walk of life to be with you. It's like in the movie Fearless, when the protagonist gets out of the crashed airplane and follows the light, saying to others, "Follow me to the light." Those who hear him follow him. They get on a wave and leave the vicinity of that disruption and chaos. They stay in order and follow the wave right home. When you're in pureness of intent, it carries everything with it.

You don't have to take unnecessary responsibility, thinking, "What if they are on my wave and it doesn't work, or I fall off," because you're cooperating with your decision to live your design and to do it fully. You're not looking over your shoulder at what others are doing. The people who come to be with you do so because they observe that the union you have with pure intent is clear and real. It offers so much that they're going to participate. You're not eliciting their support or trying to get them to join your band wagon. You're moving forward on your own incentive, under your own steam, in your own energy field. You exemplify consciousness. Everything you have come to live is being played out by you, through you, and with you, and you're happy.

It's not about saving souls. It's about honoring a point of reckoning, passing through that point of reckoning, making your choice, and sticking to it. That isn't difficult. It's easy. You might say, "I'm going down the center of my being from my essence and my soul, and I'm going to stay in that space." You're not taking sides for or against, you're not trying to recommend anything or convince anybody that they ought to do anything. You're just saying, "This is the way I see it and this is what I'm doing."

This space of being has impact for many people. Because the systems you'll eventually work in have to do with recognizing truth, you'll find that people come to be with you who are also in some way discerning truth. They're with you because they see that you found truth. Remember that truth, no matter how many pathways it takes, ends up going in one line, in one direction, and is always about unification. People may say to you, "This is what is also in my own heart, this is also my pureness of intent." Because you've looked at yourself and looked at your back, you know what you're up for. So there are no surprises. You are here to bring truth. You hold the space so that truth can create itself, and the value of total consciousness can be expressed.

Many of you are changing gears. You're finished with certain parts of your life, parts of your thinking, parts of your process, and you're ready to open the closet door, throw it all in, close the door, and blow the closet up. Done with that! You're birthing yourself in a new way. You work from the zeal center, unleash the spiritual forces, open the pureness of intent, see your whole being and essence, and say, "I want to see who I am," calling it out and calling it out. That makes a foundation for you that's very beautiful and supports you in ways that thinking about support wouldn't work.

You will feel stronger than you've ever felt. You can manifest your own destiny. Say to yourself, "Who am I really in terms of my work? Who am I really in terms of what I'm here to provide the world? Who am I in terms of where the world is ready to receive me? Where are these pieces now available? How can I create my next step in the world?" It's very important that you reach inside yourself and draw this out. "I see who I am—as a teacher, as a provider of services, as an example, as an embodiment. What is the easiest way for me to see that part of myself and create the design that is going to make this manifest?"

Every time that you work these dimensions together and experience reality in a beautiful sense of union, there is a coming together that supports you. You live pureness of intent in the world. It isn't separate from your job. It isn't separate from how you orient your time and reality. You take the shrouds off, the parts of you that have been steeped in whatever tradition, and say, "Who am I really? If there were no system, what system would I create? What could I establish that would make a difference for the planet?"

COMMIT YOURSELF TO YOUR CALLING

You can play around or you can get in there up to your elbows! The important part of your job now is to stay with that pureness of intent as if your life depended upon it, because it does. Instead of thinking, "I'd like to do that, but it's not time yet and the world isn't ready for it, and we'd have to get approval for this or that," you just decide what this pureness of intent wants.

Your first statement is, "I want to see myself. I want the pureness of intent to foster itself, so I look in the mirror and see who I am, then look at my back." The second thing is, "What am I here to do? Let me do it." You are ready to leap and the directions you leap in are safe. The direction your pureness of intent wants to take you to is a very big leap. And it's the only place you'll find fulfillment. A job and fulfillment aren't the same thing for you. What the pureness is leading you toward is your calling. "What am I here to do?"

The "how" question is big because as soon as you see what your pureness of intent wants to convey, you ask, "How could I do that?" Remember: If you have the thought, the world is ready. If you have the urgency, it's time.

If you want to make dynamic new models of reality for the children of this world, it's time to start. If you wait for something, whatever it is, it'll be too late.

Foster in yourself discipline and commitment to the calling. It's not about worrying. It's about allowing the calling to surface, giving it energy, staying with it until it does surface. It's taking all the "how" questions and putting them into pureness of intent and saying, "The pureness of intent will show me how, and if I stop myself by thinking, 'I don't know, it might not work,' I'm out of pureness of intent." The foundation that you're working from, as long as it's pure, provides you with every answer you need.

The essential place that you hold is the expression of your core essence and its connection to the truth that you carry. Anything in your system that isn't real, that doesn't reflect truth, falls away. Because it's such a little thing that you're letting go of, you have no charge on it. What you've got planned is whoosh! gone!

Where's your excitement? Where's your life force? Many of you practice many times a week to vitalize your life force through yoga asanas, for example. What are the asana postures for? They are to vitalize the force of life and spirit in the body. When you vitalize the life force of the body and bring spirit and form together, you are the edge of the blade of the sword, and you cut through illusion and manifest truth. You're here to do that.

You're not here to be railroaded or crucified or burned at the stake! You're here to create models of birth, of life, of health, of joy, and of communion. You break down the barriers of perception people have against life, and that's a challenge. They may say, "It's okay the way it is." You're aware that they are talking about supporting death because it's safer. Supporting death means slow, laborious lifetimes with boring experiences and rigid belief systems and authoritative control. So what! You say, "This is who I am, and this is what I'm doing," and you watch how that pureness of intent calls the life-seeker out.

So you get excited, and more excited, and then you have a pathway, and the people will follow that pathway with you. They will! Because you're leading them out of the darkness of a boring life—a life filled with diseases that don't need to be there, fears that don't need to be there, separations that don't need to be there, perceptions that are separating. It's your time. There's nothing to worry about any more. Nothing. It's a done deal.

FULL PRESENCE

Go inside yourself and feel the flame! Imagine that you are opening a gate, then feel the flame start to move. Sense where it wants to go. The flame is the truth, and where you end up is what truth is seeking and where you want to be. You're doing this as a visualization. Write it out, then follow it with your feet. See where it takes you. Play with it often. Where does the flame want to go? It is going to come out, it's going to express. Why is it not possible for you to create a miracle next week? No earthly reason. Why don't you do it? Fear? No, it's not fear, it's the lack of full presence. That's all it is.

It's not some psychological problem. It's that your presence is incomplete. All you need to say is, "I have the love. I have the intention. I have the clarity. I have the capability. I have the vision. I have the heart. I have the stamina. I have the discipline. I have the intelligence. I have the education. What's stopping me?"

Give yourself permission. It's the vibration of saying "yes," being in the vehicle that will make it manifest. The three points (past, present and future) are of the same vibration. When they are of the same vibration, there is an experience of instantaneous manifestation. You instantaneously manifest your presence.

Where you end up is absolutely alive, like a flame burning, so that everybody around feels that flame. You're not hiding your light under a bushel basket, waiting for somebody to give you permission to do anything. You're going for it as if your life depends on it! The flame of your essence burns away the resistance. You show people that everything is possible when it comes from the flame of intention.

Drop every perception you have about yourself. That's important, and that's what the flame does. As these perceptions drop away, you have no limits. This is very important, and valuable enough for you to share it, to speak about it, and for you to empower other people to live the charge of their own consciousness, whatever that means to them. Start stating what you want, start stating what that pureness of intent is telling you. State it everywhere you go, whether verbally or nonverbally, however is appropriate, but state it.

You have exhilarating conversations, charged with life and energy, hope and inspiration, and the effectiveness of truth. When you say, "I don't know if I can do this." Where's the truth? How do you feel inside when you will not allow or acknowledge the truth is there? Because the truth is, you know exactly where you're going, and exactly what you're going to do, and nothing is going to stop you. Isn't that true? When you say, "Gee, it's going to take time," it's like dividing your being in half. It is a procrastinating device. It holds things separate and creates life that's very drab and boring.

TEACH OTHERS TO BE VITAL

Your presence at this time in this world is very important. We would recommend that you not waste one second of it and that you teach this. Teach people how to be vital. If you teach others how to be vital, their births will be simple. Their rapport with their children will be exciting. They will know exactly what their child is doing. Teach vitality, teach essence. That is what tones the being. Tones the muscles.

Your wisdom comes from your flame. It says, "I am life. I have always come here to bring life. Now I bring life in a different way than I have before, and my premise is that life creates union in and of all time, and when union is created, and oneness is experienced, there's peace on this planet, and that's what I came to bring. "

Peace means enjoyment of life, peace means experiencing union and happiness, peace means no war, violence, or killing. When you are supporting life, what happens? You diminish death. You diminish violence. You diminish the illusion of separation. Imagine the changes in your society when a mother can feel union with herself and then with her child. The child knows what union is before it gets out in the street.

Whatever you know, let it be born. Develop it freely. Let yourself experience the flame of your calling. The pureness of your intent brings the calling and the knowing into being. The world awaits the knowing that you are called to bring.

Birth the flame. Live it now. Now is the time!

Chapter 16

Living as a Master in the Fluids of Substance
The Importance of Intention

We would like to speak with you about the field of intention and how it affects the outcome of everything you do and everything that is fostered on your planet. Intention is the wave that the soul initiates from free will. When you make an intention, it is the expression of and characterization of creation as it is unfolding, and you are in a trajectory with that which is fashioned through the wave of thought.

It is important to understand how intentions work, where they come from, and how they are orchestrated. Time is accelerating at such a rate of speed that it cannot be contained. This is why many times when you try to create something, you either over-shoot or fall short of the mark because the movement of consciousness is so rapid that unless you are on the wave with it, you do not necessarily understand where you are in the process of manifestation or creation.

Intention is a way in which the wave can be a part of your system and be unified as a consistent field of force. This allows for the experience of oneness while one is processing reality, determining outcome, and receiving fulfillment or solution from the future. It is the way in which you can say, "Yes, I need money now, and I don't have time to work with 'future-future,'" or, "I don't understand how that works, and how I can make it happen so that I can experience it rather than just hope it occurs. How can intention be like a fishing pole reeling in the fish? How can I call it in closer to where I am and feel the substance of that which I yearn for?"

SUBSTANCE CARRIES THE INTENTION

Substance is the food that feeds consciousness and the universe at large. Substance is like your breath. Breathing calls you to life. It holds you and sustains you in the field of life and order. Substance feeds the dimensions and the firmaments. Substance is fostered from universal knowledge and comes into the physical experience through breath.

An intention you might make is, "Substance embodies my essence." Breathe that, feel it, and fill with it. The substance associates you with the fluids. You ride the wave and the future is the present. The consciousness of that intention is bringing you the rhythm and cycle of your own unfolding in connection with what is ready to happen.

As you become conscious beings, as you look at how you fit into this big design, you know you are greasing the wheel. Everything is interrelated, and you feel capable of living your divinity and destiny now. You switch tracks from human to cosmic consciousness, and substance becomes your food. So you are being fed by that which feeds creation itself.

Creation works by filling a need that no one has yet expressed. It's ahead of its time because it has already anticipated what is necessary and provides it, and at the exact moment it provides it, the need is there, and the two come together in a marriage. So it isn't about getting an idea and saying, "I wonder if this is marketable." It's about actualizing the process, placing it in a container of energy supported by and surrounded by substance, and having everyone participate in it. It's a different model.

It is a systems theory approach. Individuals come together as a whole mechanism of response to something that serves everyone, rather than just serving one person. What you are seek to create, the resources that you need, and the participation of those who will make that possible, all coincide at the same moment. This is the foundation that you have come to work with in this new time. As you unfold each of these moments and bring them together, there is a sense of expectancy, meaning the excitement of knowing that what you are involved in creating is all that is possible at that moment. It's like riding the highest wave crest and seeing where you want to go because you have the vision to see where you need to be and where you need to end up. You are in a space of consistency and constancy with that which is waiting to be born.

Creation is much like a birth. There are waves you can ride which sustain themselves from substance and require no physical energy. The time is coming when you will not need your physical energy in the same way. The circuits of your body will be working completely from substance, and the physical experience of your electromagnetic fields will be an adjunct to the substance and not the primary place from which action happens.

Changing from a will-driven muscle to a substance-embodied wave is, conceptually, a movement from masculine to feminine. It is a movement from stamina, drive, practicing, habituation, and training to receiving, unfolding, enlarging, unifying, and to manifestation through consciousness.

IMMERSION

Intention is very important in moving from human to cosmic consciousness because it helps one design a space, a manual, or an instruction booklet for putting the pieces together in order and balance. We recommend the experience of immersion—going into fluid, into substance and feeling oneself as a fluid base. Put the issues, areas, problems, concerns, worries, and thoughts of your life into the fluid with you so that everything is balanced in the wave of creation and there is nothing on your mind. Let it all go. Live instead in the space of determination.

When one experiences being in substance or fluid for large amounts of time, it is challenging to return to a model where one reacts. It is easier to dissolve and allow and support the resolution that happens once everything comes into the water and settles out. One sees where everything is and how it all comes about. Instead of having the emotional reaction or the trauma of an experience, or to be over the hedge row not knowing which side to land on, or how to get over the hedge row to begin with, one feels the power of the essential being in substance rising, opening, and expanding. The being is taken care of. The fluid and the substance become an environment for growth, supportive expansion, and nurturance.

EXPRESSION IS SUBSTANCE IN MOTION

Feeling substance being expressed is the point of life. You can have all kinds of abilities and capabilities, but if you're not expressing them, you will feel less than whole. Expression is substance in motion. As you think about what you intend, it's very important that your intention be aligned with who your expressive nature says you are. That expressive nature might tell you you're an artist, painter, child care worker, carpenter, or a designer of models for future realities and relationships. Whatever that expressive place in you wants to do, it can be aligned with the intention so that substance can bring that experience into being. This is how creation works.

If you were thinking from the linear model, you might say, "I want to be an artist, so I have to take a class, buy supplies, practice," whereas, if you were experiencing the expressiveness of your nature in substance, you could make a picture from pine cones, nuts and needles, and glue them all together, expressing in that substance something that you had never thought of doing before. Whatever your intention is can be supported by the ability to use the tools around you substantively, so that you feel connected to the creation rather than to the normal patterns. You express naturally, which may or may not deal with those supplies, thoughts, and ideas that have been entrained by the culture. As you create from this spontaneous place, you actually feel linked to intention. You're on the wave and it begins to unfold.

Riding this wave of intention is not based upon what you're thinking is meant to be manifest. It comes from the substance around you and through you. So it is not about yearning in the sense of, "I think I want to do this, or I've trained for this, or my mother taught me this, or this is where I fit into society." It is from a deep level. It creates a context through which the foundation of the wave is the impetus. It has very little to do with thought or idea from the level that you're used to living from. That's why, so many times, one is unsure or unclear about how to ride that wave.

The experience of riding this wave is proliferative, expansive. Instead of doing things in the same way, you express creation in ways that have never happened before. It is like creating a piece of music. It is authentic within itself, although it has the same keys, time signatures, and notes that people have used for many millennia. You are simply expanding the context through which creation occurs.

The new models of the future will come from tapping the sources of substance. It has very little to do with what has been, so it is a completely new arena. This is where the excitement, the expectancy, the sense of being fresh, of being collaborative with the nature forces, the elements, and the experience of spirit exhilarate the being.

When you follow the calling there is a flame, a place within you that is charged so dynamically that you need very little food, sleep, companionship, or love in the old ways.

There is a space for you in the world that has your name on it. Things move aside and allow your emergence. They respect and honor you. It isn't about proving it, it's about the vibration of substance making its own place in the world.

You continually fulfill yourself. When you are one with the God or Source of creation, which inexorably fulfills itself, you are always fulfilling. So it is a different track from preparing to create, from preparing to decide what you're going to do. It is about allowing.

The vibrational field of each person will be marked. The fields will be very intense, very obvious, because as individuals become substance in expression, they are vehicles through which creation occurs multi-dimensionally. They are absolute. Wherever you are, you're spontaneously able to bring forth the expression, regardless of what tools you have with you, which gives you a freedom that has not marked the experience of humanity. There is sensitivity to being creation instead of creating something. It's a very different frame. It's about honoring the essential part of you instead of the formed part of you.

Instead of formulating a design in your mind and then executing it with your will, you say, "I'm going to draw a picture, write a story, create a garden." You invoke it and call it forth, and in the choice to allow it, creation emerges.

This has to do also with Soul Recognition* workshops (*Soul Recognition: See Glossary) and classes. As you ride the wave, you never know what will be said or done. Continual co-creative energy is facilitated in each of the mediums that is explored. What it involves is a simultaneously receptive and expressive nature. It means flowing with and having all parts available to you, instead of only some parts.

One of the people who demonstrated this spontaneous, creative capacity to its highest degree was Walter Russell. He decided he wanted to sculpt, or paint, or make a sacred garden, and he just did it. He was not dependent upon his past experience. He delved into creation. Think of him taking both hands and immersing those hands in substance, and then integrating substance through different mediums. He and the substance were the same. This is your objective.

LIVING AS A MASTER

When your circuits are charged with light, creation, substance, and riding this wave of creation through your expression, the dynamics shift so markedly that you are unlimited in any capacity and you can do anything. You can take apart an engine you've never seen before and never understood before. Even if you don't know where the parts go, there's a sense of symmetry to it. You can fix plumbing leaks, and nurse children, and foster whatever is needed in the moment. If milk is needed, you produce it. The foundation which you have come to experience as normal is being overturned.

We talk about this time as the Coming Together of the Ages. There is accessibility to every skill or capacity that you have ever mastered in any lifetime. And because of morphic resonance, you are also able to express whatever anyone has opened unto at any time.

We are crossing over from a lineage of, "This is my karma, this is my experience, this is what I understand," to, "I am a part of the whole, and anything that has ever been created by the whole, or will be created by the whole, is accessible to me."

This not only honors the divinity, opens memory, and elicits innate wisdom, it is also mastery. Mastery is a way in which the wave of substance and the wave of creation are always available to you.

Mastery is the space where no containment is possible. When you wake up in the morning, you look at the day as if it is a masterpiece waiting to be created. Whatever comes through the proliferative force of your life field can be implemented in form.

When you are in substance everything has a reason for being. When you walk in the forest, you are able to determine the interrelationship between all the points of reality that exist in that forest, and you can replicate this and represent it. You can take parameters of reality and study them, comprehending them completely, not because you've learned them step by step (which is the linear way) but because you have made the consciousness of that space available to you.

The fundamental message about intention is to provide you with a linking system whereby creation is constantly present with you, rather than something that you're waiting for. Intention is a wave that has already completed itself, and because it is completing in substance, you can organize and express the details in a natural, spontaneous way.

Mastery is the experience of total recall and total orientation to being, cellularly. There are no edges to mastery, no places forbidden. One has the capacity to be all, because the capacity from all has already been received. So mastery is a state of acknowledgment and a preparation for instantaneous responsiveness.

IMMERSING IN THE FLUIDS: AN EXERCISE

Step into the fluid. Immerse yourself in a pool of water that you might see as a beautiful forest stream coming together in a place where the water deepens. Physically experience this in a hot tub or bath tub of warm water, or just close your eyes and visualize being in water. Immersing into the space of substance, with the intention of surrounding your essence and body with fluid, provides you with a pathway to ride the wave. This experience provides you with a conscious understanding of where you are in relationship to creation. When you're sitting in the pool you realize, "I am creation." Instead of the linear process of thinking that you have to wait for something, or that something is going to come to you at a certain point of readiness, you just step into the pool. By stepping into the pool, you validate that the readiness is now. Each moment you nurture this experience, the reality becomes more strong.

The wave is underneath you and moving from you into the future at the same time. You're moving toward the future, and yet the wave that you're riding comes from the future. So as you experience this fluid movement, you begin to feel as if you're in the womb again, as if you're a part of what's being created, and yet the fluid is where creation is happening also.

You sustain yourself in the experience of being accepted, of belonging. This experience is very important because many people feel that they do not belong here. You do not feel as though you are waiting for something. If on any level you're waiting for anything, it's procrastinating rather than bringing it in, procrastinating instead of creating. When you immerse yourself in the fluids, you are in totality and whatever you've been waiting for pops up to the surface.

When you're in the levels of the substance, your physical, emotional, mental, and spiritual bodies come together and vibrate at the same rate of speed. When you are in an oscillatory wave, like the fluid, where all the vibrational parts of you are synthesized and balanced, there is no disease, because disease means that the energy levels are vibrating at different rates of speed.

Another way of fostering this absoluteness is to imagine that all parts of you are vibrating consistently at the same rate of speed as your creative consciousness. As this substance of fluid is unfolding you don't have to go anywhere, learn anything, remember anything, because it's all present.

When you're lying in the pool, all your cells, levels and frequencies are attuned to the experience of mastery, oneness, and creative substance. Not only do you feel nurtured, but everything in this cellular and organic process, even the DNA itself, is reminded, refreshed, renewed, and revitalized with the energy of the fluid. When you are cellularly bathed in the absolute level of creation, the distinctions which come from thought and emotions, and which may ordain certain patterns like loss of hearing, loss of balance, loss of integrity of tissue and tone, aging, chronic fatigue, or whatever are reversed. You are taking your consciousness to a place where it is being fed. The spiritual component of each cell (every cell has a spiritual, mental, emotional, and physical component) is activated. This is why people meditate, do processes together, go to church together, or have dinner together, because they are bathing their cells in a certain frequency.

The fluids are a threshold for the advancement of consciousness. So people will run faster and jump farther. They will have more stamina and more conscious awareness of what's going on in their bodies, much like yoga, where spirit and breath move energy into the muscles. Any physical experience becomes differently oriented when it is fostered from substance because substance is a natural, fluid space and has no boundaries. So you can literally move a couch by yourself. You can ordain any reality you want because you are becoming one with everything that is in that environment, and the experience is a combined effort. The couch helps you move it. You don't have to do it to the couch.

FORMING AGREEMENTS WITH THE KINGDOMS

You experience communication and agreement with all life, material and immaterial, all kingdoms. Those agreements are set and accorded. When you want to accord something for a particular purpose, and your intention is felt through substance, the foundation becomes available to you for that experience to happen. For example, if you want to walk on water, you talk to the cells, the molecules of the water, and say, "My intention is to unify with your essence. This is my purpose." Then the water will change its consistency to support the movement of your feet upon its surface. It's an agreement between you and the water. Much of what happens as you ordain your life system through substance is that you make life agreements. Life becomes sacred. When you spend time in substance, it becomes vital to you to stay connected.

It becomes a knowing rather than asking yourself if it's going to work, or if you're strong enough to do it, or light enough to walk on water, or if you have enough courage. These questions would be asked from old linear thoughts. Once you're in the environment of union between substance and form, agreements are made from such a deep space that the questions cease to be there. Questions are only there when you start, to lead you to the answers. When one is in substance, the answers are provided continually and questions aren't needed. In the linear, polarity initiates movement. Because there is no separation in space, there doesn't need to be polarity to initiate movement.

Change is usually initiated because something needs to be attained, whereas in the substantive space the agreement is already there. As you enter into this field, you experience that there are no more questions about how. That's when you and the outcome are the same.

This takes time out of your equations. When you keep all the steps of order that you need to create something, and allow the communion and agreement to be intact, upheld, and nurtured by the experience, time is unnecessary because you have kept the order of being intact.

It can be like a lasso where you pull all the steps closer and closer together. You're not seeking them or trying to find out what the steps are. You're in completion when you start. That's what substance assures you of, that it will nurture the outcome. This is where miracle happens. The more miracles that happen, the more consciousness will change on the planet, and the critical mass will build to support the experience of miracle. You are in the wave of intention, and the result is miraculous!

STAYING CONSTANT

Holding the space is also of critical importance. The agreement is that you will stay as stable and as intentioned as the universe is staying. Sometimes things get disrupted because people change their minds. Have you ever had the experience of affirming that you're going to receive a certain amount of money by a certain date, or a certain job offer by a certain time, or make a deadline? As that time comes and goes, you say, "It didn't happen, so I must have done something wrong, or the universe doesn't really work that way, or I wasn't really heard, or something was out of kilter, or maybe I didn't affirm enough."

238

What really happened energetically is that there was a wavering in your intention because intention is based on getting a certain result, and you did not forge that agreement prior to setting the date. It's as if you are all by yourself making up your mind, and the agreement that could be substantiated in the universe is not taken into account. When people stay alone while going through these paces, they have a lack of faith in their ability to create certain things. Each person yearns for that which is the calling, and yet many times does not know how to manifest the calling in reality.

Making an agreement, holding the container, and staying in substance to feel the foundation move through you, sets it, holds it steady. If you have a doubt, say, "The doubt indicates that on some level I am changing the agreement, questioning it, or that I'm not quite sure of it." So doubt or questions in the beginning, when you are practicing and moving through immersion, mean that the immersion process might want to go deeper, be clearer, and more agreed upon. So you put your energy back into it. When you're starting a company, you don't deplete all your assets. You put your assets back into the company to help it grow. The same thing happens in the immersion process. You put energy back into immersion when you want to grow. You do not hedge your bets and say, "I don't know if it's going to work. Maybe I should try another alternative while I've got this going, just in case it doesn't happen." You become, instead, a part of the system that's creating what is intended. That's the key to it. If you still see yourself as separate from it on some level, then you thought you made an agreement, but you really didn't.

It's about an absolute commitment to agree to sustain yourself and the ecosystem that you're in as viably as you can all the time. Your presence is absolute. That's why we spoke to you about presence, because if you put your fullness into this, make a clear agreement, and foster a reality that is consistent with your creative capacity, then it's a sure thing. Your level of commitment is the wave of life itself. You're not just putting in an idea, i.e., "I want to have X by X time." Instead, you intend, "I am the wave. I am the creative moment. I am the system through which the substance is infused. I am participating in the creative means through which this universe is emerging."

At no point do you stop and analyze, "I can feel that I'm creating now. What's my medium going to be? Should it be chalks, or acrylics, or oils, or pastels?" What it's about, when you're in that expressive moment, is to stay in that space of substance rather than taking what is emerging and designing it from your mind.

At each step of the way it's a commitment to stay immersed. The first few times you do this, you may find you're jumping out of the wave or out of the river, out of the pool onto the shore, and looking back and saying, "What's going on?" Then you realize, "I just stepped out of the pool, and now I'm qualifying everything, quantifying everything, defining everything, I'm analyzing everything. I'm feeling lost as if I don't belong anymore, as if I'm in it alone, as if I have to do it by myself, as if I don't have enough money, time, energy."

Whenever thoughts come up, you are not being nurtured by substance because you're in a different place, that's all. So you jump back in the pool, and proliferation starts to happen!

Expectancy is not to expect a certain result. Expectancy is being on the edge of knowing what is about to happen.

And so you're always on the edge of the blade of the sword of truth, always experiencing that the foundation you live from is supportive of you completely with no conditions. This is unconditional love, unconditional receiving, unconditional creation, unconditional mastery. This is the super-human coming into super-consciousness and living from viable means of support that nobody can see.

You are in a sacred place of balance between male and female, between what gets created and expressed in form and what is the invisible, nurturing space that provides the conditions for this to occur. This unconditional place is where you will be living your life in the future. You will support new models that will improve the condition of humanity in terms of happiness, comfort, intention, and invocation. What gets invoked? What has value? What is paid attention to? In the systems of creation only those aspects and experiences which foster life are invoked.

THE CONTINUAL CHOICE

Each of you has a choice continually about making this agreement. To make the agreement unconditionally is our suggestion so that you're putting apples and apples together and meeting the universe where it wants to meet you.

The Earth has agreed to nurture and sustain your physical form, to give you a place to walk, to give you resources to eat and drink from, and to find shelter and warmth.

The universe has supported you by agreeing to nurture your essence, your invincibility, your creativity, your divinity, the space of oneness with all things spiritual—that is, union.

If you look to earthly things for spiritual union (and that of course includes other people) you will come up short because spiritual union doesn't come from other people. You can experience spiritual union with other people, but it isn't coming from other people. That's the distinction. When you come into immersion you grasp that if you expect something from your life, you will find disappointment. If you live on the edge of expectancy, you will receive unconditionally.

When you understand these dynamics from a literal perspective, knowing what exists where, then your natural evolutionary step is to know where to go for what you want. You don't go to people for unconditionality. You go to spirit for unconditionality. You go to humanity for companionship and for the walking together that supports human exchange in a more natural way than ever before.

Until everyone is immersed and coming from that same space of knowing, oneness is an ideal. Once everyone comes from that level of unconditionality, oneness is the experience.

STATEMENT OF INTENTION

Our recommendation is to make the intention to ride the wave of your own creative expression in substance every moment, proliferating your own space of being, expressing yourself as fully as possible, in whatever system you find yourself, for the good of all, in all time and from all time. And in those moments you will receive, unconditionally, the consciousness through which this expression will work.

It happens as soon as you feel yourself in immersion—as soon as the water and fluid and substance surround you. This is where you can relax, be fed, where you can know your true essence. It's like being in a beautiful pool, and you realize that you're in motion and going toward the world. When you're going toward the world and you stay in that motion or that wave, the next steps happen from you. Instead of thinking about what those next steps should be, and jumping out of the pool, wondering what you should do next, you stay in the pool and the expression comes naturally from you. Agreement is made with each new biosphere or ecosystem or environment in which you find yourself.

That's how you learn about force fields, biospheres, ecosystems, environments, species communication, creativity, being creation, proliferating energy where there is none, and about how you call up energy from the Earth to assist you. Because when you're walking the Earth, when you're in the situations that require something of the substance, the substance knows it. And that's why you're there in the first place.

It's the agreement of your presence that fosters the result. You don't have to know anything or do anything for that to happen. You only need to be fully present.

Step by step, honor your own being. Intention, foster, support, receive, and be fully present—make agreements, stay expressive, open out, and see what happens. You can recap at night, just by way of seeing your progress. "What did I do for the last twenty-four hours? What agreements must I have made to be able to do these new and very natural things? Where am I now in that process?" You can look retrospectively at the last day or week and see how it is emerging. Yet when you begin the next morning, you're just in the fluid and not trying to discern how your progress is advancing because that would take you out of the fluidity.

There are patterns that you can adapt to serve you in this—ways you can foster each reality. Fundamentally what gets provided for you is a path, and once you look around and say, "Where was I?" you say, "Yes, it's a path. Now I see the coincidence between these things. I see how this was happening for me in a spontaneous way. It was because I was present in that moment, and the fluids were there with me. I was one with everything. Now I fully and truly grasp that my invocation has brought me here. It is my agreement to be a sacred part of the ever-expanding pattern of life."

That is your intention, your invocation, and your agreement. When you feel that within your being, it is accorded you in the twinkling of an eye. And that is written; that will be the experience; and that is also natural. If you were never taught to be afraid, never told there were limits on what you could do, this would be your natural way of being. So you are returning to naturalness. Commitment, agreement, intention, invocation, sacredness, movement, substance, flowing, essence, fluid. It is all the same. It is creation in expression.

In the truest words, that is why you have come here. And that is Heaven on Earth. We invite you to participate fully in the substance, to invoke it, to make life sacred here, and to make mastery the normal way of being.

The Bridge of Light
and The New Society

From this time forward, you will be working from the core of your being. You will find yourself saying, "My strength comes from my core." You will also see each other from a point of view that has no reference, no context, and no belief system, but a consciousness that everything is light, regardless of what it looks like.

You refine your energy core by grounding your energy, drinking fluids, keeping your protein level constant, and resting. The "self" ceases to exist in a sense, because it gets so much attention that it is satisfied. Now, you can move on to "we-ness."

This age is about coming together to affect the most monumental, pivotal, span of consciousness that has ever been accomplished on this planet. We call it "The fulfillment of a million years of dreaming." The child within you remembers the design of oneness. You have the consciousness that knows the truth of all being. In this time your potential has its best opportunity to be actualized. You cannot go astray because the truth is louder than the dichotomy, and the union is more present than the separation.

Because there are no parts within you that are resisting the process, you can fortify, integrate, and unify all aspects of your being so there is no separation between your levels. Your mind, emotion, spirit, and body dance together in the cells. You feel vibrant and alive.

The beautiful thing about this is that you don't have any "reason" for feeling it. You can't say, "I'm happy because of this or that." You just feel joy and nothing else except knowledge, because knowledge is joy in action.

Decide that "no thing" matters. Then you will see that everything matters, but in a different way. You have everything and nothing. That is the point of the Monad or God. It's all one. You are not attaching yourself to anything and there is nothing you need.

Nothing is sacred to you other than the essence of oneness. The false gods of the material plane, and the things that are taking attention, are held up to the light of truth. They dissipate because they're not based on anything. So you are finding out what's real and what isn't, and everybody knows what's happening—everybody.

Feel the oneness of light, of intellectual, spiritual, emotional, and physical bonding, so that none of your levels are in charge of any other levels. Your mind comes together with your heart, and your heart comes together with your soul. This catalyzes your memory so that you know where you are and what's happening.

You are here to bring forth the destiny of your planet. You all love your planet very much, or you wouldn't be here. She is not only your mother, she is your friend. So not only are you actualizing your potential, you're actualizing hers. This parallel reality is important to understand and actualize.

Take a chisel and hammer, and chip away everything that doesn't come together in oneness. What is left is the seed with your destiny encoded inside it. When you wake up in the morning, you don't think about who you are. Instead, you feel how you are living your potential. Excitement and momentum build inside you through concentricity—that place where you touch everything in the universe from your seed core.

Decide. "I want to live my destiny, completely. Who I am is the fulfillment of my potential, and what I believe is light. I am only light, and that is all there is." Make bridges to the light through your intention. Feel the essence of light inside you and know its point of origin. You're not alone, and your sight is expanded. Everyone you see is also light.

You are here to bring the Kingdom of Heaven to Earth. We are going to create this kingdom by the year 2016 so that the etheric potential destiny of the Earth (which is like her spirit) and her physical level (which is like your physical level) come together.

YOUR DESTINY GIVES YOU JOY

You're walking into your destiny. Everything you've ever wanted from your soul core is going to be waiting for you because you've already created it. That's why you have such a longing to connect with it. It's already there!

You will get refined and you won't even know how. It's going to seem like a miracle, but it's designed. It's in accordance with your divine right to chose through free will what you will experience. What that means is that it's easy. Say it! "It's easy."

You get your joy back! You're not looking at people any more and wondering, "What do they think of me? How are they looking at me? Are they judging me? What should I say and do? Maybe I should keep this job I don't like because I need the money." You do not have to conform any more. When you look at the world, the greatest secret is that nobody likes what's going on, but they keep living it because they don't know what else to live.

The models of the Piscean Age were instilled in you through your mother at birth. When the cord was cut, six generations of belief systems were bonded into your psyche. That is why the belief system has been stronger than the vision.

But now you say, "I'm getting this joy thing! Maybe I'll pick the smallest thing in my life that I want to change and change it right now." It's time for you to be happy. It's time for you to remember that the only thing that's real is light. Live your light.

In this new world everybody's prosperous, everybody's healthy, everybody's equal, and everybody remembers. The children belong to everybody. There's no color, no separation. You remember all this from your future, which is telling you everything that you long to experience.

Walk out into the dawn and place your life in the pathway of light. Live the knowing that you have brought to the planet, which will catalyze its creation. The concepts that you know, value and recognize will be possible because they have already happened. You have come to bring the memory to humanity, and there is nothing you have to do to get it, because it's who you are.

LIVING THE HOLOGRAM

Everybody has come here to help everyone remember. So you recognize each other. You place the hologram of your microcosm (the fulfillment of all your learning and consciousness) together with everyone else's hologram. Your pieces start to fit together, and you have the experience of fulfilling your destiny.

As you come together through we-ness, it is like a beautiful fairy tale. You catalyze for each other the foundation of the marriage of male and female, which is union. You walk in union with yourselves.

You serve and create. This becomes clear in the crystal ball of your future, the hologram of your divinity. Perhaps you have an idea from your essence, "I want to write a book." You believe in light taking you to this destiny because you are intending it from your essence. It's a movement from your sacred space, the core of your being, your matrix. Say into the trajectory of light whatever you want to do. "I want to write a book." Place that there and wait. Create a see-through ball in your hand, in your consciousness, and watch your destiny shape itself in front of your eyes. As it resonates to what you feel inside, you get turned on. You say, "Wow, it's getting clear to me exactly what I want! "

It grows and grows, and you get more information. More pieces come together. You're going to get the "how" piece as you watch the energy formulating. Bond and unify with your destiny in a way that accelerates the continuums. There is the feeling of being drawn. The more you visualize, feel and unite, the faster your potential will be actualized. There really is no time, so go for it. You'll get pieces that are fascinating because you have specific things that it's your turn to do.

Some of you will have the job of holding the holographic templates so that all the workers begin to understand how to come together. Some of you will raise consciousness, and some of you will condense consciousness, bringing events into the framework of union. What might normally take five hundred years, such as for one race to stop hating another race, can be created in a consolidated point of fifteen years, maybe less.

Watch the miracle from the hologram. Incorporate it cellularly.

As you're watching, you are creating a bond with what you're seeing, which makes it happen. That's how your destiny comes to you, and that's how you're going to create changes that everyone is predicting in terms of union for this planet—as a symbol that the free will experiment worked.

If you can see something with your eyes closed, do it. Begin to see what we're saying on the screen of your awareness. There is no separation between any dimensions, and in any moment you can come together with everything that you are in all time.

Breathe and move into the dimension of light. The events of the next two thousand years will start playing across the screen of your awareness. You'll say to yourself, "We can create union. We can bring it all together. Now is the time. Now is the time." As you watch your hologram, everything that you know and are becomes present within you.

Create resolution in the evolutionary spiral so that all pain is erased from all time. Each of you will erase it from your memory banks, and then when you see people, you will not identify with the illusion of their pain. You will identify with the reality of their divinity. You will lift them into that divinity because your vibration is very strong. Your knowing is stronger, and your memory is even stronger.

You outgrow illusion and you are free. That freedom allows you to gather all your knowledge and wisdom and joy and place it within the core of your being. Radiate it every single day from the part of you that remembers joy.

CREATING THE NEW SOCIETY

Where does oneness start? Right here. With you. Practice oneness by merging and blending your edges. Feel each other, allow each other in. Feel what happens. Everybody's in, everybody's together, everybody's one. Flow together so that you don't have beliefs, separations or judgments. You're just together.

You are going to create a new society. People who are here to bear the light are going to be family! Creating a new society means that because you are physical, anything you visualize becomes physical with you. That's the rule. Everything's created through the physical from the metaphysical. Put your focus on creating the new society rather than trying to change the current society. Take your energy and place it where you want it.

As you are visualizing the new reality, grounding is imperative. If you don't ground, you'll become a bundle of nervous energy because you're running so much current. If you don't ground, your life won't change. You've got to trust your body with your spirit.

In order to ground, put your feet flat on the floor or on the Earth, shoulder width apart. Anchor the light of oneness through your cells and into the core of order in the Earth. Feel roots coming out of the bottoms of your feet.

Everything that you are creating in your new society is cooperative, because you are all pieces of the hologram. Health clinics, educational systems, governance, restoring the environment, all that you want to establish makes its way into this planet.

You have focus and vision with no limitation. Every time you anchor your energy through concentric circles, sending out your point of light to all points of light, you make a space on the Earth to house your vision. The Earth wants to house your visions. She wants you to live your potential because it's like rooting for her, "Yes Earth, we're with you. We know that you are perfect, you are Divine. You are absolutely Divine."

You don't look at her anymore as if she's in big trouble. Please, look at her in her Divinity. There is nothing wrong. There is nothing to fix. All that you are here to do is live your destiny, and by living your destiny you change the world.

You are zinging and feeling alive. You're out hugging oak trees and picking up leaves and playing with dogs, and just living your life. You are happy. When, through intention, you enter the divinity of the Earth's destiny, you are also entering the dimension of creation. When you enter the dimension of creation, there aren't any rules! In the dimension of creation you feel at peace. You feel connected to the Design, to integrity, to order and balance. It will straighten out everything in your life, including your checkbook, so that it reflects that order. You are connected to everything that you are.

We recommend that you make tee shirts and signs with wonderful sayings like, "I live the fairy tale," and "The dream of we is in me." People will respond with the consciousness of the dolphin. They will listen to the words and imprint the experience. And like children they will be awake for the next moment and the next moment. Nothing matters and everything matters. When everything and nothing matter, you're connected.

The Model of Cooperation is the basis for this new society. It is in synchrony with what we call the "fiber of being." The fiber of being is the current, the thread that links everything into unity. When you look at the species of the Earth and all aspects of the universe, they are in phenomenal order. You wonder who created this because it's really cool. Everything knows what to do. Everything is in its place. Animals know what to do because they know their script and their essence. A duck is a duck.

When you are in connection and living your essence, you function with this fiber that creates the current of union between all things. You're taken care of because you belong to the family of life. You experience miracles because you are held in the hand of the universe. You are precious. You are the only one of your kind. And when all of you in your individuality and in your power unify, watch out!

SUBSTANCE, PROTOPLASM, AND CREATION

When you work in this new etheric level of consciousness, you are working in substance, protoplasm, and the invisible. This is a feminine space. That is why for this age to occur, there must be union between male and female. What you are creating is not masculine because it isn't knowledge. It's creation.

The knowledge that has been structured into your planet is being released. So the masculine level is taken care of. That's why your mountains are opening for you. That's why there are many people walking the Earth to bring forth the knowledge. That's why you're going to places that are pulling your strings and calling you, "Please come, please come." You say, "How?" and they say again, "Please come." And you find a way to go.

The etheric, substantive, protoplasmic level has one purpose, and that's to serve the Design. So if what you do is in accordance with the Design, creation will serve you. That's a geometric or algebraic equation. Practice anchoring into your body as much substance as you can. When you do your grounding, experience the protoplasmic substance in every cell of your body, and unify. You synthesize substance. That's how you get prosperous, how you feel healthy. Everything you're doing incorporates substance on a cellular level.

You think differently. You experience light differently in your body. You imagine that you are see-through, like cling wrap. You do not have form. Then you can transmute form, which is what many of you are here to do. You are not confined to your physicality. You can live it energetically through substance and go everywhere in the universe, attending to the business of unity.

People will want to know who they can trust with their soul. They'll be looking for you, and you want to be transparent. They will see your essence in substance, in balance, and in harmony with the fluids of the universe, creating without limitation. They'll identify with the fulfillment of your potential because that's what they want more than anything. Everybody is growing toward the light.

Do not define your relationships by your similarities, but by your core essences. As you experience who you are, your relationships heal because you experience substance, which is the feminine. The feminine is the nurturance that creates life. No matter how masculine you are, your compassion and sensitivity will expand.

The masses will say, "We've had enough of the structure," and will look for ways to create alternatives. Instead of going against the government, for example, people will create something alternative and take their energy out of the structure. When you don't give energy to a structure, it will have to change or die. People will say, "We want models for cooperation and sharing and resource connection."

It's very exciting because you're doing what you came to do, and you're not having to convince anybody of anything. Nobody has to believe anything. You're making money at this because people are intelligent and are not putting their resources into something that doesn't work.

When you cross the bridge of light, others see that they can do it, too. It's the morphic resonance, the hundredth monkey syndrome. People say, "There's this light coming from you. You look excited, and I feel depressed. What are you doing?" And you say, "I'm Being." They say, "Is there a recipe?" You say, "As a matter of fact, there is." And you end up taking them across the bridge of light.

People will generate enough consciousness to create long-lasting changes in your systems. Your job is to magnify the substance of the feminine so that the union and bonding shake the foundations. Then the restructuring can occur. Hold the point of unity and build the bridge. When you do that, you can find each other and work together.

The gridding of the planet is happening etherically. People who are working in that space are examples for others who say, "I see what they're doing. They're taking the poles that are opposite and bringing them together and are creating resolution. I see that my intention is to work with racial clarity so that people understand that clarity and do not see any poles, any color." If that's your job, you're attuned to the people and situations which bridge that continuum and come together to create union.

DREAM YOUR DESTINY

Ask to have a dream about your destiny. Ask that the dream be clear, concise and to the point. Ask to see the steps that you need to take in your consciousness to cross the bridge of light. Ask to be shown those experiences and dimensions in yourself that will be refined for the learning and integration to be accomplished. Every day go outside for five minutes and tell the Earth that you have chosen to help her manifest her greatest destiny. Ask her to show you what it is that you are here to do.

The fundamental shift that you have been waiting for, for millenniums, is that you will no longer be concerned about your own survival. As long as you are concerned about yourself, you are not seeing the big picture, the great Design of which you are a star player.

Everybody is waiting for you to assume your role. "When is he or she going to get it together?" Because they see potential, they see your light, and they see that you're struggling with those dynamics of how, when, how much?

As you decide to make that conscious choice, you begin to live. Your life is dynamic and vital and sexy and beautiful. It's the fiber of being, the dance of the mating, the call of the wild. It's very wanton, and very essential, full of integrity and union and completeness. There's nothing else you need.

MEDITATION

Breathe in the substance of the universe. Link it in the center of your body to your vibrating chrystallis of being in your Seed of Light in the center of your chest in the xiphoid process. Feel alive inside your body.

Breathe it in. Breathe in who you are, and what you know, and where you come from, and the Design you've come to affect. Breathe it in.

Now feel a softening right in the center of your body. You're planting a garden here. These are seeds. Feel them. They are beginning to break through the Earth of your essence. They are beginning to grow. Soften. Feel the energy growing inside your being. Now feel how your heart is opening. Feel how the love is generating. Keep softening, relax, let go, soften, breathe in the substance and soften.

In the beginning was the word, and the word was God, and there was no form. And the people rose up to create a form to journey to a land where they could find their God again. Now is the time. Feel within you the end of your journey, feel the softness of your being wrapping itself around the reality of your divinity and the visions of your calling. Feel yourself merging within your being with all time.

Let yourself go now, into the universe. Feel the bridge of light taking you where you are recognized, where you are seen, where everything that you are is visible and there is no fear. The light is within you, opening all the doorways, every part of you, in every way, in all time.

And it is a blessing, for you know everything you need to know. You are wise in all moments. And the resonance is oneness, and the vision is unity, and the society of light and order is now accorded in all dimensions. You are now unified. There is no separation.

Open and soften, open and soften. The light of the substance is now before you. Open your cells and receive the consciousness of the one. Soften, go deeper. Now you will see the image of the people dancing in the world, hand to hand, circling the world with joy and light and love. You will see the peace of a million years of dreaming. Look and you will see it. Breathe it in. Fill yourself with it. There is no time, the union is now, choose it. If you wish to, state "I now choose the union," three times. Now say it in your heart slowly and silently three times.

Know that your choice has been accorded in the dimensions of consciousness. It has been so recorded on your records, and in this moment you are given the power to fulfill your choice. And it is so. We bring for you the greetings of light from all the places of your being. We honor your choices to be the instruments of peace for your planet. We honor your destinies. We are loving you very much, and we share with you the blessings of the universe. For you are now truly the workers of the universe.

THIS MESSAGE OCCURRED AS A GROUP CHANNELING, AND QUESTIONS FOLLOWED:

Question: How would we grid the etheric level of the planet?

Answer: The fundamental concept is that as the Earth moves and rotates, and as her consciousness evolves, there is a consolidation of union which is placed within her etheric body. This is in reference to her job, which is to nurture and sustain all the life that is a part of her system. So in her etheric level, it is recommended that she have the experience of order and balance instead of dichotomy.

Those who grid the planet create union through her by designing reference points so that the Earth understands where she was and can transform into where she is. As gridding occurs, it is a shift of consciousness for the Earth, and it is also physical. The gridding reflects balance and order onto the Earth.

Question: Does this also signify that there will be geological and physical changes in the Earth?

Answer: You will find that the physical changes that have been predicted are going to happen, but perhaps differently than has been experienced in psychic representation, because the consciousness of the Earth must understand what it is to merge.

Her dichotomies and her poles must switch, but at the same time they must unify. They can switch in a moment of consciousness. You might go into the etheric level and say, "Earth, you've got to understand what your opposition is, what your polarity or dichotomy is. We can bring that together quickly so that both poles reflect union."

Then, on the planet, the shift occurs. You may find that somebody remarks in the newspaper, "This amazing thing happened. There was darkness for five seconds and nobody knows why."

Earth changes are not something that can be predicted because matter is always affected by consciousness. The greater the consciousness, the less matter has to shift in order to create the union that the shift was intended to create in the first place. If you cooperate by choice and not disaster, then you don't need disaster to create cooperation.

You are what you are, and the process is what it is, and it's all fine. The shifts are necessary to formulate the awareness on some human levels of consciousness. Some people will need to have physical loss, or some kind of situation they consider to be irretrievable in order to find themselves in the core of their being and live according to that dimension.

Question: What is the Hierarchy of Order? What is its purpose and task? What is your relationship if any, to the White Brotherhood?

Answer: We are speaking to you from the Hierarchy of Order. The Hierarchy of Order is the body of light that holds knowledge for all of the continuums and dimensions. Many of you are actually born from the Hierarchy of Order. You have been around for a long time and have come into a body to live out the destiny of light through form. You are our hands, our eyes, our hearts, our souls. Your destinies fulfill our destinies.

If you come from the Hierarchy of Order, you are interested in three things: truth, order, and unity. There are essences also that are part of the hierarchy or a part of the order, and some of you come to represent them. They are love, beauty, harmony, understanding, wisdom, and knowledge. Many of you play many different roles—have many different hats.

Our purpose is to hold the order of all dimensions constant. That's why many of you can come into the world and hold order, or the template of order, constantly. You are an adjunct in physical form of the light body that we're holding in etheric form. We are doing what you are going to do. We are holding for you what you will hold for the Earth.

When you communicate with us, you are communicating with the aspect that is guiding the process. The process becomes very clear once you're in essence. Essence is the way that you link to creation, and creation inexorably fulfills and fulfills and fulfills. When you are linking in, you are creating constantly, so you are unified.

The White Brotherhood is an embodiment of consciousness that has taken the framework of the dimensional universe and crystallized it into knowledge and experience so that people can activate themselves through that connection. People need something they can see, something they can identify, something that makes sense to the brain. The extension of the Hierarchy is the White Brotherhood. The White Brotherhood creates a crystalline structure so that you can experience it most easily. But of course, since we're all the same, all of the levels are one, so there is no separation.

Question: Is it necessary to go through economic chaos?

Answer: Of course not. It's a very good question. Economic chaos can be interpreted as denial of substance. What you are really asking is, "Do we have to deny our substance to find our substance?" The answer is no.

Sunlight on Water

Appendix

Sunlight on Water

Aggregation

Your holographic self is the aggregation of all the coordinates of your total self through all time. Access to this integrated aspect of "you" offers the opportunity to unify all aspects of yourself and bring your future into the now. Aggregation brings understanding so that you can put all your pieces together and solidify your potential.

We suggest that you foster a relationship with yourself that is designed from the future, yet has accordance with this time. In doing this, the pieces of your life will relate to each other and all dynamics are available simultaneously. The foundation you're carrying in your body, the psychic energy around you, and your spiritual connections fit together.

You work from a creative capacity that is deep and clear. You look at the world without filters. You see the design as it's meant to be lived. You function as if you are a delegate of the cosmic in form. You see your future clearly. You see the rules which people play by to bring you into the experience of rapport and relationship. You know where things belong and you see correlations. "Core-relation" puts things into relationship from the core. Understanding these processes is necessary for your life, your design, your purpose, and the fulfillment of this holographic process.

Create a design that simplifies your relationship with your calling. Think of it as a puzzle. You have all the pieces, you can see the design, and you know what belongs where.

ASSEMBLE THE PIECES: AN EXERCISE

This is an exercise to collect and unify the pieces of your life's design. Begin by assembling small pieces of paper, magnets, and a magnetic board. Write your dreams, ideas, visions, yearnings, and longings on the papers. Put the pieces of paper together so that you can move them around on your magnetic board.

Decide that you're looking at your total consciousness—your

holographic self. You want to support this self. Take the pieces of paper that you wrote your ideas on and see the correlations—the core-relations. Where does each idea fit into the bigger picture? In the beginning you will get the bigger picture. Then the bigger picture will come in closer. As you bring it closer, you see how to create the larger. You see the circle in concentric waves: the outer periphery, then the inner dimension, then back out to the periphery.

You can know the future and see the correlation between everything that is important for you to know. Your choice is to act from total knowing, from a place that synthesizes, organizes, and puts things into place.

As you put together the ideas, dreams, thoughts, and processes of your life, you also begin to access resources. This is most satisfying because when all the dynamics at play in your consciousness begin to aggregate, they solve their puzzle. They appear together as one picture so that you know the relationship between those places, points, people and ideas. The resources to create your projects— money, ideas, commitments, connections, and fulfillments—come in. The universe will speak to you about how the design will be created, and the resources will appear.

Magnify your intention through the universe. Go out to the periphery, bring it back to yourself, go back out, bring it back to yourself, and then go back out. You are amplifying ideas, sending out the vibration, creating a charge of consciousness, and putting pieces into perspective. They organize themselves so that you simplify your life, simplify your connection with creation, and place yourself in a pivotal point where you can orchestrate this creation.

All the pieces fit and are magnetically attracted. Play it on the board first by putting the pieces together so that there is no more separation in any context. It's aggregating the whole, or total consciousness, so that it doesn't have any boundaries.

The basic model is union. As you create a system where aggregation becomes the experience of truth, you see the wave of the future. This is where the models are going to come from. Instead of trying to create from a linear model where nobody knows how to "do" the future, you're using the hologram, where all the pieces want to serve all the other pieces. You feel fulfilled and validated because you find ways to accomplish the impossible. You see that when you live from the hologram, you can express your total consciousness.

Aggregating goes on even when you're not aware of it. Holographic dynamics support you while you work, make your bed, and do other daily things. It's not what you're doing. It's the container you're carrying, which is continually building, organizing, and supporting itself. Nothing in you creates set-up situations or delays. Whatever you are interested in is evoked, and the response is instantaneous.

KEYS TO MANIFESTING

For manifestation to happen, three things are necessary:

1) having an intention, 2) maintaining the vibration, and 3) focusing on the outcome. The outcome and your vibration are the above and the below being consistent. The intention is for the hologram to manifest through you immediately, distinctly, and clearly. If you have the intention, the vibration, and the manifestation all at the same frequency, manifestation is instantaneous. That's the secret.

Manifestation is no longer material work. Until you feel you have finished the material work, there is a separation between what you manifest, what you are living, and what you want. So remember that part of your affirmation, your intention, and the field of energy you vibrate with is that your material work is finished. You no longer have to do X amount of work to get X amount of dollars. It's a different mindset and vibrational responsiveness.

When you think in the old way, you separate the material world from the resources of the universe. You make a circle and cordon yourself off from the universe. When you create the magnetic board, however, you put the pieces of your reference system together so that you create union and cease having the old thoughts. Manifestation becomes the aggregation system rather than the linear system of push and pull. I do this—I get this back.

You stop thinking that there is a direct connection between work and money. Instead, you create a context that has to do with re-Sourcing the universe. You create a union of time and space. Relationship, manifestation, resources, health, anything, can manifest immediately. That's why you want to get sections of consciousness onto the same board.

You have an intention for your life. What does the vibration of that intention feel like? Bring that vibration into your body. Vibrate the intention in your cells. Then feel yourself moving out into the "future." What does it look like when it's done? Have the outcome vibrate at the same rate of speed as the other two coordinates. Then bring them together so that they become the same.

This is the way the holographic design gets lived. This is the way we function. The foundation of life is organized differently than from the mind.

Regardless of what shows up on your holographic screen, it will be earmarked vibrationally to show itself to you in terms of your intention. It may take a construct that was made millions of years ago, and say, "This is the construct. In this century, this is your vibrational intention. We'll put both together. We'll frame it so that it can express itself to you. It can show itself in this language or this picture or can show up in this dream." You can actually receive input from parts of yourself that you don't speak the same language with or have the same orientation with, yet are in your vibrational field.

Aggregation is the way union fits together through all the individual psyches and collective consciousness. You receive your instruction manual. You can design, clarify, and unify through all the projects you set into motion. At least once a week you say, "I want to look at all my projects and see how they take me to a higher level. I want to see how they fit together, and what they're telling me about my next step."

Go in and out from the cosmic point to the personal point and back to the cosmic point. The faster you do that, the greater the growth will be, the faster the results will happen, and the easier will be the process of transformation. You can say to yourself every day, "I know what is being created and sustained here. I can challenge myself if I want to create higher, deeper, broader results."

As you aggregate your consciousness, the pieces come together to bring you the totality of what is and what is possible. There are no unknown areas. Nothing is left to chance. Aggregation unifies all aspects of your being and provides a doorway to your fullest expression and knowing.

Sunlight on Water

Model of Co-Operation

These principles for living in cooperation offer valuable guidelines for living in a natural state of oneness and harmony with each other. As people give their gifts, they also receive what they need. They experience the abundance of the universe.

THE PRINCIPLE OF COOPERATION

The first principle we want to discuss is cooperation. When you practice the dynamics of cooperation, you create layers upon layers of union. You gladly share your gifts, abilities, and knowledge. Each person knows something different from the others, but you may not know that that is. So your first exercise might be, "What do I know that is valuable? What gifts might I share?"

If you write down your gifts and make them available to others, people will come. There will be sharing and connections. People will feel the magic because they can find exactly what they need when they need it. They have access to information, understanding, experience, knowledge, and resource—practical things that they don't have otherwise. They stop feeling alone because they are part of a beautiful network.

NO BELIEFS ARE NECESSARY

People do not have to believe anything to belong to this network. They only need something to share. There are no religious, demographic, cultural, racial, or educational considerations. The only thing a person needs is a life force. They simply have to be alive, breathing. Each person has something special, but so many people don't think they are special. You know that being in the human body is not all there is. But many people don't know that. They think that this world is all there is, and it's a pretty bad experience for them.

You cannot teach them through education. You have to teach them through the heart. You have to teach them through a cross-cultural vibration that transcends the barriers of separation imposed by people on the planet. All of you have a design that affects other people. You are not individual souls only concerned about your own evolution. You are here for the experience of oneness. Nothing else really matters.

It doesn't matter what you think. It does matter what you believe, though, because if you believe something, then you attend to the details of the external world, which creates separation. So believe nothing. When you believe something, a judgment is always attached. Your beliefs have a way of etching themselves into your psyche as truths when they are really not truths at all. They are just things that have been appropriate for you to do in response to stimulus that you have received on the level of the five senses. If you don't believe anything, and you're running the fiber of being, and you don't have any context for anything, then you can live what you know.

Everything you know has been given to you from your soul in order to express your essence. When you go into essence, you're in the fiber of being, which connects everything. Your essence is out there like a neon flag and you continually live your potential.

When you reach people from essence and potential, they get it because it's nonverbal. You are transmitting the fiber, and they feel re-energized, alive, and honored. They feel that you have taken time to be with them in the space of union, and they bring forth their gifts. For example, maybe all someone can do is wash dishes, and they do this really well. If you look at them with your essence, from the fiber of being, you see that their hands are golden and their soul is full of light. You need someone to wash your dishes, and you know this person will do a very good job and won't break your dishes. You don't have to do them yourself. When you honor each person, they can bring forth their gifts and share them with others who are looking for those gifts.

THE HOLOGRAM IN ACTION

This is the beginning of the hologram in action. It is micro-and macrocosm. You have a purpose, and your purpose fits into the whole, the hologram. Your purpose and everybody else's purpose merge. You are all there in love and harmony, and you fit the purpose of your soul into the manifestation of your destiny.

The intermediary step to fulfilling all of that is this Model of Cooperation. You are sharing things that you care about because they help your life work more easily. As you come together and share, unify and experience the fiber of being together, you create a hologram that works on a practical level. It works with language, and it is sustained without language.

You might start your network with 10 people, then go to 20, 50, and 500. You don't need meetings, although it might be a nice idea. You have core people who radiate the energy. Every time you are in the fiber you are with everybody. But you do want to have times when you experience merging your edges and feeling union. The union creates energy, which creates action.

THE PRACTICAL PARTS

You have a data bank of information, and it's available all the time. You might have positions where people fill the roles of entering information or answering the telephone. What they get in return is what they need. That's where the universal design comes in because you will attract the people who have what you need.

The question is not, "How do we start?" because it's already started. Your question is, "Will I make the commitment to be in union? Will I share my experience with other people and think about my uniqueness, write down who I am, open my heart in every situation, so that there is no longer any separation?"

If you open and do not separate, and you unify with the fiber of being, you join together with those people who come across your path. You don't have to reach out. They'll come right to you. If you open your eyes and listen with your heart, the people who come across your path will have something to exchange with you—

something very important. If you are open to that exchange, you have just created another person in your network.

You say to them, very excited, "You know what? We're just starting this group! And we need your skill. We need your gift." How many times in the week does somebody say to you, "I need your gift"? If someone came to you with a very open heart, vibrating with the fiber of being that binds all life together, and had angels and realms around them, and said, "You have a gift to share, and it is very special," how would you feel?

Be a light. Shine in a way that is very different from recruiting and the normal processes of establishing something with people. You really don't have to do anything. People will come as long as you are in the space of cooperation. People will be attracted to you and will cross your path. You'll get used to seeing their gifts. You might say, "I know you can do something very special. I know what you can do, and I know that it is needed over here." And it begins to happen.

You will change the dynamics of human conversation, of human interaction. Society will be bonded through potential. The action is the extension of the energy of potential. So it's a quantum leap of experience. You don't have to wrack your brain to have something happen. All you do is place yourself in a vibration, which we are calling the fiber.

As you place yourself and the group in that vibration, you affect reality through concentricity. It's like dropping a pebble in the water. Ripples of circles go out from where the pebble dropped. The waves of union that you send out connect to everything, and all that you need comes to you, individually and collectively.

EXPANDING THE NETWORK

If you share this with 10 people and they share this with 10 others, see what will happen. Not that you get on the horn and convince anyone! Simply say, "I open myself to 10 people. May they cross my path when it is appropriate. May we see the light in each other, and may we share resources, and may we add this momentum and energy to the union of cooperation, to the model of everybody working in harmony. May we trust the design that we are creating that everything is perfect, and everything we need is right here."

Whoever crosses your path is connected in whatever way they need to be. And you do not have to structure it. You bring everything into a framework of holographic design, which means that it doesn't have one point of initiation. It's like taking the group and dividing it into a million pieces, and then giving a piece to everybody.

You become known as a group that shares. It has no name and no place because it's everywhere. It doesn't confine itself to anything because you go from washing dishes to car mufflers to doing surgery. It doesn't matter what the skill is. It doesn't matter what is being exchanged. It might be human labor, human compassion, anything that is needed and can be shared.

Everything that would become a task in any other organization, everything that you don't look forward to, you don't do. Create something so different that it's exciting. Trust the process to the point where you no longer consider normal options.

So there is trusting, receiving, balancing, union, sharing, excitement, and joy. Touching becomes an ordinary occurrence. Touching a life, making a difference, having someone come into the fold. And not worrying. When you stop worrying, you start creating. This is a monumental, pivotal point in evolution. *People are beginning to think about something other than themselves.*

It is important that there are pioneers in consciousness who are not interested in profit, glory, or publication. They are interested in consciousness because they understand that the only way to heal the world is to raise consciousness. So let the fiber and the light be your focus.

The fiber does not have language, so you can join with the fiber of a hummingbird, or a bee, the moon, a beam of sun, a star, a drop of rain, a bird, a leaf, or a tree. It's not just a nice feeling of bonding. It's, "What is your language about? What do you need?" You establish a continuum of experience broad enough to encompass interspecies communication. People are able to understand what the language of BEING is.

SYNCHRONICITY

The excitement is that you know as others cross your path, there is a reason. If you find out why, you'll be richer, and they'll be richer. Then everything you touch is rich because you are living the magic.

You'll experience simultaneous points of reality, coincidence, and synchronicity pouring through you at a rate of speed that makes things happen. People who are drawn to you are ready to live the magic with you. Never question that, regardless of their education, or what they look like, or what their prejudices are, because it doesn't matter.

This is the point where you stop separating, and start being. Your work is clearer. It's faster. It happens like "that" because you are no longer thinking, "How can I do what I came here to do?" You're doing it. It doesn't have to be logical. It only has to be the truth of your essence so that everybody you talk to will recognize it and trust you. Think about that. They will trust you.

LIVING FROM YOUR ESSENCE

It takes your ability to see something that is not there, to dream of something that has not been seen, to know in your heart that why you are here has more to do with what you are than with what you do. So call forth your essence and live it. Everybody who crosses your path is destined to influence your reality and you theirs. When you do that consciously, you stop having "accidents" because when you cross each other's path, you acknowledge.

This is what the Coming Together of the Ages is about. Everybody is rich, happy, loving, coming together. You can have power at the same time I have power. A man and woman can each have power and still be married. Children can have power at the same time their parents have power, so that they all live in harmony. It changes everything. It's simple, fundamental, and it doesn't cost anything!

Be accessible to people, animals, elements, essences, everything. Make yourself available. A doorway will open up in your psyche and all the gifts that have been crammed in there and not used since you were two years old will fall out. You'll recognize who you are and what you have to give. Nine times out of ten, what you think you have to give is more fundamental than you have imagined.

As you develop the experience of giving, of opening, you receive in an exact increment to what you give. You will get exactly what you give. Exactly. It will be balanced infinitely. So you give over here; you will receive over there, in balance. You will not be drained. You will be affirmed. This is because you are available for the work of the universe, and therefore, you receive what you need.

You will receive in the amount that you have allowed yourself to be opened. If you don't think it's enough, then you're not opening enough because it's always in exact balance. When you live in the fiber, the wave of creation, everything you need comes to you. If someone needs something, and you're the right person to give it on whatever level they need it, they will ask you for it. You will know as they speak to you what they are really asking you for, and you can give it to them—a piece of information, a bit of time, an apple, whatever it is. It works 100 percent.

You will receive many gifts. Sometimes it will be a smile of a child, or a grimy apple that you would like to wipe off. But you take a bite of the apple anyway in gratitude that someone gave you something that they don't have very much of.

People will say, "You know, there is this diffuse group of people who are all working in harmony with very little strife and very little communication. Everybody seems to know who to call for what, and where to go for what. And what's interesting is that no money is being exchanged. Nobody is really in charge. And they are making it work." That's the way the new society is going to be based.

When you start living in harmony, it becomes magic. People know that there's a God out there, a Source that cares about them, because they are getting taken care of by human beings.

Your hologram is very specific for you. If you need a banana, your hologram has a banana in it. It has a sunset in it if you need a sunset. Your hologram is complete. When you allow yourself to live it fully and open to receive and experience from the fiber, whatever you need will be right in front of you. That straightens out your health, your love, your awareness and your life. You don't have questions any more because you don't have any considerations. You are living your purpose. That's what this is about and why it's so important.

WEAVE ONENESS

So weave, weave a pattern. If you bake a loaf of bread and give it away, the person will feel in you God, Jesus, Buddha, Mother Theresa—whoever they idealize in their frame of thinking, perception, and experience. You won't care what they think. Then they might stop feeling that idealizing is real. When you don't care what they look like, and you just feel their essence, they will give you their essence. If a teacher knows that a child has a special gift and tells the child, the child will give the teacher the special gift. *It is the intention to find potential that actualizes potential.*

All you have is your potential. You sense what you would be like without it—how dead you would feel. When people do not have a knowing of their potential, they act dead because they don't believe they have a potential. That becomes truth for them.

So you are missionaries. You can actualize potential by living in the fiber of being, by weaving the thread of oneness. If you go into a situation with someone you do not know and cannot relate to, either through language, experience, or race, whatever the dynamics might be, and you are in the fiber, they will feel and see the sunset in your body. They will say, "Can I come and sit in your garden? I feel good when I'm with you." The important thing is this: when you stop separating from anyone or anything, there is no separation. What you experience is created from what you believe.

One day you might say to a friend, "There's somebody's name I need to give you." You do it, and then you allow. They come back to you and say, "That changed my life. I didn't even know what to ask for, and that person was the key."

Don't believe in anything. Just be in the fiber of being because there is nothing that separates you from anything. Nothing. You are a butterfly, a cloud, a rock. You are freedom.

When you see someone, you do not judge. You do not separate. You do not categorize. You open yourself. Practice, because you weren't taught to do this. Maybe you are standing next to someone in the supermarket and you talk about tomatoes. "Is this one ripe? It looks a little green. It doesn't smell very good. What do you think about this one?" You give them the fiber wherever you are. "What day do you shop? I shop on Wednesday. Maybe I'll see you next week." And you hand them a lovely tomato. And in the tomato you place the fiber. They share the fiber with their family, and they all have the fiber. It doesn't matter what you think happened or what they do with it, because that's in Divine Order.

Let go and let God. Trust. Give up your power so that you are in the power of being. Know that you don't know enough to analyze anything. The interesting thing is, that tomato wasn't yours. The tomato was there and you gave it, but you didn't give anything that was of yourself. And yet you gave everything from yourself. The tomato was there as a way to bring together this union.

Use the resources that are available to you. Remember that everything belongs to everybody. Once you believe that everything belongs to everybody, you don't have to worry any more. Everything gets taken care of. All the pieces fall together. Whatever you need manifests. And you give thanks. Everything you are, all that you know, and everything that comes from your Akashic record is available to you.

This model of cooperation is a model for the future. Start it now. Speak to the people that you care about, the ones you want to have with you. If you are going to have a meeting of this group that shares and you want someone to come, call them, but don't say, "I want you to come to a meeting tonight at 8 p.m. Will you come?" How many people are asking for others' time? Call them and say instead, "I really want you to be there. This fiber thing is important, and I care that you're there with me because when you are, it's easier for me. Your specialness is helping me feel my specialness." Say whatever is true for you. Be real with each other.

People will come. It's such a strong experience that even though it may be two weeks or two months before you do it again, it sustains you by magnifying the energy of concentricity. The microcosm flows into macrocosm.

You are creating a very beautiful concentric crystal that accelerates and amplifies the energy of manifestation. Being in the fiber makes this easier. It brings the connection into focus so that being here is the experience of oneness again. Remember that you do the work of the universe through the vehicles of your expression and your being.

HOW TO RUN THE FIBER IN A GROUP OF PEOPLE

Begin by sitting or standing in a group and holding hands. Remember that running the fiber is not a meditation or focused exercise as much as it is becoming the fiber that flows through all life and brings it together in sacredness.

To become part of the oneness of all dimensions, breathe together, flowing the breath between and among you for a minute or so. Sense the flowing and movement of your consciousness as it merges and mingles together.

Begin imagining that you are at your favorite place for watching sunrises or sunsets. If you have a memory of a particular place, a particular sunrise, return there in your mind. Feel the sun's rays rising or falling above the horizon and imagine that you are at one with the rays. This is the important piece. As you visualize and experience the rays moving, your consciousness will move with the rays and begin to touch the whole planet, filling it with the fiber of being.

As you continue to hold the space with the group, you may feel a deep, warm, tender awareness forming in your body, usually in the area of the sacred space, (the heart, the soul seed, and the solar plexus.) You may feel your body relaxing and moving with the sun's rays throughout the universe.

Be in this space together for about ten minutes. This will allow the osmotic blending and melding of your knowledge and information to touch others. You will experience the fluids of being, the universal substance of the feminine, filling the cells and tissues of your body. You will feel a sense of balance and peace.

When it feels comfortable, someone can suggest using your awareness to come back into the room. Gently bring your consciousness into your body again. When you feel ready, share whatever you are moved to communicate, spontaneously, without thought.

Running the fiber gives you the opportunity to flow in union with other people, with the Earth, the sun, the universe, and spirit. Sharing spontaneously brings you the experience of oneness with the point in the universe where oneness originates. Have fun!

Understanding Community
Welcome to Heaven on Earth
July 25, 1994

Your purpose is to create a space that is called Heaven on Earth. There is really no other purpose for anything that you do while in community. To create this space on Earth means that each individual has value, each individual has a particular part to play, and each individual is an intricate link in the outcome of the total. No one is considered more than another, and each of you considers each other more than yourself.

You will do your best to always honor another before you honor yourself in the outward sense, while maintaining an inner honor that fulfills what you need. So when others honor you, it is the icing on the cake. Their honoring you does not fill a place that you need to fill for yourself.

SELF-RESPONSIBILITY

There is work to do in an individual sense to make sure that you are honoring yourself in a way that supports the total. If you work toward the total and have not honored yourself first, and filled in all your own spaces and gaps, then you are always going to want someone else to do that for you. In a beautiful way, you are responsible to do that for yourself first.

The core of what you are creating, your model, is that you have honored yourself and filled in all your blanks, and you do not need that experience in the group. If you need that experience, we recommend that you not be a part of a group.

We say this so that this message can go out to anyone who is considering being in a group. The consideration about who is to be in the group is based upon individuals being responsible for their own wholeness.

If one does not know how to honor oneself, then it is put on the group to do that. That's the old paradigm: the group takes care of its people and tries to make it all work. When this happens, however, there are no magnets for creating wholeness. This is the first question to ponder in your internal dialogue when you have interest in joining a community.

LOCATION

The location is not as important as the intention and knowing what needs to happen. Having said that, the most viable place to establish a community is on a vortex where the threshold for the future can take seed in physical form from an etheric level. It's like creating an etheric city first, and then the land will support that. It is not the only location that will support it, but you are drawn to this space because of the vortex.

The etheric level needs to be fed by intention. Intention manifests the linkage that will designate the space vibrationally, and that becomes the magnet for the physical body. Honoring the self becomes the magnet for the emotional and spiritual bodies. The practical elements and plans become the magnet for the mental body.

ESTABLISHING INTEGRITY

When you establish a community, you are establishing integrity. If you don't establish integrity, it won't hold together. You are building bridges between the old and the new, which means that you want to preserve the things that function well from the old paradigm and use the new paradigm to accelerate the momentum.

The energy, funding, and capacity are there before you begin. You know that, so you are not worried about those things. What you're logically setting down are your foundations. They may be people, processes, proposals, connections, or bridges. And they need to be covered before you'll feel comfortable.

When you begin anything, if you feel uncomfortable about it, say, "Wait a minute. We need another foundation point. What is it?" Open to get your holographic picture and start plotting. Plot it circularly. When you're finished, say, "Does it feel complete?" Your logic will let you know if it's complete or not. You're learning to see what you want to create holographically so that the whole picture is always present. Then logic can fill in the details. But you're always in the creative mode.

If you want to act holographically, all parts of the self have to be married. You're learning to do that as you marry your power and your gentleness, your force and your trajectories, with your open expansions. You're learning to marry your logic with your absolute knowing.

Take care of your honoring first. If you don't, the community is going to feel it. If one person does not honor the self, it will become a community issue. Instead of creating all that could be created, there will be the consensus that he or she will have to be dealt with in some way by the whole community. That's the old paradigm—that the community is there to heal you, to listen to you, and to support you because you don't have what you need. If you make a community based on that, it takes a lot more energy and time to create. Creation and survival are dichotomies. If you are worried about surviving, then honoring is taken away from the self because the self does not believe in its own ability to create.

CREATING THE RESONANT FIELD

How do we function in this place? We function through knowing that our lights are necessary. We function through knowing that we are truth—that we don't have to find it, we don't have to remember it. It is what we are. Each time one of us speaks, or we speak as a group, a resonant field is conveyed. Your intention is to convey a resonant field all the time.

It is an opportunity for each of you to take a flashlight, open your being, and shine the light in, saying, "If there is darkness, pain, anything in here, I make it light." It's not that you need to do deep processing, necessarily, although some of you might need to. Come to glory and to grace with those parts of yourself. Say, "You are my teacher. How do I honor myself at this moment with light?"

Co-dependence is fostered at birth when the emotion responds to the mother's sensations. It is also fostered when the mind begins to understand humanity's belief systems. Co-dependence is engaged when one desires to be acknowledged through the human factor.

You are yearning to find the congruence outside the human factor, and then live it in the human factor. Each of you has an assignment to become completely self-sufficient. And in becoming self sufficient, the irony is that you will choose not to be alone—you will choose to be with others in an environment of support.

Being in an environment of support doesn't mean that you find ways to oneness through human interaction. It is one way, but not the desired way to do it. The desired way is to find it yourself through the fields of order (the realms of nature), through the connection with your own guidance, through the experience of your own sunrise and sunset. You activate your independent God space and assist each other in maintaining that. That's what you want to be together for! That's what co-creation is. And it's important that those distinctions be honored.

If you make yourself responsible for and responsive to that frequency, you are creating a model for your time. Anything else is already lived in other kinds of groups and communities. A challenge goes along with this: you have your own closets to look at, but this is model will help change your world.

The laser beam that comes sometimes through us to you is that there is a path, and that path has millions of people in it. It is not a belief system, and yet there's a path, an energy, a frequency, a guardianship. We're charging you with that guardianship because there is a difference between this and the other models that have been lived in the world.

ALL FACETS OF ONE GEM

If you live it as you are intending to, you'll see the facets. Each of you has a facet. On the inside is the place where you connect with each other. What shows outside is the wholeness of the facets as they blend together to make one stone, one gem. You are all one. The distinctions are so deep inside that they cannot be found, and yet the distinctions are what make the facets. These kinds of awarenesses are new to humanity.

Each facet honors its need to reflect and refract light. As it comes in to the center point, pieces are forged together. That space shines for the totality. Each of you flows through the other to make the wholeness happen.

It is fundamental that each of you do your work, and then practice bonding with each other. Practice bonding with the larger group, then practice the resonant field.

ALWAYS UNIFY YOUR FIELD

Before you do anything, unify your field, individually and collectively. Actively unify all the time. This is a formula that we would recommend for everyone, no matter what group you're in, who you're with, or where you're living. Unify with yourself, then with each and every component. The integrity that you're holding is a charge from all the firmaments and dimensions.

Your souls have been honed over time. You have had the capacity many times to live this kind of union, awareness and synthesis. But when one of these components was absent or delayed, it did not come about, because it wasn't supposed to happen in the design. Each of you has a knowing of why it didn't come about for you. That's the honoring again—finding that place and saying, "What is my link in affecting consciousness?" In other words, if you were to look at your conscious and unconscious points from all time, what would glimmer? Look at it until it's not there anymore, until there is a resonance in your field so that you can be resonant with others' fields.

If one person in the group is not resonant, the whole group is not resonant. That's where you each have infinite power. If you're resonant, the whole thing magnifies your frequency. If you're not resonant, you take away from the magnification of the total frequency. If you're resonant, then you are like 500 or 5000 people. If you're not resonant, you bring energy toward yourself, and the whole dynamic goes off course. So take responsibility for being resonant.

Let everybody know that your group is practicing being resonant, practicing union, practicing your core work. You're creating something at the same time that you're practicing. Don't wait until you're perfect to start the community because that's not the point. We are being realistic about these things so that you don't set yourselves up. You know many communities, groups, and organizations that have set themselves up. They have wonderful ideas and great visions. And yet they cannot get past their personalities. You don't want to be another one of those. The personality is your responsibility. Nobody else's.

WHAT DO YOU WANT TO CREATE?

FIND YOUR CONGRUENCE

See what the similarities are, and write them down. Have a playing and brainstorming session where you have beautiful pink or purple paper. Stick the papers all over the wall and look at them and say, "This is what we want. Yes, there are 10 things that we agree on. There are a lot of differences on the edges, but let's focus on what we want." Then the concentric circle will give you your next circle, and you're on your way.

People usually create things in a parliamentary process by taking their pros and cons and addressing everything. They give as much weight to the cons as they do the pros. In the holographic design model, what is congruent gets the energy. What's incongruent doesn't get the energy.

The incongruent doesn't like that very much. It comes out and becomes a squeakier hinge. Don't give it any oil. Focus only on what you want. Create the intention to focus on the things that you come together on. If you can't meet physically, email each other and have conference calls. Communicate your ideas. Have somebody agree to be a central clearing space if you cannot all get together.

If five of you out of ten can get together, do it. A lot of people will find that when it comes to honoring the self first, they still need to do that somewhere else. And that's fine. It is no reflection on anything. You just keep going with what you've got. If you end up with three, you end up with three.

You will get so finely tuned that the three of you will be like an instrument playing the same note at the same frequency. Then that magnet will draw the next three. Maybe they won't be the same three you thought they would be. It doesn't matter. If you have an attachment to who's there, it's probably not serving congruence. Just work with what feels congruent, and then if somebody doesn't fit, fine, keep going. Just start. "Three of us got together. This is what we feel." Take your next step, regardless of who's there.

CREATE INTO NATURE FIRST

When you create in etheric dimensions, you always want to create into nature first. You do not want to create into human consciousness first. If you create in the fields of order (nature) first, you magnify the fields of order. If you magnify order into a situation where there are lots of people first, like a city, you can have chaos.

Your commitment is to create Heaven on Earth so that people can come and feel it palpable in the land. They feel it in every breath they take, in every twig they step on, every piece of moss they see, and every leaf they see falling.

You function through a creative framework that allows people to be responsive to it. They respond in the way that you do. Set parameters in place and measure them by your sensations, feelings and harmonics. Then when people come into this space they will say, "This was already thought about, already taken care of. I don't have to worry about that. The space has been prepared, and I am ready to enter. I am being received." Creating the harmonic dynamic cuts in half the time you need to prepare people to be on the land.

Learn by your mistakes. Take responsibility for your own honoring. Always honor another more than yourself in each situation when you can. If you do the honoring consistently with each other for twenty-one days, it will never be an issue again because it will be recorded in the psyche. None of you has had this experience in the world, and that's why you yearn for it.

So be powerful. Honor yourself, honor each other, and it will be a done deal. Then wherever you are, you don't create stuff with anybody. You are just present. It all flows around you, and it all functions through you, and it's an absolute space of truth. That's what you really want.

Get together in small groups and practice. It works easier in small groups. It's when you get in large groups that things start to come apart. So learn to listen and adjust.

Adjust with yourself first, and then enter the group. Try that instead of adjusting to each other. You've learned to adjust to other people—the way they think, the way they feel, the way they talk. That doesn't work because you spend a lot of time and energy just trying to adjust. And then you can't create. Stabilize your field. Then enter other fields that are stable. Learn what that feels like. It becomes a normal, natural part of your evolution.

THE WORK OF THE SOUL

Please put the work of your soul before your location preference, job preference, or life preference. This has never happened before! This is your next step, and it's the next step for your world. It doesn't mean that you have to live in a community. Just think about your life differently. Someone is born, they grow up, they get married, they have a family, they have a job, they stay together, they don't stay together, the children are with them, they aren't with them, and then they say, "Now it's time for me to live from my soul. What's my soul supposed to do? Where should I go? Maybe if I go someplace, my soul will follow. Maybe if I'm in a relationship, I'll be able to feel my soul." Change the human evolutionary pattern that you have been conditioned to live and go to the place of your heart and soul. Birth it in any way that you can.

This is the rock hitting the water that sets up the wave that will touch the whole planet. It isn't the only rock hitting the water, and it isn't the only place in the world to be. It isn't even the best place in the world to be. It is the place that you designated that you belong. It doesn't mean that it's your home and it doesn't mean that you come here only on holiday or for retreats. It doesn't mean anything. The way you live the form will develop out of the intention.

Community is based upon the spiritual premise that humanity can live in oneness. An experiment is taking place and order is lived through the people, the processes, the buildings, and the experiences that are created through this experience.

Anyone who wants to be a part of that can be a part of it. The rule, number one, is one must honor oneself first. And then honor the others. This is not a community of people who don't have any place to go. It's a community of intention. If what you see when you look at someone is that their light is diminished by their need, then it's not the place for them to be.

How does that get determined? By structuring a design that reflects the hologram. You fit your piece into the hologram when you acknowledge that you have a piece. You make an intention and implement what your piece tells you. You act on the blueprint that's in your soul. Then the universe opens to you and everything is known. Everything is given. It's about choice.

That means that if someone comes into the community, and you know right away that they need something from you, you give them the choice. You say, "Can you fill that need yourself, or do you need us to fill it for you?" We will be glad to welcome you when you can fill that need yourself.

You have made the choice to fill the need yourself. There will be times when each of you forgets. If you have already made the choice, then someone can just hold up a mirror and say, "Make a choice now." A person can choose to leave, and that's fine. It's not failure. It's staying resonant.

You can be mirrors for each other, but you do not fill each other's needs. It's very clear from the beginning so that processing is at a minimum. You go out in the woods and process yourself. It doesn't mean that you do not receive healing from each other, and help, and guidance, and support, and love, and affection, and anything else that you desire. That's agreed upon. It's that until you take self-responsibility, it's not a community. It's a welfare state.

The intention of this community is to serve only light, not the people. The souls are there to serve the truth, and not each other. In so doing, everyone can co-exist, and the truth can be supported.

There is the intention to live from the fluidness of the breath, of the spirit, of the knowing, and of the truth. There are no promises in a community like that. You don't promise anybody anything. "Come here and you'll find oneness. Come here and you'll be accepted. Come here and you'll be loved. Come here and you'll be taken care of. Come here and we'll give you a job and a roof over your head." It's not about that.

It's about sanctifying humanity, which means that every living organism in this space has divinity and is honored. And it's not religious, so nothing has to happen to create the sacredness, but you do have to ordain it.

Each of you is going to add an ingredient to the environment to make it all happen. And that's what has to be respected—that if you're sitting under a tree doing nothing, maybe you're making the whole thing work. And nobody knows necessarily what anybody else is doing to make it work.

The checks and balances are energetic. They're not task-oriented, and they're not verbal, which means that there is an honor system. It is knowing that you are the one who needs to honor the self, which means that everything else falls into place.

Sunlight on Water

THE BIRTHING

Excerpt from
I Remember Union: *The Story of Mary Magdalena*

I rode swiftly, urging Saschai onward into the cool, damp darkness of the midnight sky, for I heard the calling in my mind and answered it.

There was one, a woman, coming into her time, and I must be there to assist her. The cycles and the rhythms of her birthing were unbalanced, and the body and the soul of the unborn child were, as yet, disconnected. If there was no one to bond the spirit to the body at birth, the soul would have no grounding place and would bind to the mother and to the patterns of man, and the beliefs of fear and judgement.

This was a special soul, one who would help to lead the people after I had gone, and it had been appointed that I attend it. I would teach it the ways of the Earth and reinforce the pathways of its calling, and that was why I must assist in its coming forth.

I was almost there. I could feel the energy of the coming, calling me forward.

When I arrived, I took my pack from Saschai and left her to graze, knocking upon the door frame of the small home before me.

The mother answered the knock, not appearing surprised to see me, relieved at my presence. She remarked that she was alone now. Her man, a shepherd, had gone with his flock, and she said it was good that I was there to be with her. She was older and seasoned, her face rich with experience and tempered with time, and this was her first birthing.

She invited me within and we sat in the way of women. I listened to her passage. She told me of the days of her life and the ways of her learnings, and I was aware of her fears and her strengthenings.

After a time she relaxed, telling me of her dreams, and then finally, of her saddenings. At times we laughed together, but always quietly and softly, as if honoring the presence of the unborn child through the whispers of our caring.

And after a time, when I knew that she was ready to listen to me, I told her of why I had come.

I reached within me to the core of my memory and began to speak:

"There is a place called the Hierarchy where there is no hatred or fear or judgement, the place of the source, from which all souls are born.

The truth is born with us from this space also; the truth of who we are and where we are from and why we have come here to learn. But we forget this.

"When we are born on the Earth, if those who birth us do not tell us this truth, we do not remember it.

And therefore an amnesia is born and we feel separation from the truth and from the Gods.

The ways of humankind, the greed, the fear, and the judgement, are because we do not remember that we are all from the same place, that we are all the same.

The forgetting causes pain and then, after a time, the pain is expected.

When the children are born, they are taught that the pain is a part of life, and that the separation is a part of life, and the competition and the fear are a part of life.

And then, sometimes, there are souls born who come to the Earth to help the people remember the truth.

Your child is such a one."

I paused a moment and let the words stand between us, giving her time to take in what I had said.

After a moment, I continued:

"Your child will be a girl.

She will remember what the people have forgotten and will

teach them. She brings hope and will speak to them of the truth and the oneness which they seek.

She will remember that she is one with the Gods and will act as such, healing and standing as a guide to the people on their inner journey.

She will help the people remember that they are divine, that they are light, and that they come from the truth and will return to the truth."

I stopped my speaking and rose to add wood to the fire. Then I moved the water to the heat and began preparing some steepened brew.

I did so to give her time, for the tears were standing as droplets unshed in her eyes, and her memory was stirring, but not yet ripe.

"Why do you tell me this?" she asked.

"I tell you this because of the child," I answered.

"As she is born, it is important that she remain at one with the Hierarchy and the Earth at the same time. This will help her remember."

I paused and then continued.

"During her first years it will be necessary to teach her and to remind her so that she knows her calling and remembers who she is and what she has come to do."

She waited, as if weighing her words before she spoke.

"I am seasoned, as you know," she said.

"I have wondered for these months of my confinement why, now, I would conceive to bear a child. My husband and I, for many years, have had no life between us, and now. . . ."

She paused, looking away from my eyes, and then, after a while, meeting them again.

"Is it so?" she asked.

I heard the unspoken questions between us.

She wanted to know if her destiny was tied to the unborn child and if bearing her would help to bring a change in the ways of the world.

She asked me if the child was her contribution to the unity of which I had just spoken and if she could find this unity through the passage of her calling into motherhood.

She asked the question each mother asks silently before that moment of birthing. "Can what I now create bring the love and unity I have sought but been unable to find?

"Can I love this child enough to change the patterns of what is and create here what I know can be?"

She asked me if the world could change and if there could be love and if there could be acceptance, and peace, and the remembering.

As I heard her questions, I knew I had asked them also, as does each woman at the moment of procreation, and I answered her very softly, "Yes."

We looked at each other then in complete understanding, and I said, "It is time to begin."

She nodded and moved slowly and deftly to the stove where she finished preparing a brew of strong herbs and leaves to see us through the long night to come.

I watched her as she made me a small meal of bread and figs and meat.

As she moved, I saw that she was more assured, the fear gone— a new determination showing in the carriage of her body and within her womanness.

It stirred me deeply, for it affirmed my calling, and I was well rewarded.

I let her prepare the food even though she was beginning her rhythm and the cycle of birth was upon her. This was the only way she could repay me, and it was a point of honor between us.

She gave to me the food, and I ate what she had prepared.

She nodded to me then and said, "I am now ready."

I began to speak.

"The child is now moving into the tunnel.

The vibrations of density from the Earth are now affecting her memory, and she is seeing only the light, forgetting the calling, and where she is, and why she is moving through the dimensions."

I paused and drank some brew and felt the knowing come into the mother, and then I continued.

"The pattern of destiny is encoded into the soul, but for the child to remember it, she must be connected again to the memory as she is born.

I can do this for a time, but it is your calling to instill the knowledge of divinity and the memory of her origin into the consciousness of your own child.

When the child's soul is honored and upheld from the time of birth, there is much joy, for there is no experience of separation from the knowledge and the unity within. The child is happy, well contented, fulfilled within, needing nothing in the way of the human to give her dignity or self-worthiness.

The child creates from the inner potential and remembers her design. When this memory is real to the child, she has a sense of belonging and knows the angels as well as her physical playmates. The world is a beautiful place of discovery and creation. This is the way of the calling."

"How can I do this for my child?" she asked.

"Close your eyes and place your thoughts in the Seed of Light in the center of your body, in the place where your ribs come together in a point. There, yes, right below the heart.

Breathe there, and you will feel your knowing.

Ask that your light and the light of your child now be one.

Imagine a light in the place where you hold the child in the womb.

Now, as you feel and remember unity, expand your thinking to be a part of the light which your child brings. Feel your lights as one.

Yes. Now as the rhythms and cycles of the child are felt in your body, you will feel the quickening more strongly, and the time between cycles will be shorter. Stay at one with the soul of the child now, and the birth will be easy and quick and clear."

We moved to the place which had been prepared for the birthing, and I continued to instruct her in the breathing and the merging.

I told her I was also bonding with the child, and we continued for some time, feeling the soul of the child approaching now, more completely.

I instructed her to breathe into the light of the union between her and the child and to form a bridge of this light between her womb and the outside world. This would lead the child through the canal and into the world in light.

I asked her to keep the image of light inside and outside of her body at the same time, so that the child would see no separation and would be born in unity, remembering that the universe is a safe place to be.

Just before she was born, I sent out the call to the child and anchored universal light in her consciousness helping the mother to bridge the span between dimensions.

I showed the child the light of her calling and led her out of the womb into the density of Earth affirming her divinity:

"You are spirit, and so you shall remain," I said over and over again.

"Your truth shall be honored here. You are free to create from the design within and live your potential and hold to the memory of your knowing."

When the mother had fulfilled the birthing, and the cleaning and ordering had been accomplished, we sat, the three, and bonded the light between us once again.

I instructed her, and she began the ritual of the birthing of light into form.

She began connecting her seed with her child's seed again, feeling the bond between them.

She then brought light into the top of the child's head and drew it through the small body, creating a waterfall with the light. She did this several times until she felt the light steady and constant throughout her child's body.

She then took the child's small feet in her hands and held the bottoms saying slowly and distinctly:

"You have chosen to come into form.
You have chosen to come into form.
You have chosen to come into form.
I anchor you into the mother Earth.
I anchor you into the mother Earth.
You have chosen this form.
You are light.
You are light.
You are light.
"You are light and light you shall remain.
You are light and light you shall remain.
You are light and light you shall remain."

She said the words of the affirmation to her child with intent.
Then she placed one hand on her heart and the other hand on her
baby's heart, speaking in the child's ear and saying:

"The bond that we have is through love;

what I teach you I teach from love;

what is not of your truth,

I give you permission to release.

I acknowledge your divinity and your spirit.

You have arrived on the planet Earth, and you

are a part of our family.

Know that you are creative and can achieve and

accomplish anything that you desire and that there are

no conditions on my love for you.

I will love you, always, without question."

As she finished the ritual of the birthing, she drew the child to
her breast and they continued the joining.

Since she was more open in the first forty-eight hours after her birthing than at any other time in her life, I told her it was important to run the light of spirit through her body before she held the infant so that she would be filled with light when she held her. I also spoke of the need for her to be with her own spirit, while cherishing the bond with her child.

I instructed the mother to spend some moments each day joining with her child's seed of light and going with the child into the light of the Hierarchy and the place of truth. Since the first twenty-four months establishes the foundation between the hemispheres of consciousness, I told her that every day for two years the child would need to hear an affirmation that she is light.

I stayed with them for six months following the birthing.

Each day I instructed the mother and sent the child a validation of her purpose and spoke to her the affirmation of light.

I grew to love the girl child and her mother, and we spent many hours talking, sharing, and loving.

I told the mother of the future of the child and gave her the teachings of the soul to share with her when she was older:

To always uphold the creativity of the child and encourage her uniqueness, affirming her child's divinity daily.

To listen every morning to her child's dreams and, at night before bed, to listen to the experiences the child had that day. This would help to integrate the unconscious and conscious processes of the child every twenty-four hours.

To have the child express all of her feelings without judging them and to give the child an example of this through her own honest expression of emotion.

This would explain the ways of the world and the laws of man, telling her why things are as they are. This would give her the understanding necessary to live here and respect others. If the child respected the ways of others, then others would respect her ways.

I spoke to the mother about the Earth as a learning place and about the lessons the child's soul had come to learn. I told her to teach the child that the lessons did not have to be learned through pain because pain is man-made and is not created from the Gods.

I instructed her and the child in the ways of the heart:

To love unconditionally,

To ask for the memory of the design,

To join daily with the Seed of Light of those you love,

To spend some moments together in dreaming and being.

I stayed because of my calling, yes, but also because it was a respite from the travel and the aloneness of my outer existence.

I explored the hills and valleys there and took the child with me, explaining to her about the Earth and the elements and the force fields. We went into the wind and the rain and under the trees and the stars. We touched the living things of the Earth every day, and the child learned about life.

And as I was preparing to leave, I told the child about the truth within her; telling her of why she had come and of why I must go. I spoke to her as if she were of my years, sometimes using my tongue and sometimes using my mind.

She would listen, now barely sitting by herself, propped against the rocks beside her earthly home.

She had clear almond eyes which reflected the memory of her inner truth and the knowledge within her soul. She was happy, smiling often, and content to be here.

When it was finished, we stood together in the door frame, the three as one—one in our calling, one in our being, one in our intention as women to create the wave of truth.

I knew we had done well and I smiled, kissing them on each cheek. I mounted Saschai then and rode forward, even now feeling the next calling. I was going in a direction, a direction which would bring me to Christ, for we had so appointed it.

It would take many Earth years, and yet I did not sigh, for I was well contented. There was no place of lack within.

The child had filled me again with the presence of home, and it was fresh in my memory, as was the image of the prophecy and light the child had chosen to bring to the Earth.

As I rode away, the sun came over the mountain, and all the memories of all of the sun's risings came with it.

GLOSSARY OF TERMS

Used by THE ONES WITH NO NAMES

We are bringing to you the essential points of order, or structure which uphold and engender the universe of your experience. This is now proof that you are ready to know the full magnitude of your own capacity to create and engender your universe, to uphold your own life support system. We are revealing the truth in essence to validate your readiness to participate as Gods and Goddesses in the unfolding of a design which has been held away from you for the purpose of drawing you toward it, a way of urging and evoking a response and memory.

Now that you remember, there is no need for the mystery to surround the process. It is time for the clarity which you seek and the unfolding of a greater frame of acknowledgment and union. We open the mystery to you as proof that you are now a God/Goddess of creation. Use the truth as a pattern to approach the words described below, as a key system which lies before you as a gemmed or jeweled city of lights.

The words are lights which trigger your excitement and initiative. Share now, more than ever before, the creation of your light, also, so that the knowing and the participation and the acknowledgment are the same. As you share in your knowing and your learning and your remembering, there comes an invocation, a calm acceptance of your place, a fulfillment of yearning.

This is also about trusting each other with your ideas and secrets and gifts, knowing that no one can take a gift away from you, that essentially you are the same and that all is truly one. This is what you are practicing now.

Know that there are no longer lines of division within your structures, and that this is what the ego may be resisting. Trust yourself to have the place necessary for your fulfillment, and each of you will unfold as your light joins the others, and the whole city, or system, of light is then awakened. Begin afresh to honor that the design guides you forward and yet, you are now seeing so much of the design that you no longer need to believe that it is taking you anywhere. You are already there.

Rejoice in this and know that this is the Kingdom of Heaven, now among you.

THE ABSOLUTE:
The Absolute is a space of infinite creation, where the beginning and ending are known, the design is accorded through truth and the soul is the element of creation which engenders life itself. All other creatures are, in a sense, examples of the power of creation so that you can see what is possible. All life and all essential places of creation exist in the Absolute. If we say that you are representing the Absolute or are bringing absolution, it is because you are full of the awareness that there is no right or wrong, that there is no way for the separation to continue and knowing this brings freedom from guilt. Those of you who know the Absolute, are, in a sense, the messengers for humanity. The holographic principle of oneness is held here.

ABSOLUTION:
The result of being in the Absolute is to experience absolution, which is the removing of all karma (grief, guilt, fear, and separation). Knowing the divinity within is the result.

ABSORB:
To receive and integrate through the circuits of the body so that you realize your connection and linkage with something.

ACCELERATION CURVE:
The wave of energy which coincides with and therefore measures the expansion of human consciousness, or the raising of human vibration and awareness. This is the way Spirit can tell what is needed for the next step. It is like opening a door and looking outside and sensing what you need to cover the body on a certain

day, perhaps a raincoat or a sweater. The curve tells anyone who is attuned to it that there is a process underway which indicates action and participation.

ACCORDED:
Acknowledged, upheld, recognized or affirmed.

AFFIRMATION:
1) To make firm, as in a verbal statement to provide intention.
2) To give honor or credence to, to accord. If you affirm something, it is using free will to align your intention with your outcome.

AGGREGATION:
To put all the pieces of the puzzle together at one time so that they fit; to collate and order all events and aspects; a preliminary exercise and experience to show how the hologram was initiated and designed. Practice putting the pieces together and you learn what it is like to create universes.

AKASHIC RECORDS:
The "Library of Congress in the sky," where all the choices, aspects, and learnings of humanity are recorded. This is where all beings are made real, in a sense, because the record is the essential "proof" of life. Those who tap the records are accessing the design level, the level of the Council, for this is the Council's journal. Perhaps an example would be that if you decide to create a universe, you will express the creative intent in some way and follow its progress; it's that simple.

ALIGNMENT:
Alignment is the sequential ordering of the circuits in the body and the pathways of the psyche so that there is an agreement about the resonance, frequency or vibration being experienced. After the agreement, the other part of alignment is that, spontaneously, the person then feels or experiences a connection with other beings, and states of being, which are sensed as oneness, i.e., attunement.

ALTERNATIVE REALITIES:
Realities linked to your current reality through the pathway of soul, but not usually perceived by the current reality. These realities are accessible from soul through intention.

AMNESIA:
The state or condition of not remembering truth. In most instances, human birthing produces amnesia by separating the human being from its spiritual essence and soul.

ANGELS:
Angels are the messengers of the Council, who provide a link or connection between humanity and Spirit. Angels know the design and see the holographic plan and in literal and sensual ways, provide a message to assist you in taking the next step. Their messages take the form of synchronicity and coincidence, which are the angels' signals. Angels are created by the Monad for companionship and provide an intercessory level to sustain the invisible. Angels travel in pairs and, although they cannot change your mind about something, they will gently prod and encourage, particularly while you sleep. They thrive on gratitude, so it is recommended that you communicate and say "thank you" every night. They will work with you, and you can develop a system of communication if you desire. State the intention that you want to receive the guidance of your angels, ask for a sign or signal of how they wish to communicate with you, and then be alert for the fulfillment of the signal. Then ask for help in certain areas and stay aware of what happens. Talk to the angels in your mind and prepare to receive great union, for this is the angels' purpose in being.

ASPECTS:
Aspects are points of reality which are born as souls into this dimension. Before and during the time of Christ, many souls chose to incarnate together, to participate in the experience of this dimension in groups. Some souls after that point also incarnated in groups, although the design has been to incarnate as individuals, for this is the experience of creating unity from different bodies

and "souls," and provides more in-depth learning. There are 144 aspects of Christ, for instance, which means that 144 souls created the personality of the Christ.

ATTACHMENT:
The response of the emotional body to external experience, people, structure, or events, resulting in a separation from self.

ATTUNEMENT:
The place of vibrational balance in the levels of the being.

AWARENESS:
The experience of perceiving and bringing that which is perceived into the senses for acknowledgment.

BALANCE:
Balance and alignment are basically the same thing: a point at which all comes together and nothing can be differentiated. An example is when the pendulum stops swinging: that is balance. In the being, it is when there is no struggle, only acknowledgment.

BEING:
The state where there is no thought. This is the most direct way to know God. It is to feel as if the material concerns and normal necessities are a long way away, and you are self-sufficient and safe and know no limits. It is the state where what you usually require is on the back burner and you know the gas is off, and you can relax. Make it simple, because "being" is an important piece in remembering that you are important to the design. For in the state of being, there are no questions, only essential knowing. When we say "the total being," for example, we refer to the total organism: body, mind, emotion, spirit, soul, and psyche.

BELIEFS:
Ways of perceiving and interpreting "reality" which usually separate people. Things that you believe, are held in form in the mind and usually contain judgment. We would recommend that there are no beliefs in your psyche, only truth from the Seed of

Light. If you have to believe in something, we would suggest that you believe only that there is light.

BILOCATE:
To be physically present in more than one place in one moment of time.

BLUEPRINT:
The etheric structure in the soul which holds the choices for the life made in the Swing Between Worlds. When read to the soul, the blueprint elicits and charges the vibration housed in the soul's structure to assure its remembrance of choices made before birth.

CAUSAL FIELD:
The level of energy in the firmament which restructures and realigns physical matter. Asking to use the causal field or level of energy brings the capacity to realign broken bone, for example, and re-establish order in the physical system, because it is matter.

CHAKRA:
A Sanskrit word which means energy wheels. Designates major energy vortices in the body.

CHOICE:
The single most important step in creating your reality is to choose. Nothing happens without choice.

CHRIST CONSCIOUSNESS:
The union of oneness in form as ordained through the essence of the One.

CHRYSTALLIS OF BEING:
This is the soul's recognition point, the place where the soul is born—the energetic and vibrational resonance of the individual soul's birth.

CIRCUITS (CIRCUITRY):
Circuits are the pathways that run through the body and are aligned with spiritual intent. Much like highways which connect

your cities, they are the frame upon which the movement of consciousness is based. Developing and maintaining the circuits is a primary focus of importance as you live the blueprint of your design, because the circuits are what carry the charge of light and build the vibration to house the truth within you. If your circuits are developed you have a vital life force, are open to creation, and are balanced within and without. To balance and align the circuits is to order the being and place all the diverse human and physical points into the same intent and focus, providing access to the universe.

Water is essential to running the circuits, as water supports the current that actually flows through the circuits, to expand them. So drinking plenty of water is a way to accelerate the amount of charge you can run. For starters, add one glass of water per day, gently working up to 11 glasses per day. The current will take the extra water from your cellular body if more is needed to run the circuits. If you are consciously working with the circuits and feel like you have your finger in a light socket, or feel queasy, your body may need more fluid. Some of the circuits are physical and correspond to the ley lines and meridians, and some of the circuits are etheric, lying right above the body.

CLAIRAUDIENCE:
Clear-hearing; hearing words from the invisible.

CLAIRSENTIENCE:
Clear-feeling; sensing or feeling the invisible.

CLAIRVOYANCE:
Clear-seeing; seeing or vision of the invisible (see Vision).

CLONING:
The word used to most clearly explain the process of imprinting which occurs from the mother at birth. The six-generational bonding of information, belief, fear structure, thought process, and memory into the circuits of an infant at the time the cord is cut from the mother.

Co-creation:
Creating with others simultaneously.

Co-dependence:
Co-dependence is set up at the moment of birth with the cloning process of information imprinted into the soul of the child (see Cloning). As information is passed to the mind and emotion from the six generations of heredity (mom, grandmom, great-grandmom, etc.) the concept of separation is set into the psyche. The mind and emotion then feel the separation and become co-dependent on each other to translate the reality of experience, setting up union between their two points. They depend on each other for responses, decisions, and perceptions, relating from this co-dependence to everything that is lived and perceived. When the being senses something, the mind immediately checks the subconscious for a record of how that experience "should" be translated or perceived and sends a message to the emotion and the emotion responds. The emotion is most times dependent upon the mind to give the appropriate reaction, and the emotion is therefore using the mental instead of responding totally from its essence. The experience of having one part of the being decide what the reality is, and then influencing one or more other parts of the being to determine reality instead of having the whole being respond, is what makes co-dependence an uncomfortable and self-limiting process. The concept of co-dependence is then taken to other experiences, such as family relationships, intimate relationships, issues with substances, or beliefs.

Coincidence:
Events happening in rhythm with your experience which feel natural and synchronized with your intention, your direction, or your path.

Comfortability:
All vibrations, impressions, experience, memories, and yearnings are in balance in your being. There is no need.

Coming Together of the Ages:
The age of remembering; the time when the veils are thin and allow access to all information from all time. A visual for this is a

slinky. When the slinky is open, there is space between the coils which could represent "time" and when the slinky collapses, all parts of evolution are open for perusal because all the coils, which represent experiences in simultaneous reality, are close enough together to be available.

CONCENTRICITY:
A circular wave of expanding and unfolding energy initiated by an intention which is grounded from truth, as in the sharing of a common center by the circles emanating from a point where a pebble has been dropped in water. Christ consciousness is concentricity. This is how critical mass is begun, how worlds are formed, how creation is expressed.

CONDITIONING:
That which you get used to and think is real or the truth.

CONDUIT:
A channel or pathway for something, i.e., consciousness, light, order, etc.

CONGRUENCE:
The place where it all comes together. A point of balance attained through union with all components.

CONSCIOUSNESS:
God's rainbow. The visible, yet invisible pathways through which creation links and expresses. Your communication with the fields of order aligns, unifies, and includes you as one with all things, and is a way to practice experiencing your consciousness.

CONSTANCY:
Maintaining the point of congruence.

CONTINUUM:
A circular path of reality created to embody truth, universally; a circular representation of a universe or universes; the point at which universes spin and differentiate; a circular frame which

moves life through its courses and holds it intact at the same moment; a container for life, life systems, and creation (See Twelve Continuums).

COSMIC:
Deriving its essence from the invisible; pertaining to that which has not been embodied physically.

COUNCIL:
The body of light, order, and truth which emerged directly from the Monad to direct the free-will experiment. The Council is God's/Goddess' right hand organization, contains 12 original points of reality, and is the sustaining body, so to speak, of your universe. The Council is your energetic stability, that which provides a knowing of "home."

CREATION:
The expression of truth in form. What you create expresses your truth and allows you and others to be aware of your part in the design.

CREATIVE CONSCIOUSNESS:
Creating from the awareness of all dimensions.

CRITICAL MASS:
Critical mass is the combined molecular wave form, comprised of many singular points, which moves consciousness, energy, or form. When many singular points of consciousness join together and create in the same wave or thought field, the corresponding answer or return from the universe is to join these points together and respond. As you put out a message, the universe listens. As a response, it is generally a creation index, or an answer that is held as a thought form. When many begin to put together their ideas for oneness, union, order, or truth, there is a critical mass or molecular level of impact reached, which then goes out into the universe. The returning response, as well as the initial wave, is what is meant by the term critical mass—a level of impact that sustains a promise.

DERIVATIVE RESPONSE MECHANISM:
The organic response of the hypothalamus to light and the accompanying synthesis which allocates light to the cerebral tissue, catalyzing functioning.

(THE) DESIGN:
The original map or plan for the free-will experiment. The design guides anyone who chooses to participate in its memory, to live according to laws and frameworks which instruct and unfold, without pain. If you are experiencing pain, you are outside of the design. The design always works for all aspects of life, for all people and situations. It always works perfectly, in alignment with everything, for the purpose of creating oneness in form.

DESTINY:
That to which you have been called, the outcome you have chosen in the Swing Between Worlds, is your destiny. The individual design or contribution is the destiny. So you are individually called to fulfill this, because it belongs to you, and it is necessary for your part in the hologram to be played out.

DIMENSIONS:
Levels in the firmaments which house different aspects of total consciousness. These levels are invisible and were created as crucial foundational points for the integrity of life in all places.

DIVINITY:
The divine is the sacred from origin, the holy, respectful place of honoring and yet, non-distinguishing. When one accesses one's divinity, all is accepted, including the self, and there is no judgment or separation. When one acknowledges one's divinity, one then acknowledges being an emissary for the Monad. Another way of saying this, is that when one acknowledges one's divinity, there is absolution, which results in the experience of being divine.

DOMINO EFFECT:
Used in context with the lasso and universal creation, the domino effect is the momentum or charge issued from the point where the

fulfillment of creation and the initiation of creation join. A forward thrust takes the first event or place of order in the equation and touches the second which touches the third and so forth, using this effect to continue movement for actualization.

EARTH'S ETHERIC PHYSICAL BODY:
The body of the Earth lived in the dimension of the etheric.

EARTH'S ETHERIC POTENTIAL DESTINY:
The potential of the Earth as lived from her etheric physical body. This level actually surrounds the physical, dense Earth where the free-will experiment is taking place, and is where the potential destiny of Earth and humanity will be lived.

ECOSYSTEM:
An environment for life where systems support communication and cooperation.

EGO:
That part of you which keeps you from the memory that you are one with all things. Your greatest teacher and guide is your ego. Wherever it pops up, you know that oneness is imminent and available.

ELECTROMAGNETIC FIELDS:
The subtle bodies of energy which surround the physical and vibrate at varying rates of speed and attune the physical and spiritual dimensions.

ELEMENTS:
The elements are nature's textures and fabric, such as water, rain, wind, air and fire. Elements are the signals and signs of the changing and growing communication between levels, Earth and Spirit, and bring messages and grace to you. Working with the force fields is working with the elements.

EMBODY:
To incorporate into your circuits.

EMISSARY:
Those individual souls who came on a mission from the Monad at the beginning of time to speak with the Earth about housing the free-will experiment, many of whom are here now; those now here to act on behalf of the Monad, the Council, or creation.

ENERGY:
The invisible force which is sustained by substance and expressed through form.

ENERGY CONSTANT:
Any vehicle which sustains the natural and authentic design of creation—the Silver Chalice, the hologram, truth, order, the fields of order, the fluids of being, the Absolute, and so forth.

EQUILIBRATED:
Balanced.

ESSENCE:
The essence is your particular blueprint, fabric, vibration, and frequency uniquely assembled to provide a one-universe point which can be added to the whole. In holographic terms, essence is that which comprises the whole and yet remains distinct.

ETHERIC:
Any and all points of reality that exist outside of form and yet are intricately linked with the creation of spirit in form.

EVOLUTION:
Evolution is the unfolding learning of souls. It is the upward rising spiral that represents the process of forward movement. The plan was designed so that in each lifetime and situation, when one learns, one moves toward integration, taking another step on the spiral. However, evolution was stopped as a concept at the end of 1991 because the learning was no longer accomplished. People returned to the same learning patterns over and over again, which was not the intention of creation. Remember, if you want to learn without pain, get off evolution and onto the design.

EVOLUTIONARY SPIRAL:

The path which the learning of humanity took to document and record its journey.

EXPECTANCY:

The place of excitement which generates the coming together of the wave of creation and its manifestation.

EXTRATERRESTRIAL:

Outside the terrestrial body of the Earth.

FIBER OF BEING:

The essential place from which life is generated and sustained in oneness. The easiest way to feel this in this world is to align with the sun as it rises or sets, and to become the rays as they touch all life, then you can feel the generation of life within you. This is the sound or tone of the Monad.

FIELDS OF ORDER:

The fields of order are the Monad's way of maintaining the universal order here, which is exemplified by nature and the Earth's rhythms and cycles. It has been designed so that when you enter these fields of order, you can communicate with nature, and know the Monad, or God/Goddess. The rhythms and cycles that support and exemplify order will appear to give you a message, lead you further into nature, or support an understanding to link you more closely to these fields of order, i.e., a butterfly, cloud, twig, feather, or animal. Inherent in these experiences is trust, communion, connection, and knowledge that crosses the line between species. Inter-species communication can result, as well as a sense of belonging and support from all levels of being, and a knowing of oneness with the Monad and the Absolute. So we recommend playing in the fields of order, using nature to access your true connection with the unseen.

FIRMAMENTS:

The firmaments are the levels of consciousness where the unseen exists. They surround and uphold these unseen components of the universe as we know it. This is similar to having air around you and your world. The firmaments are fed by substance.

Fluids of Being/Substance:
The fluids are the feminine manna or protoplasm which is the medium for creation, the place where truth is sustained. Substance and the fluids are associated with the fiber of being—the fiber is the etheric linking point and the fluid is the inherent medium through which this manifests. Substance is what gives form to creation, and the food that feeds the firmaments.

Force Fields:
see Elements.

Foundation:
When we speak of foundation it can be the soul as foundation for the psyche, the underlying structure of universal law which gives structure to the etheric, or your making a new structure here of the potential of the hologram so that a new model is formed to support creation.

Framework:
We sometimes use foundation and framework interchangeably. A framework is something you build around or from which houses ideas, creation, and manifestation.

Free Will:
Free will is the greatest gift to humanity from spirit. Free will is that which provides the capacity to choose and therefore create from whatever is chosen. It is the concept that whatever you choose, you create, which therefore, makes you God/Goddess. When you know this is so, whatever is chosen can manifest through substance.

Free Will Experiment:
The journey of the soul from the Swing Between Worlds to the Earth and the choice to bring those two points together through the union of all points, simultaneously. The experiment where souls in human form live the illusion of separation from God and each other until they choose to remember that truth is union. The

Earth's history is a record of this experiment.

FUTURE-FUTURE:
The ninth point of "time." Synonymous with the hologram, the point of resolution, the fulfillment of the design of union.

GOD:
God is the point where all comes together and, at the same time, where all is initiated *from*. It is the going-to and coming-from point. God is inherent in what we call the Monad, and is the first place where expression happened in this universe. As with the Monad, if you decide to be at one with creation, you fulfill yourself inexorably. This is the basis for or the example of life itself. There are no belief systems equated with the Monad or God, nothing that you have to do or not do to be a part of God. Therefore, sin is not a factor because, actually, sin does not exist. Remember that you were born as a part of a great dimension. God is the overseer of this universe, and that which holds the space for the choices of the souls of humanity to be carried out.

GODDESS:
Goddess is the part of God which brings the qualities that you think of as feminine. These qualities exist as an inherent point of balance. When souls were created as male and female, then the Monad differentiated itself as God and Goddess. There is no difference in power base (self-actualization potential) or true identity, it is just that the God focuses on knowledge, steadfastness, and expansion, and the Goddess focuses on sustaining, nurturing, and creating. In this universe, the feminine is the force through which procreation and proliferation happens on Earth, and the God is the place where procreation happens in the firmaments. This balance aligns the heavens as well as the Earth.

This sacred marriage is the example of **truth**, which is feminine because it is invisible, and **order**, which is the example of male because it is visible. The invisible and visible are unified through the Monad and are then unified in your dimension. If you want to live the sacred marriage, the Goddess intends to be equal to the

God, or there is an imbalance. One is not better than the other—both are necessary for completion to occur.

Many of you come to provide order here in feminine bodies as a way to bring balance to Earth, because then you bring with you both qualities. The male on Earth brings the knowledge and the steadfastness and this is coming forth, just as the feminine of sustaining and nurturing and procreation is coming forth. The feminine will create the new ideas, and the masculine will steadfastly hold these ideas and acknowledge them, representing knowledge again. So it is already worked out in the design. The existence of the Goddess assures balance and divine justice here and provides an environment of safety. She is the counterpart of God and is contained in the Monad. The essential nature of creation signals union as a merging which exemplifies the sacred marriage.

GREASES THE WHEEL:
That which spins the hologram into completion. See Hologram, Holographic Reality, and Holographic Wheel.

GROUNDING:
The process of bringing all the circuits of the body into alignment through the feet. Connection is made with the core of order in the center of the Earth through the feet, and the crown of the head opens to the Source above. Our favorite and easiest way to ground is to imagine that you are on Star Trek and are asking Scotty to beam you up. Imagine that your body no longer has any limits, boundaries, or edges, and is made up of oscillating, dancing cells, like sunlight dancing on water. Imagine this oscillating light coming into the top of your head and sparkling through your body, inch by inch, flowing out the bottom of your feet. Grounding is increasingly more important as old energy beliefs and systems are changing. To be connected with the above and the below creates you as the central point of order between the Hierarchy and the core of order in the center of the Earth (See chapter on grounding for information and another exercise).

HERSTORY:
The chronicle of events ordered through "time" from the feminine perspective.

HIERARCHY OF ORDER:
The Hierarchy of Order is the body of light and knowledge which sustains order and truth on this planet until the equality of balance is accomplished in the people. Then the hierarchy will, in a sense, be reabsorbed and become part of the whole again.

HINGE-LIVES:
Those points of reality which directly affect the outcome of your design in your current lifetime. They can be "other lifetimes" as you think of your past lives, or simultaneous points of reality if you acknowledge that you exist through all time.

HISTORY:
The chronicle of events ordered through "time" from the masculine perspective.

HOLOGRAM:
The point of re-union, comprised of all points of time, space, order and being, all aspects, souls, coming together in the experience and memory of oneness.

HOLOGRAPHIC:
That which can be lived or seen as a hologram and applied to the concepts of oneness.

HOLOGRAPHIC DESIGNERS:
Those souls who are choosing to assist in the implementation of the hologram now and who assisted in the actual designing of the model at the beginning of Earth time.

HOLOGRAPHIC REALITY (HR):
Holographic reality is the fulfillment of a million years of dreaming, the "time" when all souls of this level and all aspects of the greater universe are aligned through intention and action. We speak of this

at times as if it were already here, and for all intents and purposes, that is true. It is here within your knowing and, just as you became form, this will become form. What you are creating is the holographic reality. For all of you to be creators means that there has to be a place for you to create simultaneously, which will contain or uphold all these creators and creations. Your HR is the place where you can all create because the design of the HR is that when you are all ready, HR emerges as a house for your dimension to, in a sense, make a new universe. It is the coming together of all your visions in the seed of light and the fulfillment of that point of being.

HOLOGRAPHIC WHEEL:
The wheel which spins the reality of the hologram (See Holographic Reality).

HYPOTHALAMUS:
In physiology the part of the brain which regulates and balances bodily response to temperature and other bodily functions. In the universal application, the part of the being which regulates the flow of light, light synthesis, and health.

ILLUSION:
Anything that separates you from the truth and experience of oneness; anything which creates separation.

IMBUE:
To permeate or fill with, usually used with light or energy.

IMMERSION:
The process of placing all events, actions, and experiences into a fluid pool and entering the pool to merge all ideas, thoughts, and judgments, so all that remains is a state of calmness and repose. What emerges from this process is the experience of oneness with all things, and a non-expectancy which engenders resolution (re-solving) of all questions from the whole being. This is the way to practice "being."

IMMORTALITY:
The knowing that you exist now, have always existed, and will always exist.

IMPRINTING:
To make an intention into reality by merging the essence with the form and holding it until it "takes."

INFUSION:
To create an environment with thought and to place it into an existing context. Most times it is someone using their intention to initiate or maintain a field of healing, light, order, truth, or whatever, for the purpose of placing this intended energy within the spaces between the cells or energy bonds of others. It is best exemplified by the concept of absent healing. You put out your intention, then focus on the person or area to be affected, then send out your field and surround and uphold the individual or group or process, and the field of higher order enters the field of pain, disease or conflict, re-ordering or re-attuning it for the highest good of who is involved. Literally, illusion moves out of the field if order is present.

INTEGRATION:
Integration is the process of becoming aligned. It is taking the different parts and putting them together so that they form an integrity within. The result of integration is a state of flowing, so that there are no sharp edges to the experience or to the being.

INTENTION:
Intention is choosing, affirming, and implementing the energy to manifest. Making an intention declares to the universe that you are ready to receive. It is the use of volitional will to invoke a chosen reality.

INTERDIMENSIONAL SPACE:
A wave or level of consciousness which flows between dimensions.

INVOCATION-INVOKE:
To call forth from intention.

JOY:
Knowledge in action; living through knowing.

KARMA:
The device used by the universe to teach divinity. Karma is the state of balance that exists when one is learning, which provides insights and awarenesses about the relationship of thought and action to truth. It is called the law of cause and effect because it seems that what you do causes what happens (See Law of Cause and Effect). There is really, at this point, no more karma (See Evolution).

KNOWING:
The union of energy, thought, and intention in the being.

KNOWLEDGE:
The infinite order through which all things are born and have their being. Knowledge is the way of truth, which means that knowledge knows of its own divinity and importance and has taken its place as a structural component of the greater universe. This means that knowing or knowledge is a primary point of creation of the Monad and existed before life as we know it. There are no separate places in knowledge, there is only congruence. That is why when knowledge is present, everyone listens and stops what they are doing, and there is respect and honoring. It is not about knowing facts, it is about remembering being, and therefore it is sanctity.

LASSO:
A concept used to assist in manifestation. Take all the events you would normally see necessary to create an outcome and begin by placing them on a line, from the first event, to the last event necessary to complete the outcome. Then bring them together using a needle and thread or thought wave. When you have threaded all the items, bring the beginning and the completion together by making a lasso. Energetically this speeds up

the process of creation, brings the excitement of completion to power the initiation, and uses the domino effect to catalyze the movement of each item to the next.

LAW OF CAUSE AND EFFECT:
The universal law of cause and effect defines the underlying relationship between creation and ordering. Creation is the cause and ordering is the effect. The effect is where creation happens in order for what has been chosen or designed to be accomplished. It is different on Earth, and the law of the universe has been translated so that it applies to karma, which was not the original intention. On Earth, the Law of Cause and Effect is usually lived as the opposite of the "Golden Rule." What you do unto others comes back to haunt you.

LIGHT:
Light is the experience of being. Light is the primary source which the Monad utilizes to expand (masculine) and sustain (feminine). Light is the primary source of growth and was initiated by the Monad, created, in a sense, because organically, cellularly, all creation came through this experience of being. Light is the medium for birth. So you all remember light as an innate and long-awaited promise.

LIGHT BODY:
The physical representation of light in form.

LIGHT FORCE:
The unified field created when intention and light join together.

LINEAGE:
Your place of origin in the unfolding of the design. Identity with and experience of the Monad in the beginning which attends you and aligns your course.

MACROCOSM (IC):
The cosmic or absolute reality—the larger picture and the experience of all parts being equal.

Magic:
Changing consciousness or perception at will.

Master Plan:
The great design hatched at the beginning of Earth time.

Mastery:
The acceptance of your rightful place in the universe. To be a master means that you are aligned with your true essence and live it regardless of your surroundings or the illusions of others. You live in a sacred alignment with all life and know that there is no control necessary or actually possible, and so you shape and guide and nurture, rather than proclaiming. In the same way, there is nothing to be master (or mistress) of, in reality, because it is all one. So a master lives the oneness.

Matrix:
The energetic house of your soul, essence, and vibration, within which the embodiment of your dreams and visions begins. Located in the central area of the chest.

Metaphysical:
Beyond the physical.

Microcosm (ic):
The individual point of union with self which establishes the basis for interrelationship of all parts of the whole.

Miracle:
Creating from order, outside of time. To create a miracle simply decide what you want to make, gather together the ingredients, and then bring them together without time involved.

Mission:
Your mission is your calling in expression, the reason you have come, the design in personal/microcosmic perspective.

Model of Cooperation (MOC):

The concept that everything belongs to everyone, everyone gets what they need, and there are no places where separation exists. The MOC is a way to practice being in the holographic reality of the future and provides literal concepts you can study and familiarize yourself with so that you think differently about your existence here. The MOC, lived very literally, would be Heaven on Earth. So you can begin anytime (See Appendix for transcript).

Monad:

(Monadal) The source of creation, the initial point of recognition which emerged from the Absolute. Sometimes called by humanity God and/or Goddess.

Morphic Resonance:

The tuning fork concept; sharing knowing and creation and vibration within your species through frequency, which brings the knowing into this dimension of Earth; vibrating at the same rate of speed, which imparts knowledge.

No-thing:

The void and the place of the Absolute.

Oneness:

Oneness is the incentive to learn, the reason you are here, and the fulfillment of the journey, all at once. The experience of being unified with, the memory of being loved, accepted and honored in infinity, and the incentive to go forward, even when you want to quit. The free will experiment is based on the return of individual points of consciousness to one point of consciousness, or oneness. You came from oneness and so you will return to oneness. It is the experience of no separation.

Ordained:

Held sacred by all points in the universe.

ORDER:

Order is the basis of the universe, the sacred honoring of the individual and collective place of creation. Order establishes the inherent balance which is how light, growth, knowledge, and sustenance exist. In a sense, order is the food of all components, the fertile bed through which the Earth and her gardens in nature are completely balanced. Order calms and brings peace and fosters awareness and encourages expression. Order exists through the Monad and is upheld by the Hierarchy and exists in each person's matrix as an inherent knowing. When one opens to the matrix and makes the decision to see and know the soul, order begins to "come out" and be remembered and expressed. This makes the society more functional, because more and more people begin to live and create through order, which means they are living and creating through the Monad. Order and the wave of order is the primary way in which the critical mass of consciousness will be opened out unto the Earth.

ORDER WAVE:

Since order is the basis of this universe, to harness that wave and to direct it into the Earth's field, can provide extensive changing of the consciousness and experience of those here. Order and truth waves are what is colloquially termed "critical mass." The order wave is a very important way to acknowledge and expand the existing reality and to create unity.

ORGANIC:

Organic or organicity means innately unfolding from within, responsive rather than planned, being in the fields of order rather than mental decisions.

OSCILLATE:

To vibrate.

OSCILLATORY FREQUENCY:

A vibrational wave or pathway.

Osmosis:
The process of becoming one with something and exchanging energy on the cellular level. All consciousness is gained, accessed and experienced through osmosis, i.e., prayer, meditation, etc.

Osmotic Fluid:
The cellular fluid which is used by the body to run the charge of light through the circuits.

Paradigms:
Structures, models, and frameworks to build reality and creation from and into.

Parallel Reality:
The counterpart reality to this dimension. Here one can create at will by crossing the barrier of perception and merging the two dimensions.

Past-Past:
The original point of creation, the Absolute, the point where the free-will experiment began.

Past, Present, Future:
The way reality is divided into separate experiences.

Potentiation:
Energy moving toward its fulfillment.

Power:
Self-actualization potential, which is housed in the solar plexus chakra. Power is seen as the ability to live one's fullest potential in the world.

Pre-knowledge:
The space where pre-original consciousness exists and is maintained. Before the Monad split into God/Goddess aspects, there was pre-knowledge. As creation and the expanding universe

became "defined," knowledge was born and carried through all aspects of the Monad's expression. Since knowledge was changed as it was recorded and utilized, and, to some extent, altered and compromised, this pre-knowledge has been held away from humanity. Those coming from the pre-knowledge space have made the commitment to live from that point and bring it to this dimension when the acceleration curve indicates that it is time for the pre-original knowledge to become accorded here.

PRESENT-PRESENT:
The moment where you are now, that you identify or perceive as your current reality.

PROLIFERATION:
The feminine capacity to create and grow life with no boundaries. The energy of complete union in expression. WOW!

PURE INTENT:
The choice to live from the heart of the one for the highest good of all concerned in each moment.

RAYS:
Rays are focused beams of intention which provide different energetic and relational guidance to access consciousness.

REALITY:
The experience of union and oneness.

RECEPTION:
The act of receiving, being a place where receiving is possible.

REGROUPING:
The choice to re-order or re-calibrate the system, experiences, or energy of a situation; learning, relationship, or the process of coming to center; breathing in resonance with pure intent, grounding, or any means which will assist you to see a situation more clearly.

Rendering:

The time of rendering is the time of choice. Each of you will be called to make a choice as to whether or not you want to stay here and fulfill your part of the design. Sometimes we speak of it as if the time of choice is about choosing love or fear. Actually it is more accurately whether you will choose to fulfill your potential or not, and then, of course, it is the same thing. (For more information on this refer to The Bridge of Light.).

Resolution:

Re-solving; coming back into solution; finding the experience again of being fluid and in oneness with no edges and no separation.

Resolution Constant:

The Silver Chalice is the resolution constant in the universe, or that which brings the coming together of balance in and from all dimensions.

Re-Sourcing:

Receiving again the connection with Source.

Response-ability:

The ability to respond; the intention of the universe is that you respond instead of being responsible for.

Seed of Light:

The seed of light is located in the soul under the xiphoid process, the pointy bone in the center of the chest. It is your individual and collective vision of your purpose and the part you play in the greater design. The vision of the seed of light, when tapped, provides guidance for actualizing your destiny. The seed of light is a primary source point in the body and is sometimes called the Source chakra. Opening the seed of light enables you to see the pictures of what you are going to do and safeguards the total design by showing you what happens when everyone lives from their truth, and how that collective truth looks and feels.

SELF:
That which you identify as you, and which carries the identity of your psyche. The self is a space that connects the body and spirit.

SEPARATION:
The state of amnesia which defines things as separate and unrelated or outside of oneness.

SHAPESHIFT:
Changing form and shape through the molecular movement of energy and substance.

SOUL:
The microcosmic dot of the Monad which is on a journey to experience itself and then to reunite with its source. The soul houses all memory of all time and space and order and being. The soul is derived from truth and light and carries knowledge and all the incredible seeds of unfoldment. The soul cannot die because the whole universe is its home, so no matter what happens, the soul is always alive.

SOUND/TONE:
Essence communicated through vibration.

SOURCE CHAKRA:
See Seed of Light.

SPIRIT:
Spirit is the essential way in which the Monad exists in all dimensions. A part of the Monad is expressing as invisible to open the pathways of communication with itself. So in a way, spirit is the messenger of the Monad, a way that we come to know the original through intercessory points. Spirit is the air in the balloon. Spirit is the way in which the Monad communicates, gives messages, and sustains the consciousness of humanity without tipping its hand. There is guidance in the spiritual level which aligns and calls each soul to remember the Monad, which is the point of it all. So spirit is the intermediary between soul and

Monad. Spirits come in all shapes and sizes, all levels of remembering. Spirit is also defined as an essence which inspires hope, because when you are in touch with spirit, you live in a closer way to the Monad.

SUBSTANCE:
See Fluids of Being.

SUBTLE BODIES:
The levels which surround the body, make up your "field," and have dimension in the etheric and invisible, encompassing all points of reality, seen and unseen, and all points of "time." All that you are is in your field.

SUSTAINABILITY:
That which has the ability to sustain all life at one moment.

SYNCHRONICITY:
Synchronicity happens when there are no thoughts, and the design is able to be lived automatically with no planning to disrupt it. Try it, it's great!

SWING BETWEEN WORLDS:
The inter-dimensional space where souls choose their incarnative destiny (This is where we know you from).

SYSTEMS THEORY:
Systems theory is the unified theory of the universe, which was the original design of the Monad. This theory includes all systems and, of course, all life. The basic principles are that 1) all life has innate intelligence, 2) all life communicates either consciously or unconsciously, 3) all life is creating the experienced reality, or is in co-creation, 4) there is co-responsibility for whatever happens, and 5) that everything is growing toward the light. In systems theory, conflict is seen as an indication that it is time for growth. There is no judgment in this system. Everything is known and unfolding. When one lives from this system, the choice is to grow rather than to fear expansion.

The Ones With No Names:

The body of light and knowledge which sustains order and truth in the universe. Amorphous light beings whose "job" is to act as Cosmic Guidance Councilors for humanity. We "live" in the Swing Between Worlds.

Time/Space Continuum (TSC):

The basis of life on planet Earth is the existence of a set of parameters that defines what is thought of as reality. These parameters make the conditions you experience and are the ingredients which you use to create and bake your cake. TSC is an environment through which things relate to each other, hold their shape and form, can be thought of as chronological, and have a place to occur. A creation of the Monad to house the free will experiment, the TSC changed its parameters at the end of December, 1991, when the Piscean age ended and began being termed "the space of order and being." Actually, what changed is the perception of life here, rather than that one continuum began and one ended, because it is the perception that creates the experience. Now people are realizing that there is no time and they are more inclined to study "being" than "space." Actually, order and being is an adjunct to time and space. All four points exist at once, and when the shift happened it was to bring these points together. Piscean = time and space experience; Aquarian = order and being. Put them together and you have technology and the heart.

Time Tunnel:

The point and location in which reality shifts from organic memory of oneness to amnesiac separation and biological conditioning. This is the place you experience just before birth, as described in *I Remember Union: The Story of Mary Magdalena.*

Tone:

See Sound.

Transcendence:

Going beyond the form to experience the essence; returning to the place of knowing and creation while in physical form.

TRANSFORMATION:
The experience of energetically matching form and spirit in the same vibration, while still in form. Union of all points while physical.

TRANSITION:
The levels between dimensions; the places a soul travels through during entry to Earth and after death; sometimes referred to by humans to indicate change in the circumstances of life, i.e., going through transition(s).

TRANSLOCATE:
To change direction or location either physically or psychically.

TRUTH:
Truth is the point which upholds life and the design by carrying the wave or energy of the essential story of creation, oneness, free-will, resolution, and therefore, the hologram. Truth brings the design into fruition, and is the incentive for each soul to live from a perspective that engenders truth, for truth guides one to oneness.

TWELVE CONTINUUMS:
The twelve continuums are the basic universes which are the experience of the total universe relating and evolving and opening unto the oneness. These twelve points are learning simultaneously from different perspectives about returning to the original point of choice, and yet are learning differently in each instance. The twelve becoming one is an important concept to remember because you will encounter this over and over again in your experience. Just as you are living in a unique and singular paradigm, so are all the other eleven continuums, having their own reality and growing toward the light in their own perspective. Some of you have come to align these twelve levels into oneness, and this will be accomplished by the year 2016. As the alignment happens here, it happens everywhere. The twelve levels will become four by the year 2011 and then unify to one level by 2016. The first order of business, however, is to align this universe.

UNIFIED FIELD THEORY:
A field of energy and consciousness that initiates oneness.

UNION:
The experience of all life as one essence or point of recognition.

UNIVERSE(S):
There are 12 universes. We live in one. Our universe is comprised of our solar system and all life forms of our physical reality, set in motion by and unfolding from the Absolute.

VIBRATION:
Oscillation, pulsation, movement of energy, usually too fast for the eye to see.

VISCERAL CELLULAR RESPONSE:
The organic response to light and truth which occurs in the cells of the body and in the circuits, and therefore establishes magnetism and presence in the physical body.

VISION:
Seeing with the total being instead of the eye. Seeing becomes more possible when you hold the images together until they become palpable. At this point, you can begin to "see."

VOLITIONAL WILL:
The intention and choice made in conjunction with free-will which charges the universe to accord the decisions of humanity. Use of volitional will is the most clear way to affect change and create or manifest when in form. To use this path, simply stand on the Earth, create a clear intention of your choosing, breathe into the seed of light to connect the intention with the truth within, and breathe out, seeing the vision of what you are sending forth as meeting the design and Akashic records.

WAVE FRAME:
The field of energy which comprises the total being, including the body, mind, emotion, spirit, ego, soul, and all points of time.

WEAVING:

The process of blending more than one aspect, energy, field, or paradigm into synthesis. Infusion is a form of weaving.

ZEAL (CENTER OF ZEAL):

Located in the back of the neck, the center of zeal is the place to unleash your spiritual force and create what you are here to express directly from creation.

Sunlight on Water

Credits

Edited by Flo Aeveia Magdalena, Noel McInnis and Jayn Stewart with final editing by Susan Quinn and Karuna Kress.

Lay out and typesetting by Désirée DeKlerk

Cover Design by Raul Chico Goler

Illustrations by Wendy Rode and Dru Fuller

Printed in USA by CreateSpace

This book was typeset in Palatino

For Information about programs that support an understanding and integration of the principles and concepts presented in Sunlight on Water, please contact Soul Support Systems.

Soul Support Systems is a 501C3 educational organization that offers individual and group support of the soul's purpose. Opportunities to deepen and expand connection with the soul are offered through coaching, readings, HeartThread sessions, Soul Recognition experiential classes and retreats, and Circuitry Alignment.

Classes and trainings in facilitating the above offerings are also offered as an integral part of the work of Soul Support Systems. Contact us if you are interested in assisting others on their soul's journey.

Soul Support Systems
18 The Square, Suite 20
Bellows Falls, VT 05101
802-463-2200
Fax 802-463-2201
Soulsupportsystems@comcast.net
www.Soulsupportsystems.org

48036933R00193

Made in the USA
Middletown, DE
08 September 2017